Praise for the original *Dividends Don't Lie* (1988)

"Geraldine Weiss, the doyenne of dividend enhancement, has popularized the theory that there is an inescapable relationship between the corporation's ability to pay consistent dividends over time and its price performance in the stock market. Her respected newsletter, *Investment Quality Trends,* employs this theoretical basis, and her classic *Dividends Don't Lie* is a primer on her theory."

—*Library Journal*

"Geraldine Weiss' dividend yield investment model espoused in *Dividends Don't Lie* is basically reiterated and confirmed. This relatively simple, straightforward strategy, limited here to 350 select blue-chip stocks, has regularly outperformed the market (as documented by Mark Hulbert, who tracks investment advisers in his *Hulbert Financial Digest*)."

—*Booklist*

"In their technically detailed, conservative analysis, the authors recommend careful study of high grade issues with steady dividend-increase records. Investors should buy shares when the stock is undervalued in relation to dividend yield, then sell (reinvesting elsewhere) when a bullish trend drives the share price up to an overvalue level."

—*Publishers Weekly*

"The first dividend accrues to the reader when you buy *Dividends Don't Lie.* It is a superb value."

—Bob Gross, Publisher,
The Professional Investor

"A lucid and powerful presentation of one of the best documented investment theories."

—Peter Brimelow,
Senior Editor, *Forbes*

"Finally, an investment book that deals with values! Values ultimately rule the market and a knowledge of values is always based first and last on dividends. This book should be '"the bible of dividends."'

—Richard Russell,
Publisher of *Dow Theory Letters*

"I have a lot of respect for the common-sense approach of an investment strategy based on dividends. There is a wonderful order and simplification in this long-term skill which tends to achieve profits by patience rather than clever short-term market moves which do not create income or build capital."

—James L. Fraser, CFA, President,
Fraser Management Associates

Dividends Still Don't Lie

THE TRUTH ABOUT INVESTING IN BLUE CHIP STOCKS AND WINNING IN THE STOCK MARKET

Kelley Wright

John Wiley & Sons, Inc.

Published by John Wiley & Sons, Inc., Hoboken, New Jersey.
Published simultaneously in Canada.

Library of Congress Cataloging-in-Publication Data:
Wright, Kelley.
Dividends still don't lie: the truth about investing in blue chip stocks and winning in the stock market / Kelley Wright; foreword by Geraldine Weiss.
p. cm.
Includes index.
ISBN 978-0-470-58156-8 (cloth)
1. Blue-chip stocks. 2. Dividends. 3. Stocks–Prices. 4. Investment analysis. 5. Portfolio management. I. Title.
HG4661.W75 2010
332.63′22–dc22

2009041771

Printed in the United States of America

V10003355_081318

To my late grandfather,
Elbert Nelson Dummitt,
my first teacher and mentor.

Contents

Foreword

It is with a great deal of pleasure that I introduce Kelley Wright's new book about the dividend-yield approach to lifelong growth of capital and income in the stock market.

This investment concept first was published in 1966 in what then was a new investment advisory service, *Investment Quality Trends.* Forty-three years and three books later, the service is still helping investors master the stock market by investing in high quality, dividend paying, blue chip stocks. It helps them know when stocks are *undervalued,* when they can be bought, and *overvalued,* when they should be sold.

The importance of dividends in determining value in the stock market cannot be overstated. The main reason investors are willing to risk their capital in *anything* is to get a return on their investment. In the real estate market, that return is rent. In the money market, it is interest. And in the stock market, it is a cash dividend.

Folks who ignore the importance of dividends in making stock market selections are not investors. They are speculators. Speculators hope that the price of a stock will go up and reward them with profits. Investors know that stocks that pay dividends go up too. Meanwhile, they are getting a return on their capital. They believe the old adage: A bird in the hand is worth two in the bush.

The legendary Charles Dow has written, "To know values is to know the meaning of the market. And values, when applied to stocks, are determined in the end by the dividend yield."

It is undeniable that many stock market investors are attracted to companies that pay dividends. Unconsciously, investors have established profiles of value for each dividend-paying stock based on historic extremes of high and low dividend yield. Those extremes of yield provide profitable buying and selling areas. A stock is undervalued when the dividend yield is historically high. It is overvalued when the price rises and the yield become historically low.

Let us examine how and why dividends create value in the stock market.

When the price of a stock declines far enough to produce a high dividend yield, value-minded investors who seek income begin to buy. The further the price falls, the higher the yield becomes and the more investors are drawn to the stock. Eventually the stock becomes irresistibly undervalued, buyers outnumber sellers, the decline is reversed and the stock begins to rise. The higher the price rises, the lower the dividend yield becomes and fewer investors are attracted to the stock. Meanwhile, investors who purchased the stock at lower levels are inclined to sell and take their profits. Eventually the price becomes so high and the dividend yield is so low, sellers outnumber buyers and the price of the stock begins to decline. A declining trend generally continues until a high dividend yield is reached that again attracts investors who step in and reverse the trend. At undervalue, the price/yield cycle reestablishes itself and the journey from undervalue to overvalue starts all over again.

It should be noted that each dividend-paying stock etches its own individual profile of value. These profiles of high and low dividend yield are established over long periods of time. There is no one-size-fits-all. Some stocks are undervalued when the dividend yield is 4.0 percent. Some, when the yield is 5.0 percent. Some will decline to yield as much as 6.0 percent or even 7.0 percent before they are historically undervalued. Some growth stocks are undervalued when the dividend yield is as low as 2.0 percent or 3.0 percent. The yields at overvalue are similarly distinctive and individual. *Therefore each stock must be studied and evaluated according to its own unique profile of dividend yield, one that has been established over several investment cycles.*

Now, here is the best part. Every time a dividend is increased, the prices at undervalue and overvalue move higher to reflect the historically established high and low dividend yields. Therefore, a company that has a long history of consistent dividend increases is most desirable. It promises steady growth of capital as well as continuous growth of dividend income. Frequent dividend increases prolong the life of an investment by raising the price/yield targets at undervalue and overvalue.

Dividends are the most reliable measures of value in the stock market. Earnings are figures on a balance sheet that can be manipulated for income tax purposes. Earnings can be the product of a clever account's imagination. Who knows what secrets lie in the footnotes of an earnings report? Dividends, however, are *real* money. Once a dividend is paid, it is gone forever from the company. There can be no subterfuge about a cash dividend. It is either paid or it is not paid. When a dividend is declared, you *know* that the company is in the black. And when a company increases its dividend, you don't have to read a balance sheet to know that the company has made profitable progress. In short, dividends don't lie.

But nothing is perfect in the stock market. There is one problem with the dividend-yield approach. Sometimes an unusually high yield can send a signal that the dividend is in danger of being reduced. When a dividend is lowered, the prices at undervalue and overvalue also are lowered and a price that previously was undervalued no longer represents good value. Therefore, it is critical to make sure that the indicated dividend is adequately covered by earnings.

One way to provide a measure of safety is to confine investment selections to time-tested, high-quality, blue chip stocks with long histories of unbroken dividend payouts and attractive records of earnings and dividend growth. The companies should have reasonably low levels of debt. The stocks should have relatively low price/earnings ratios. Such stocks have been carefully researched and are listed in this book.

The dividend-yield approach to value in the stock market can be applied to any dividend-paying stock. However, it is most successful when it is applied to high quality, blue chip stocks. The companies reviewed in this book and listed in the *Investment Quality Trends* advisory service have long dividend histories and well-etched profiles of undervalue and overvalue. Most of them carry a *Standard & Poor's* Quality Rank of A+, A, or A−. They are, in fact, true blue chips.

On a personal note, I am very proud of this approach to finding value through the dividend yield. Since it was introduced in 1966, it has helped many investors achieve financial security. It has given investors a sensible method to grow their capital and income and

Acknowledgments

Gloria Patri, et Filio, et Spiritui Sancto. Sicut erat in principio, et nunc, et semper, et in sæcula sæculorum, Amen.

All thanks to the Holy Trinity from whom I have been blessed with the gift of faith, the love and support of my beautiful wife Kathy, and our five incredible children: Trinity Faith, Keegan Patrick, Jillian Grace, Evan Michael, and Christian Blaise.

Although faith and family are sufficient to make any life fulfilling, I have also enjoyed a rich professional life. Without discounting the benefits of my monetary compensation, it is impossible to put a price tag on the affirmation one receives from providing the appropriate solution for a clients' dilemma, or a value on the life experience and wisdom gained along the way. When all these factors are considered, I am the recipient of an embarrassment of riches.

I realize that while employment, for many people, is a necessity of life; how we embrace that necessity can transform a mere job into a calling or vocation. If, as The Good Book reads, "one must earn their daily bread from the sweat of their brow," where is it written the sweat of the brow must be ordinary, uninteresting, and without joy? Thankfully it seems no written edict exists except in the hearts and minds of those who have chosen that path. As for me, I can gratefully acknowledge that my road has been blessed. I have had the wise counsel of caring mentors. The practice of my craft has resulted in relationships with truly wonderful people who have shared their hopes, concerns, and dreams with me. Lastly, my journey has been a humbling experience, because these good people have trusted me to help them transform their hopes and dreams into reality.

I am indebted to my late grandfather, Elbert Nelson Dummitt, for preparing the soil, planting the seed, and keeping the garden fertile. His innate sense of value and common sense were lessons of immeasurable worth; his love and patience were boundless. I miss him deeply.

I am also blessed with a good business partner and friend, Mr. Michael Minney. Mike is more than a wingman; he makes sure the i's get dotted, the t's get crossed and the nets are in place every time I run off a cliff before I know where I will land. You are my brother from another mother.

Last but certainly not least is my gratitude to the diva of dividends, the incomparable Geraldine Weiss. She broke the mold and shattered the glass ceiling, proving that Wall Street is no match for mom's common sense and experience. Thank you for your confidence in entrusting me with your baby, but more importantly for your friendship and wisdom. *Ad Majorem Dei Gloriam.*

List of Figures and Tables

Introduction

"Life is the best teacher, boy." This was my grandfather's way of saying that the best education is experiential. I am confident he arrived at this knowledge honestly; I know that I did.

I know this to be true as the result of almost three decades of experience as both an advisor and private investor. Experience means you have lost money in the markets, survived, and learned how to invest better. Rest assured that I have a lot of experience.

In 1988, my mentor and predecessor Geraldine Weiss wrote the classic *Dividends Don't Lie.* That book detailed the dividend-value strategy behind *Investment Quality Trends,* the highly successful newsletter Geraldine founded and that I now have the privilege to edit. Twenty-two years hence, the investment world has changed dramatically because of computer technology and the Internet. Tremendous amounts of data and information can be gathered, sorted, and analyzed in a matter of minutes. What used to take weeks or months at a library can now be accomplished in an evening; all one needs is a computer and Internet access.

What hasn't changed is the success of the dividend-value strategy for producing consistent gains in the stock market. Despite the advent of new technologies and the ability of investors to access information on an unprecedented basis, our old-school technique of using the dividend yield to identify values in blue chip stocks still outperforms most investment methods on a risk-adjusted basis.

Forty-four years after its inception, *Investment Quality Trends* continues to focus on combining sound stock selection with a long-term orientation because, over time, the stock market rewards investors who recognize and appreciate good value. In fact, the two greatest assets an investor can have are a system to identify quality and the ability to recognize value.

Although the dividend-value strategy has always had its fair share of detractors, critics and criticism have grown exponentially since the mid 1990s and the advent of alternative investments and the evolution of investment theory. Although the vast majority of these advancements have proven to be abject failures, it is still fashionable in some circles to simply dismiss the dividend-value strategy as an offshoot of the buy-and-hold philosophy.

In the simplest of terms, buy-and-hold is making an investment with no intention of ever selling and expecting financial gains into perpetuity. If detractors of the dividend-value strategy had actually taken the time to objectively study its concepts, they would find a clearly defined selling discipline based on repetitive dividend yield patterns; just one of several critical dimensions that are clearly absent in the buy-and-hold philosophy. Putting this and other fallacies to rest is one of the primary purposes of writing *Dividends Still Don't Lie.*

We believe the twin pillars of quality and value provide an investment foundation that takes much of the risk and anxiety out of investing in the stock market. We further believe that protecting principal while realizing a tangible return on investment from dividends makes perfect common sense, yet both are routinely dismissed as archaic. To be sure, disagreements among market participants are a requisite element for a properly functioning market, however, disagreements can devolve to a degree of dismissive hubris that allows for the type of irrational exuberance that brought us the worst bear market since the Great Crash of 1929. Interestingly, the current bear market has validated that our thought to be archaic beliefs cannot only survive, but prosper, in virtually any investment climate.

Well into our fifth decade in publication, *Investment Quality Trends* remains relentless in the pursuit of identifying value in the stock market and in understanding the myriad factors that influence stock prices each day. While this is a fascinating quest, it is not easy, nor are we always right. Our track record of success has been consistently sufficient, however, to affirm we are on the right path.

Although advances in technology provide investors access to more data and information than at any point in history, human nature has remained relatively unchanged since the Garden of Eden. This is to say that having more data and information has not cured the human propensity for being easily seduced by myths and misinformation, which results in missed opportunities and valuable compounding time. Investing is a business and should be treated as such. If you want to gamble, go to Las Vegas. If you have issues that need to be worked out, get a therapist. If you want to be successful in the stock market, learn how to identify quality businesses that offer historic value and then make the most efficient use of your resources.

This book is a short read by design. The game plan outlined here is based on the fact that a stock's underlying value is in its dividends, not in its earnings or in its prospects for capital gains. More than four decades of research have shown that blue-chip companies, those with long records of consistent, competent performance, are far more predictable than are upstarts or less-established companies with erratic records of earnings and dividend payments. In short, the dividend-value strategy is a proven, commonsense approach that has ultimately led to long-term results.

Although the volume may be light, the content is heavy. With all due respect to the Nobel laureates in economics and finance, the sheepskin isn't required to be a successful investor. I would suggest that you would do better to mind a good dose of mom's common sense and a little discipline. If you feel like it's necessary to do some heavy mathematical and economic lifting to get your money's worth I can steer you in that direction, but you'll probably get confused and frustrated trying to implement some esoteric investment strategy you'll never understand. Don't be intimidated into thinking simplicity doesn't work.

Most investors don't lose money in the markets because they're stupid; they lose money because they haven't put in the time and do not understand risk. If you can learn to think through your actions before you take them, you are well on your way to reaching your financial goals.

Lastly, investing is as much about perception and perspective as it is methods and technique. If your gut reaction to an event or situation is that something isn't right, for gosh sakes pay attention to it! "Opportunity," Geraldine says, "is like a streetcar; another one will come along soon."

Dividends Still Don't Lie

THE TRUTH ABOUT INVESTING IN BLUE CHIP STOCKS AND WINNING IN THE STOCK MARKET

PART I

THE ART OF DIVIDEND INVESTING

CHAPTER 1

First Things First

We don't receive wisdom; we must discover it for ourselves after a journey that no one can take for us or spare us.

—Marcel Proust

I am not a therapist, and this book is not a journey into navel gazing and self-discovery. That being said, you have to get this part right.

Investor psychology and sentiment play a significant role in how you approach investments and the investing process. In my experience the most successful investors have had an end goal in mind that they wanted to achieve, which necessarily dictated the majority of their investment decisions. This is not to say that you can't be a successful investor without having a game plan mapped out, but understanding your motivation for putting your hard-earned money at risk in the markets can help you avoid taking unnecessary risks.

With that in mind, forgive my waxing philosophical for a moment. If September 11, 2001 has taught us anything, let's hope it's that life is precious and time is valuable. If you accept this premise as true, you would agree with me, then, that ideally, we should spend as much time as possible in this life to find and embrace our passions; those activities that make our hearts swell and our souls soar.

The reality though is that we don't live in an ideal world. As human beings we have to spend a significant portion of our time providing for the *practical necessities:* food, clothing, housing, transportation, education, recreation, and medication. The means by which we acquire these necessities is called *cash.*

It's All About the Cash

Generating sufficient cash to meet your needs will be a primary objective until you die. If you have loved ones you are responsible for, they will continue to need cash *after* you die.

During the employment years, you must make wages, salaries, and bonuses do double duty, providing for current needs while investing for the future. Optimally, the invested cash will generate sufficient interest, dividends, and capital appreciation to meet your future needs when your wages, salaries, and bonuses are no longer your primary sources of income. Your long-term challenge then will be to balance your cash flow between your current cash needs and your need to accumulate cash for the future. Your level of success in this endeavor can be positively impacted by a modicum of financial planning.

Financial planning is an excellent exercise and a useful tool to organize your financial activities and to create a disciplined structure. Although some practitioners can overwhelm you with the minutia, an understanding of your current cash flow and budget is sufficient to make some reasonable assumptions for a retirement budget. This information will provide a working framework for how much you need to save, the required rate of return on those savings to meet your goals, and how much insurance you need to protect yourself and your loved ones should you become disabled or die prematurely. Armed with that information and this book, you can accomplish the rest.

Technology has changed the world, our culture, and social mores. This new era of interconnectivity has accelerated the pace at which we receive information and process its applicability to our lives. By extension, the workplace and the work ethic have evolved as well. The time when one would choose a career track with one employer or within one industry from beginning to end has vanished. Second, third, and even fourth careers are now commonplace. Again, by extension, retirement or at least the concept of retirement has also evolved. The twentieth-century model of moving from employment to the golden years in pursuit of leisure has morphed into the reality that for many, whether by choice or necessity, a portion of the golden years now includes some form of continuing employment.

The recession and cyclical downturn in housing beginning in 2008 notwithstanding, the long-term economic reality is that historically the cost of living increases year after year. Unless your cash flow increases at the same rate as the cost of your expenditures, you will have to decide between spending on current needs and investing for future needs.

Barring a major depression or the end of the world, the cost of living and the average life span will most likely continue to increase. Assuming I am correct, you need to be prepared for the rising cost of the practical necessities for a greater amount of time. This is to say you are going to need a lot of cash. Granted, we all have unique circumstances and situations, so how we approach spending and investing will vary by the individual. Regardless of the myriad factors to consider, don't just stick your head in the sand and hope for the best; hope is not a strategy for success.

The Importance of Planning

As an investment advisor, I have witnessed too frequently the stress and anxiety of investors who have underestimated their cash needs for retirement. Because retirement planning didn't gain wide acceptance until the early nineties, too many waited to properly fund their 401(k) plans, IRAs, and after-tax investments and savings, and/or they weren't properly invested. I can't tell you how many people have told me that they thought that Social Security would make up the difference. Although Social Security worked well when the demographics were more favorable, ensuring benefits for future recipients required changes in the system that were never instituted. Today we are faced with the prospect of a bankrupt program. Although there are voices that advocate long-needed reforms, I would suggest that there will not be any significant changes made to Social Security because it is politically too hot to handle. For the reader below 40 years of age this is unfortunate; I wouldn't count on Social Security being available to supplement your retirement. Let's all hope that I am very, very wrong.

Undoubtedly there are some readers who are proactive and better prepared, who embraced retirement planning early on by funding a 401(k), an IRA, and after-tax investments. By design or by luck, some will have invested well and will be on track; others won't be so lucky. If you are unsure about where you stand, don't guess. If you need help, engage a fee-based financial planner. Your tax preparer or attorney should have some ready references. Whether you go it alone or require some assistance, however, just make sure you get it done. Knowing what you need and when you will need it is critical to the investment process. When it comes to your future, don't be afraid to ask questions.

In my experience, few people have the answers to these questions off the top of their heads. It isn't that they aren't capable, but most people prefer to concentrate on activities they find more attractive. I understand that perspective because most people naturally gravitate to what most interests them. Some of us are butchers, others are bakers, and many are candlestick makers. So I say again, don't guess; find out what you'll need so you get your goals and objectives in focus, and then we can help you with the rest.

If you know what your goals and objectives are, you are well on your way to achieving investment success. At the end of the day, successful investing is realized by three activities: *know the end goal(s) of why you are investing; use an investment approach that makes sense to you and can generate returns sufficient to meet your goals; and, keep an eye on taxes and expenses.*

The three activities, shown in Figure 1.1, are nothing more than being *mindful* about your investments and investment decisions. You put thought and consideration into other critical areas of your life, why shouldn't you do the same about your investments? Think of it this way: By entertaining some mindful decision-making about your investments, you just might eliminate any fears and anxiety you may have about your financial future. How's that for a payoff?

As stated previously, little has changed in human nature. The two base emotions of fear and greed are still the most difficult challenges most investors face. The fear of losing money on a poor investment is equaled only by the fear of losing money on a lost opportunity; both are directly attributable to a lack of good information. Making mindful, long-term investment decisions is almost impossible without good information.

It is ironic that, in the Information Age, the average investor suffers from information deprivation. On a certain level this seems absurd, considering the number of investment newsletters, magazines,

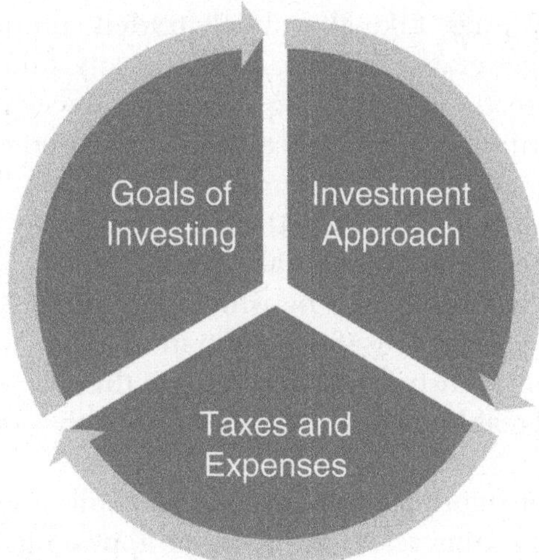

Figure 1.1 Mindful Investment Decisions

and periodicals in publication; the financial shows with which the radio waves are congested;, and the content of cable television, offering more content around the clock than anyone can possibly assimilate. Well, yes, all of these sources are readily available. But so what? The answer lies not in how much information is available but in how much is important. The investing public doesn't suffer from a lack of information; they suffer from a lack of relevant information.

Our Purpose

As the editor of an investment newsletter I don't wish to come off as self-serving or hypocritical, but there are two critical elements to understand about this point: content and purpose. At *Investment Quality Trends* we produce all of our content internally for the purpose of helping the subscriber to make well-informed investment decisions. At inception we decided that to remain independent and completely objective we would accept no outside advertising. Therefore, our revenues are based solely on subscriptions. That fact necessitates that our content must fulfill subscribers' needs for information that results in good investment decisions and profits, which results in continued subscriptions.

By comparison, much of the mainstream financial media is big business beholden to shareholders who expect its company to generate big revenues. Like all publicly traded companies, the sole function is to generate a profit, just like any other business in America. The means by which big media produces its profits *is* by advertising revenues. Advertising revenues are based on the number of people—the audience—that medium reaches. To encourage people to read, listen to, or view their medium, they have to create interest and grab the audience's attention.

Unfortunately, the means by which the audience's interest is grabbed isn't necessarily useful information. And, when questionable information is distributed by sources that are thought to be highly knowledgeable and dependable, it only compounds the problem.

On the other hand the information that will work for the audience isn't always commercially attractive or appealing. So, in wanting to be entertained, much of the investing public gravitates toward information that is the equivalent of nutritionally empty fast food, and then they wonder why they are suffering from malnutrition. The tragedy is that with vast exposure comes the mantle of credibility, which, unfortunately, often fails to result in any meaningful, long-term success. It is unconscionable that important investing information can be displaced by ridiculous though entertaining discussions that are simply useless and can distract you from the basic purpose of investing: generating sufficient cash to meet your or someone else's current and future cash needs while limiting risk.

In addition to publishing *Investment Quality Trends,* we eat our own cooking for our private capital and as portfolio managers at our sister company for endowments, foundations, and the private trust accounts of high-net-worth individuals. The proven methods found in this book assist us in making thoughtful decisions about how to invest and realize the financial goals and objectives of our clients. From experience we have learned to ignore the useless information created by the junk food peddlers because it simply doesn't work. This book will show you what does work and how to properly use it to your advantage.

As portfolio managers we are subject to stringent legal and regulatory requirements and are held to a higher standard of competence. If we fail to meet our fiduciary responsibility, we are subject to tremendous liability. Consequently, we and like-minded professionals seek out and take advantage of the best information available; so should you.

Similarly to big financial media, the retail platform of investment products and advice, although well meaning, is designed for mass consumption. In a one-size-fits-all environment, it is inevitable that the average investor will be exposed to risks of which they are not aware. This is not an indictment of any individual but of the culture, which is sales and transaction oriented, not performance oriented.

Dividend Truth

Whether you buy individual stocks, mutual funds, or Exchange Traded Funds (ETFs) you do need to have a methodology and system to follow: however, a three-minute sound bite from a mutual fund or money manager isn't useful to the investor who lacks the skill set and experience to use it correctly. Professionals have skills and experience most investors don't have and/or don't want to take the time to acquire.

A Trusted Approach

The performance-oriented approach has three areas of focus: understand what you *need* so you can establish *achievable* goals; make investments with the highest probability for meeting those goals; and limit taxes and expenses. Repeated studies confirm that the decisions you make in these three areas will make the most impact on the success or failure of your investment plan. My experience is that if you adopt these methods into your mindful investment decision-making process you will enjoy higher returns while reducing your risk and increasing your chances of reaching your goals.

The strategy behind our approach, the dividend-value strategy, is based on the Dividend-Yield Theory, a value-based approach to investing. The term *value* can mean different things to different people. To us, knowing what represents value is the key to investing in the stock market. Investing in a company when it offers good historic value dramatically reduces downside risk to investment principal while providing the maximum upside potential for capital gains and growth of dividends.

Rather than some arbitrary definition or metric, the Dividend-Yield Theory uses a stock's dividend yield as the primary measure of value. Obviously price is important, but price on its own, without some substantive context, is meaningless. Beyond price then, an investor must have a proven method to establish whether the price of a company under investment consideration offers sufficient return potential to justify taking a risk with his investment capital.

According to the Dividend-Yield Theory, the price of a stock is *driven* by its yield. We delve into this concept deeper in following chapters, but in the simplest of terms, a stock is most attractive when it offers a high dividend yield. As investors rush in to lock down the high yield, their buying pushes the price higher. Eventually the price reaches an area where the current yield is no longer attractive and buying stops. With no new buyers to push the stock price higher, inertia sets in and the price begins to decline. At this juncture the early buyers will begin to sell and lock in their profits. When later investors see their profits evaporating, they will also sell to salvage what they can of their profits and principal. Eventually, the selling will push the yield back up to an area where once again it is sufficient to attract new buying interest.

So rather than emphasize price alone or a company's sector, products, or other analytical factors, the dividend-value strategy uses dividend-yield patterns to make buying and selling decisions. By understanding the historical dividend yield pattern of a company, the investor is better informed about whether the stock offers much value, little value, or somewhere in between.

One last aside as we begin our journey together: I will try to avoid industry jargon wherever possible. The English language is broad enough to explain this method and the process in a way that the everyday noninvestment professional can understand. This should help to lift the veil of mystery and confusion to what is actually a relatively simple process.

CHAPTER 2

The Case for Investing in Stocks

October. This is one of the peculiarly dangerous months to speculate in stocks. The others are July, January, September, April, November, May, March, June, December, August, and February.

—Mark Twain

As detailed extensively in Chapter 1, we all have practical living needs that generally must be purchased with cash. At some point, typically in retirement, you will need a pool of cash to supplement your other sources of income. Unless you are independently wealthy, hit the lottery, or inherit a fortune from Great Aunt Sally, your options for growing wealth are fairly limited; in short, you will have to invest. As with any major venture, those who begin with achieving a specific goal or outcome have a much greater chance for success. Investing is no different.

The biggest mistake investors make is committing hard-earned money to investments, with absolutely no idea of why they are making those investments. Some of you are no doubt saying to yourself, "This guy must be thick. People invest to make money!" Let's agree among ourselves that that is a given. Now let's drill down to the heart of the issue: Money for what; money for whom; and, money for when?

Investment Needs

These questions are important; the answers are critical to your success. Simply plunging half-cocked into the markets with only a nebulous concept of making as much money as possible is an invitation to disaster. Minimally, you need to know two things: how much and when. Knowing how much you will need and when you will need it will allow you to devise a strategy, not just any strategy but a personal strategy to meet your specific individual needs. Trust me, without this base level of understanding you will do one of two things: shoot for the moon by assuming more risk than necessary to reach your goals and objectives; or play it too close to the vest and fall short of your goals and objectives.

When it comes to needs, there is no one-size-fits-all. Every investor is an individual with unique needs and objectives. You may have more than one objective; you may even have to prioritize among competing objectives such as education, retirement, big-ticket purchases, or even possible elder or special needs care. These objectives could be near term, long term, or a combination of the two. Your objectives may also need to be approached separately because there may be different factors to consider. If you can clearly answer these questions you will be in a much stronger position to meet your needs.

Once you have the end in mind there is only one thing you need to understand about investing: The sole purpose of investing is to grow your capital and income base to meet a current or future cash need. If you believe you might not meet your cash goals and objectives you will panic and take unnecessary risks, which generally result in loss and disappointment. So in simple terms, investing is about meeting needs, not hitting the lottery.

Stocks, Bonds, or Cash?

An entire book can be written (indeed, many already exist) on this subject alone. For our purposes I want to keep this simple: For most investors the majority of their investments will be made in the three primary asset classes: stocks, fixed-income (bonds), and cash or cash equivalents.

Cash and cash equivalents (short-term instruments that can be liquidated quickly with little to no loss of principal) serve several purposes. One purpose is to provide liquidity to meet current obligations; another is to temporarily hold interest and dividends that are earmarked for reinvestment; lastly, cash is a short-term, low-risk alternative to stocks and bonds during periods of extreme market volatility.

As an asset class, stocks can be divided into many subsets: domestic and international; growth and value; large-cap, mid-cap, small-cap; developed and emerging markets, and so forth. The same is true for fixed-income instruments: taxable; tax-exempt; Treasuries; government agencies; mortgage-backed; high-yield; international; emerging markets, and so forth.

In addition to the common asset classes just listed, the contemporary financial marketplace also consists of alternative asset classes such as hedge funds, private equity, venture capital, direct real estate, precious metals and gemstones, art and antiquities, and, of course, futures and options contracts on almost everything. The list can go on forever.

Perhaps this is part of the problem: The investment landscape has become so cluttered and sophisticated that investors have lost site of the basics. When distilled down to the most basic level, however, there are two primary choices for investment capital: to loan or to own.

In the simplest of terms, when you invest in a fixed-income instrument—a CD, a T-Bill, a T-Bond, a corporate bond, a municipal bond—whatever the case, you are making a loan of your capital to the issuer. For the right to use your capital, the issuer promises to pay you a fixed rate of interest over the agreed upon period of the loan and to return your capital, in whole, at the end of the loan period, otherwise known as maturity.

When an investor buys shares of stock, he buys part ownership of a corporation. The return on a stock investment comes in two forms: capital appreciation (an increase in share price) and dividends, which we will discuss in greater detail shortly. Unlike a fixed-income investment, common stocks pay no fixed rate of interest and offer no guarantees for the return of capital.

The asset allocation decision (the percentage of capital allocated to stocks, bonds, and cash in a portfolio) is one of the basic yet most often confusing decisions an investor must make. Generally, the role of stocks is to provide long-term total returns (a combination of price appreciation and dividends). The role of bonds is to provide an income stream.

When considering the respective risks and rewards of stocks versus fixed-income, stocks, in theory, have unlimited appreciation potential. That is, there is no upper limit on how high the price of a stock may go.

A fixed-income investor, on the other hand, generally knows the maximum return potential for a fixed-income investment, especially if it is held to maturity. Although it is true that a fixed-income instrument can sell at a premium, prior to maturity, the potential for price appreciation is significantly lower than the potential for price appreciation in stocks.

This brings us to one of the major areas of disagreement among investors, financial academics, and the investment industry: What is risk? Before I address that question, a long-held tenet of investing is that risk goes hand-in-hand with reward: no risk, no reward. Based on your definition and understanding of risk, this may or may not be true.

My belief is that, if you ask the average investor (not a professional or academic) how they define risk, they would tell you it is the possibility of losing money on an investment, meaning a partial or total loss of the original investment principal. Financial academics—and the investment industry in general—define risk as the short-term (annual, monthly, or daily) volatility of returns. The volatility of returns is measured by variance or standard deviation; think fluctuation.

Without opening a huge can of worms, what is a loss? Is it a realized loss (selling an investment for less than the original outlay) or a paper loss (holding an investment with a current market value below the purchase price)? Don't laugh; you won't believe how people can get all tied up in knots over this.

For the short-term investor who may need the use of funds today, next week, or next month, there isn't much to argue here; any definition of loss means they have less money to work with and are feeling pain. For the long-term investor who has a 20-year time horizon, it might make strategic sense to take a quick realized loss on an investment gone awry because they have time to make up the difference and then some. On the other hand, if the investment is sound but just temporarily depressed (paper loss), why get shook up over short-term market fluctuations?

For the short-term investor, then, risk is not having sufficient liquid or near liquid funds to meet cash needs at the present and out to five years. If this applies to your situation, then you don't need to be anywhere near investments that can and will fluctuate significantly over the short-term, period.

As investment instruments, both stocks and bonds have apparent risks. Stocks may not have a theoretical ceiling, but they do have a bottom: Stocks can fall to zero and become worthless. With fixed-income investments, there is the possibility of a decline in the market value due to an increase in interest rates. There is also the possibility the issuer will be unable to make interest or principal payments on time or at all, effectively defaulting on the loan.

For the long-term investor, though, fixed-income investments have a whopper of a risk that is subtle to the eye yet very dangerous; that is, inflation risk. Inflation risk is the possibility that the stream of income payments and eventual return of principal will decline in purchasing power (not keep pace with inflation).

For the long-term investor, then, neither the average-investor definition nor the academic/industry definition adequately addresses risk. With regard to the average-investor definition, much of the risk can be mitigated through education about appropriate investment time horizons and limiting investment considerations to high-quality investments that offer historic good value.

With regard to the academic/industry definition of risk, short-term (annual or even less frequent) price fluctuations (volatility) aren't as relevant to the long-term investor with a 20-year time horizon as is building sufficient long-term wealth to meet future cash needs. Secondly, this focus on volatility is almost always based on nominal returns, which ignores the loss of purchasing power caused by inflation.

For short-term investors inflation isn't such a big concern but for long-term investors the impact can be huge.

The Case for Stocks

As the editor of a stock investment newsletter and portfolio manager that specializes in blue chip stocks, I am obviously an advocate of investing in stocks. Let me tell you why.

Most investors are familiar with the concept of total return: capital gains (price appreciation) plus dividend yield. As a formula we would write it like this:

$$\text{Capital gains} + \text{dividend yield} = \text{total return}$$

Let's use an example. You buy a stock for $25 per share and at the end of three years the price has increased to $50 per share. The capital gain is $25 per share or 100 percent. Let's assume the stock paid a $1 per share dividend the first year, a $1.10 dividend per share the next year, and $1.21 per share in dividends the third year. By adding the $3.31 in dividends to the $25 capital gain, the total gain equals $28.31.

To find the percentage return, we divide the total gain ($28.31) by the purchase price ($25), which is 113 percent. This represents the total return on investment for the three years. On a simple basis, the average annual return equals 37 percent per year.

Dividend Truth

Stocks are the best investment for the investor who:

- Desires growth of capital and income
- Ignores the "noise" of the markets
- Recognizes and appreciates good value
- Has the courage to buy at *undervalue*
- Has the patience to hold until the value is fully recognized
- Has the wisdom to sell at *overvalue*

The *IQ Trends* dividend-value strategy adds another component to the concept of total return, namely, dividend growth.

Capital gains + dividend yield + dividend growth = real total return

The growth potential of real total return is the underlying reason and really, the only viable reason for investors to invest in stocks.

Although fixed-income investments offer a fixed return, it is only in a declining interest rate environment that fixed-income investments offer the potential for capital gains. Growth of dividends, however, is only achievable in the stock market. In later chapters we delve deeper into the importance of dividends and dividend growth to stock prices, but for now, know that only in the stock market can you achieve real total return.

In the final analysis, the true benefit of real total return is only understood when you consider the damage inflicted on capital by the twin evils of taxes and inflation. That is, if nothing is left to spend or reinvest after taxes and inflation, you have nothing to show for the risk you assumed. If you are putting your hard-earned money at risk, then shouldn't it be in the area with the highest probability of leaving you with something to show for your efforts?

The Growth Rates of Stocks

For the 83-year period from 1926–2008, the nominal, compound average rate of return for stocks (the S&P 500) was 9.60 percent. Twenty-year government bonds returned 5.70 percent and 30-day Treasury Bills 3.70 percent. Adjusting for a compound average rate of inflation at 3.0 percent, the real returns were 7.10 percent, 2.20 percent, and 0.50 percent, respectively.

Dividend Truth

When considering rates of returns, it is important to understand the difference between nominal returns and real returns. What you make is the nominal return; what you keep is the "real" or after-inflation return.

A simple example of nominal return is a fixed-income instrument with a 5 percent coupon. There are different ways of measuring this, but the 5 percent basically means for every $100 you invest you will earn about $5 per year.

Real return is what you earn after subtracting the rate of inflation. Using the above example, if your fixed instrument pays you a nominal rate of 5 percent, and inflation, or the annual increase in the cost of living, is about 3 percent, your real return is about 2 percent. It is the real return that you can spend or reinvest.

After you factor in taxes, 30-day Treasury Bills are a virtual wash and 20-year Treasury Bonds are only slightly better. Only stocks have historically provided real, long-term growth of capital.

Now to be fair, nobody has an 83-year investment time horizon. There is also the argument that historical returns are irrelevant because those economic conditions are not applicable to today's—maybe, maybe not. What I know about the stock market though is that it takes everything into consideration: the past, present, and as a discounting mechanism, the future.

Without the benefit of clairvoyance, we have to look at what we do know, and that is the past. Although the past guarantees nothing, it does provide insight into how investments have performed under various economic conditions over varying time frames.

The common trap when looking at the past, however, is to cherry-pick the data that supports the thesis. Indeed, there is an entire body of investment theory that is based on torturing the data until it confesses; I won't be a party to that and you deserve better. That being said, it is reasonable to review holding periods that are representative of those of the average investor so we can find some commonality for returns.

Let's start with a very reasonable time-frame of 20 years as shown in Figure 2.1. In the 64 rolling 20-year holding periods from 1926 through 2008, stocks (the S&P 500) outperformed fixed-income (20-year government bonds) in each instance except two: the 20 years from 1929–1948 and 1989–2008. Let's put that into perspective: Stocks outperformed bonds in 62 of 64 20-year periods, or 96.8 percent of the time.

That is a pretty high batting average, which almost begs the question of what happened in the two periods when stocks underperformed bonds. For the period beginning in 1929 the answer is fairly simple—the Great Crash of 1929. By the time it ended in 1932, stocks had declined by almost 90 percent. It takes a while to dig out of a hole that deep.

For the 20-year period beginning in 1989 the story is a little different. Instead of stock prices declining at the beginning of the period, as in 1929–1932, the declines came at the end of the period: 2000–2002 and October 2007 through the end of 2008.

Per the norm, analysts and economists disagree about the reasons for the declines in these two periods. In the final analysis, the only opinion that matters is that of the investors who did the buying and selling. In both periods, however, there is a strong argument that valuations were excessive. From 1926 through 1928 stocks increased by 120.40 percent on a nominal basis, a simple average annual return of 40 percent per year. From 1989–1999 stocks increased by 221.40 percent on a nominal basis, a simple

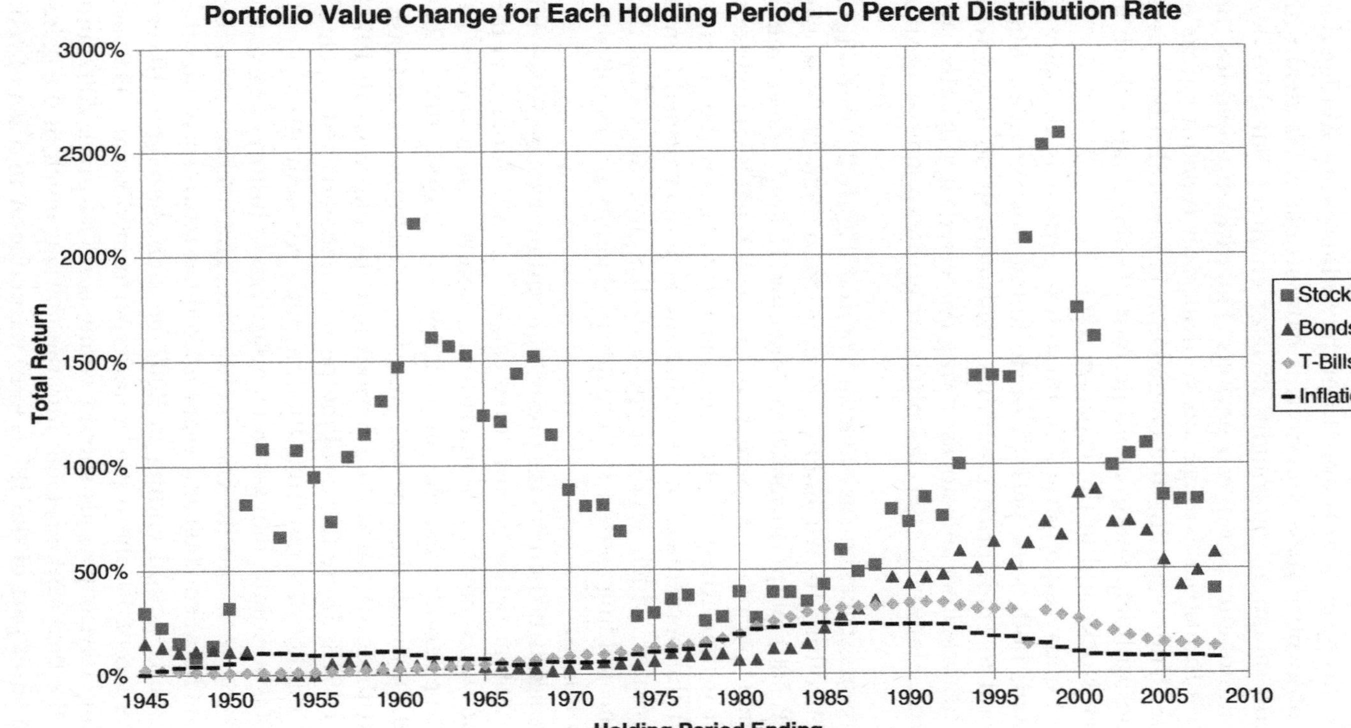

Figure 2.1 Rolling 20-Year Holding Periods from 1926–2008

Source: *Stocks, Bonds, Bills, and Inflation Yearbook,* 2008, Ibbotson Associates.

average annual return of 20.12 percent per year. A 20 percent return in any given year is not out of the ordinary—to average that for 11 consecutive years, however, is extraordinary. We deal with values and valuations thoroughly in later chapters, but there was some commonality in the two periods. The dividend-yield for the Dow Jones Industrial Average was at historically repetitive areas of overvalue. Understanding the connection between dividend-yield and values will help you to avoid periods of overvaluation both in individual stocks and in the broad market.

That bonds outperformed in these two periods is also easy to understand; both were periods of declining interest rates, when bonds tend to enjoy price premiums. With current bond yields at or near historic lows and stocks having corrected significantly, you have to consider which asset class offers the greater potential moving forward.

If 20 years strikes you as too long a period, Figure 2.2 shows that in the 74 rolling 10-year holding periods from 1926–2008, stocks (the S&P 500) outperformed fixed-income (20-year government bonds) in 64 periods or 86 percent of the time. What is immediately apparent is that, when the holding period decreases (20 years to 10 years) the percentage of time that stocks outperformed bonds also decreases, which lends support to the argument that the longer the holding period the greater probability stocks will outperform bonds.

Once again, 86 percent is a pretty high batting average. As we did with the 20-year periods above, what can we learn by looking at the 10 periods when stocks underperformed bonds? The first four 10-year rolling periods were the ones that ended in 1937, 1938, 1939 and 1940. Obviously these periods were impacted by the Great Crash. The next three 10-year rolling periods are also interrelated: 1974, 1977 and 1978. These three rolling periods encompassed much of the bear market that ran from 1966 through year-end 1974.

In 2000 one of the longest bull market runs in history came to an end with the tech and dot-com meltdowns. The declines over the three years between 2000 and year-end 2002 were so severe that the 10-year rolling period ending in 2002 became the eighth 10-year rolling period of 10 where stocks underperformed bonds. The last two rolling 10-year periods should come as no surprise: 2007 and 2008. As the bear sank his teeth into the markets much of the gains from the latter part of the 1990s were washed away in a sea of red.

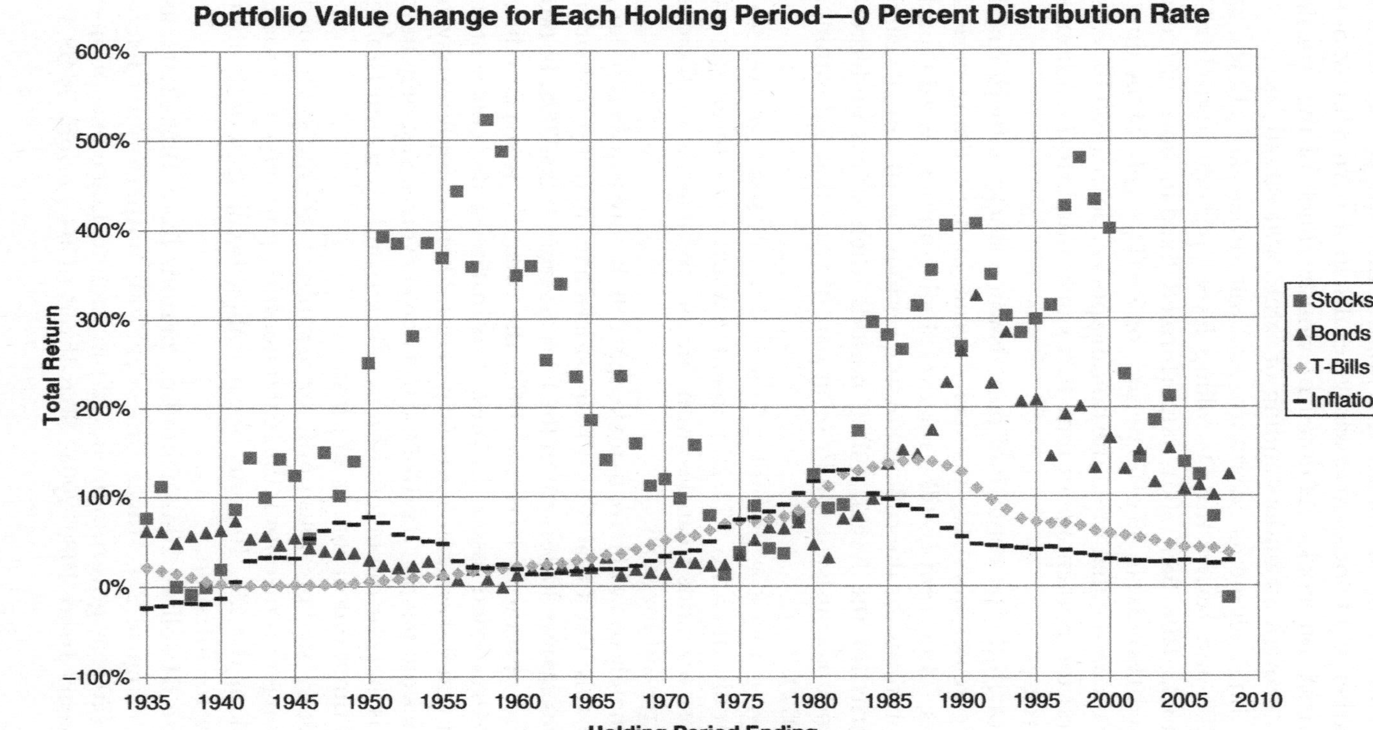

Figure 2.2 Rolling 10-Year Holding Periods from 1926–2008

Source: *Stocks, Bonds, Bills, and Inflation Yearbook*, 2008, Ibbotson Associates.

What should be obvious at this point is that any period when a bear market is in force necessarily results in a period of underperformance for stocks. As noted previously, much of this can be avoided through an understanding of values and valuations.

The final segments of returns we will review are shown in Figure 2.3 and review the 79 rolling 5-year periods from 1926–2008. Stocks (the S&P 500) outperformed fixed-income (20-year government bonds) in 58 of 79 periods or 73.41 percent of the time. Once again we see that when the holding period decreases (10 years to 5 years) the percentage of time that stocks outperformed bonds also decreases.

Although the percentage of periods when stocks outperformed bonds decreases when the number of years in the holding period decreases, 73 percent is still a relatively high number. As we found with the returns for the rolling holding periods for 10 and 20 years, the returns for the 5-year rolling periods when stocks underperformed bonds consisted wholly or in part of years that fell within a bear market.

Knowing investor psychology the way I do, some of you are undoubtedly thinking "73.41 percent is darn near three out of four; those are odds I can live with. Maybe five years is a sufficient holding period for stocks."

Ultimately you will have to make that call. Before you do, though, consider this: On a real return basis, stocks have had four calendar year losses of over 30 percent in the 83 years from 1926–2008. In two of the four instances, 1931 and 1974, the calendar year preceding each also recorded losses. In these two instances the consecutive calendar year losses totaled over 50 percent. There's simply no way to put lipstick on that pig. If two of the five years in your investment time horizon is that one out of four when stocks go south, you aren't going to think three out of four is so great.

As I suggested previously, where the rubber really meets the road for the long-term investor is the real (after-inflation) return. As such, let's look at the 20-, 10-, and 5-year rolling holding periods after adjusting for inflation.

In the 64 rolling 20-year holding periods from 1926–2008, as shown in Figure 2.4, stocks (the S&P 500) outperformed fixed-income (20-year government bonds) in each instance except one: the 20 years from 1989–2008. Sixty-three of 64 periods is 98.43 percent.

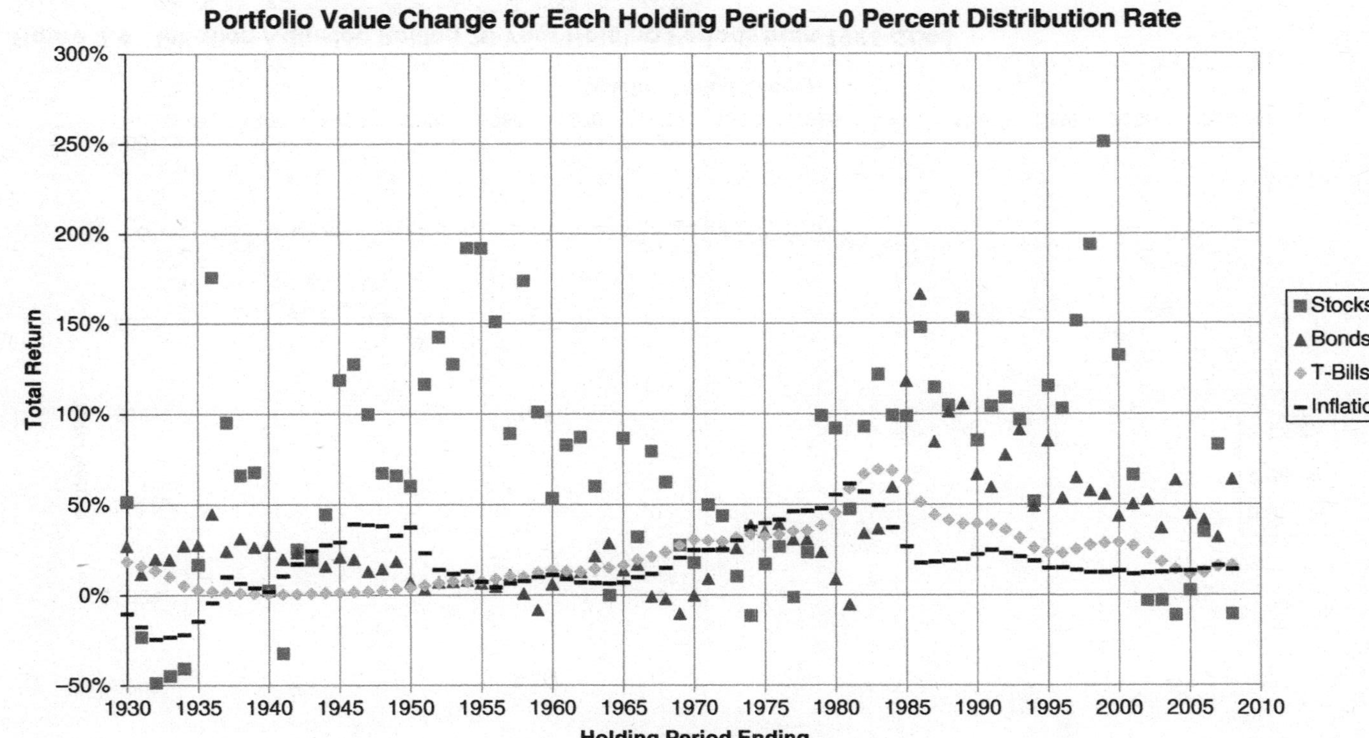

Figure 2.3 Rolling 5-Year Holding Periods from 1926–2008

Source: *Stocks, Bonds, Bills, and Inflation Yearbook,* 2008, Ibbotson Associates.

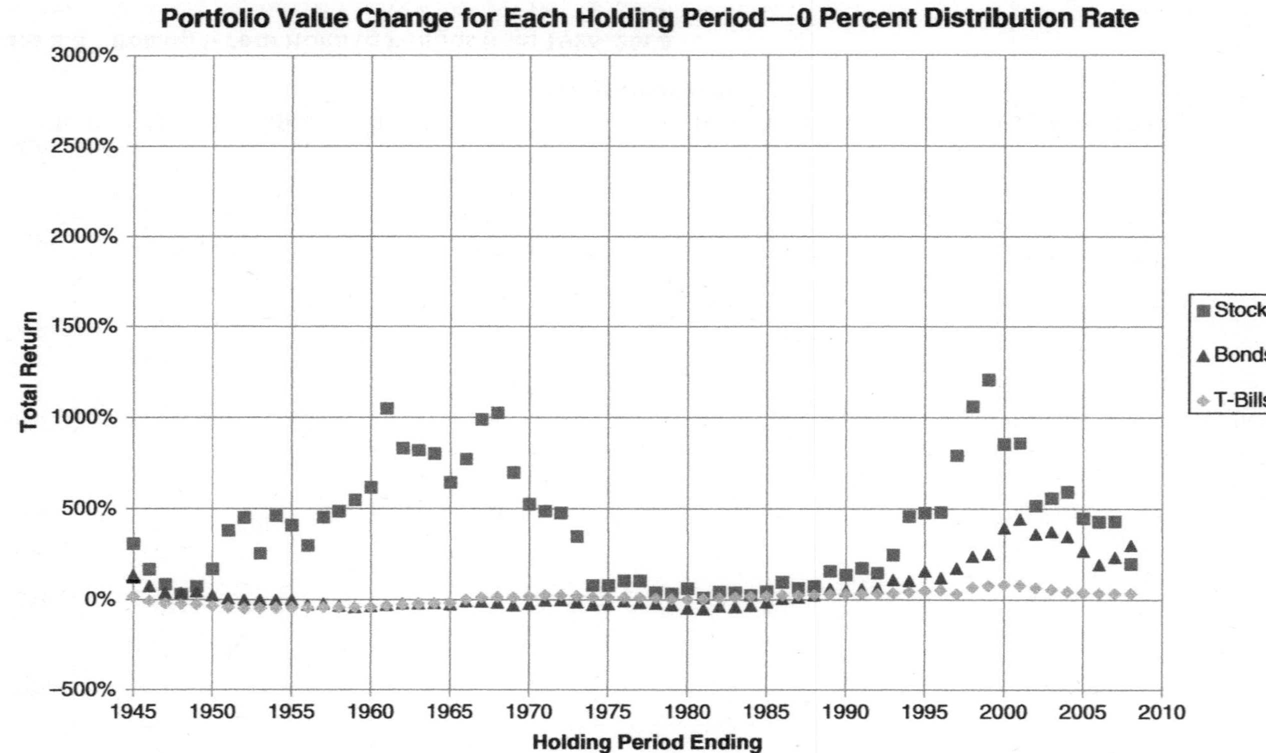

Figure 2.4 Inflation Adjusted Rolling 20-Year Holding Periods from 1926–2008

Source: *Stocks, Bonds, Bills, and Inflation Yearbook*, 2008, Ibbotson Associates.

In the 74 rolling 10-year holding periods from 1926–2008 as shown in Figure 2.5, stocks (the S&P 500) outperformed fixed-income (20-year government bonds) in 63 periods or 85 percent of the time; that is one less period than on a nominal basis.

In the 79 rolling 5-year holding periods from 1926–2008, as shown in Figure 2.6, stocks (the S&P 500) outperformed fixed-income (20-year government bonds) in 58 of the 79 periods or 73.41 percent of the time; these are identical to the results on a nominal basis.

Knowledge, Strategy, and Tactics

We have covered a lot of ground in this chapter, so let me summarize the most salient points. Inflation is a constant in our capital system. As such, the cost of the practical necessities will probably continue to increase over time. In the event you don't earn, inherit, or win a fortune, you will necessarily need to set aside and invest a portion of your capital to build a pool of cash and stream of income to meet your future needs.

The major risk for the short-term investor is a capital loss. The major risk for the long-term investor is inflation and insufficient capital growth.

Of the myriad asset classes available for investment, most of your investment decisions will be centered on the allocation of your investment capital into the three primary asset classes of stocks, bonds, and cash.

Bonds provide for a specific rate of return over a specified period and a return of investment principal upon maturity. With the exception of a period of declining interest rates, the potential for capital appreciation is minimal. The apparent investment risks for bonds are interest rate fluctuations and credit risk. The less apparent risk for bonds is the long-term loss of purchasing power due to inflation.

Stocks do not provide for a specific rate of return over a specific period nor for a return of investment principal. Theoretically, stocks have unlimited potential for capital appreciation, but they also have a bottom; they can go to zero and become worthless. The obvious risk for stocks is short-term volatility or price fluctuation. Last and most important, stocks are the only investment vehicles that offer the potential for real total return: capital gains + dividends + dividend growth.

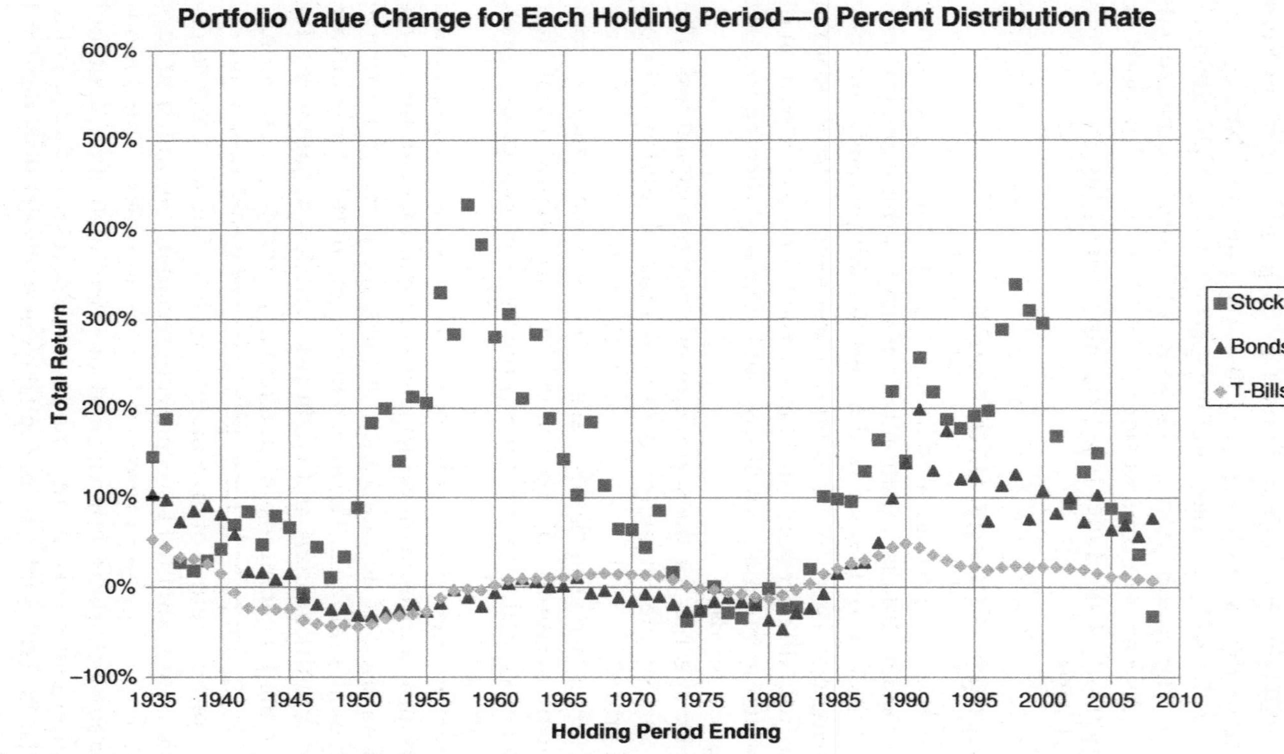

Figure 2.5 Inflation Adjusted Rolling 10-Year Holding Periods from 1926–2008

Source: *Stocks, Bonds, Bills, and Inflation Yearbook,* 2008, Ibbotson Associates.

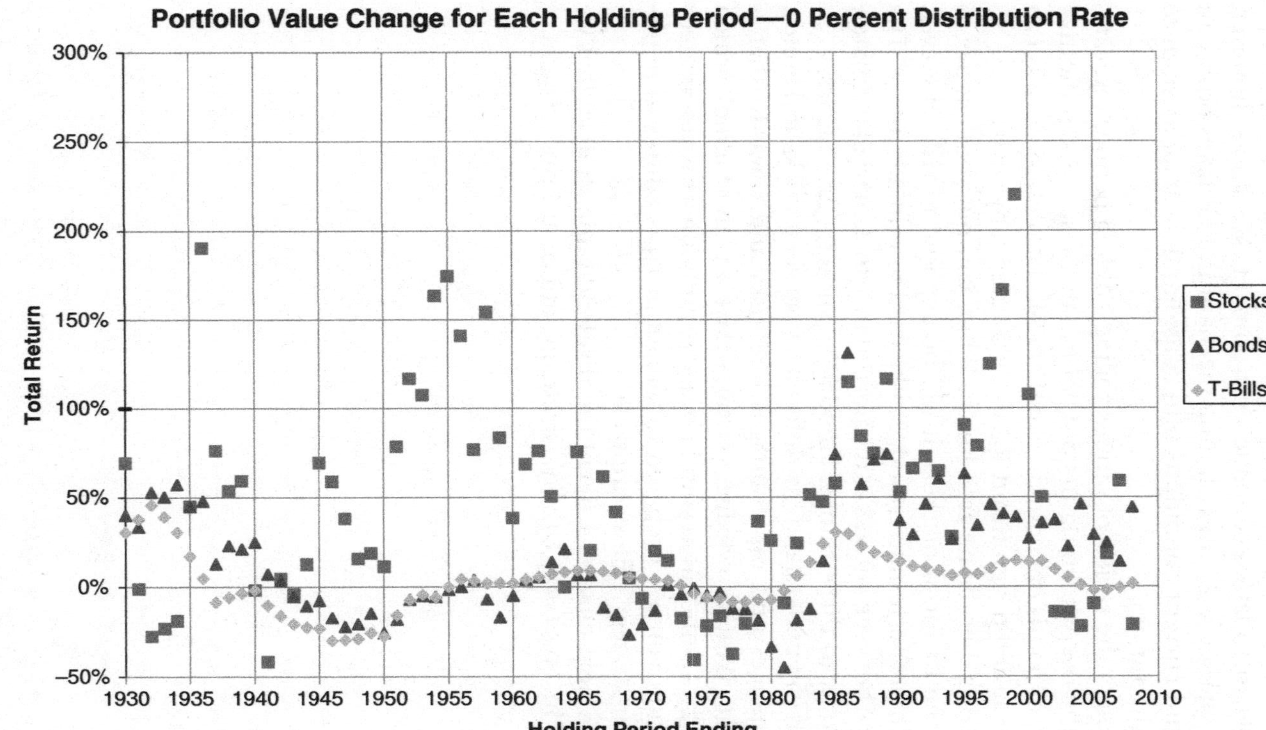

Figure 2.6 Inflation Adjusted Rolling 5-Year Holding Periods from 1926–2008

Source: *Stocks, Bonds, Bills, and Inflation Yearbook*, 2008, Ibbotson Associates.

No one has tomorrow's newspaper, so the future is uncertain. What we do have is historical data, which may or may not be applicable to today's economic environment. We know, however, that the markets are a discounting mechanism that takes both past history and current conditions into consideration in an attempt to discern the future.

Although the review of various rolling holding periods indicates that, in the overwhelming majority of instances, stocks significantly outperform bonds on a nominal and after-inflation basis, stocks can and have suffered significant losses on a calendar-year basis.

In short, there is no free lunch. When you put your money to work in the financial markets, it will be exposed to risk. However, risk, when properly understood, can be used to your advantage. The difference between success and failure in the stock market ultimately comes down to three things: knowledge, strategy, and tactics.

When you understand the differences between stocks and bonds, the advantages and disadvantages, the risks and rewards, that is knowledge. With knowledge you can devise a plan of attack, which is a strategy. Confident in your knowledge and with a proven strategy at the ready, you are prepared to initiate the procedures to implement your strategy. Those are tactics.

In the next chapter I detail the dividend-value strategy that we advocate in *Investment Quality Trends* and utilize at Private Client.

CHAPTER 3

The Dividend-Value Strategy

If you don't know where you are going, any road will get you there.
—Lewis Carroll

Any serious student of the stock market and investment history is undoubtedly aware of the vast collection of colorful characters that have achieved either fame, infamy, or both for their spectacular successes and/or even more spectacular failures. Many of these stories are true; an equal number, perhaps more, are myths.

Whether these stories are true is unimportant, what these characters represent is: winning and losing. Everybody loves a winner and more often than not we in the United States turn them into heroes. When it comes to investing in the stock market, however, many investors can more readily identify with the losers than the winners, which is unfortunate.

Losing money hurts more than just the pocketbook; it vexes the soul. When you take a loss in the stock market, it is not uncommon to feel a variety of emotions: anger, guilt, perhaps humiliation. The fact is that, if you invest long enough, you are going to take your share of losses; nobody gets a free pass.

No matter your level of intelligence, success in the stock market can be elusive and transitory. Over the course of my career I have met many people who were flat out brilliant in their field of endeavor, yet who were completely hapless when it came to investing in the stock market. In many cases, these brilliant people, who in the rest of their life have experienced nothing but success, have chosen to throw in the towel and just give up, which was unfortunate and entirely unnecessary.

What few investors understand is that the stock market is the grandest of competitions, the game of all games, played out on a global scale. As anyone who has ever competed on any level knows, every game has its rules! In the stock market, as in any other competitive situation, the best players—the winners—are those who have knowledge and a strategy. Winning, not surprisingly, is much easier with the right strategy.

Obviously there are some major differences between investing in the stock market and a simple pastime. For one, the stakes are higher—the potential loss of hard-won earnings, savings, and security both now and in the future.

But for the winner, the rewards are also higher. Beyond the gain in wealth, few things are more satisfying than the thrill of the hunt, the joy of discovery, and the lasting satisfaction of a victory that is heightened because of the importance of this endeavor. And winning is much easier with the right strategy.

The Two Paths of Stock Return

Most investors who buy stocks do so with the hope of realizing a good rate of return. Hope, however, is not a strategy. For the investor who chooses the stock market as the avenue to grow their wealth, it is important to understand the elements that comprise the return on investment in stocks. More often than not, the most tangible element of return, the dividend, goes underappreciated.

All stock investors want the price of their stocks to increase, but stock prices don't rise because of simple desire; they need a catalyst, a reason for investors to buy and push the price higher. The underlying premise of the dividend-value strategy is that the dividend yield is the major driver for the price of a stock. Think about it: All things being equal, when is a stock most attractive to investors? When its dividend yield is high.

An attractive dividend and high-yield is all but impossible for savvy investors to ignore. As the lure of securing a high yield attracts investors, the price of the stock begins to move higher. As price and yield have an inverse relationship, climbing stock prices result in declining yields. When the yield declines to a level where it is no longer enticing, investor interest, and therefore buying, disappears.

Without investor demand, the price of the stock will begin to decline until it reaches a price point where the yield is again sufficient to attract new buying interest.

When compared to the analytical systems that focus on price patterns, a company's products and services, price/earnings to growth (PEG) ratios, earnings yield, or a host of other measures, the elegant simplicity of focusing on the dividend yield emerges. That is, knowing that a stock is attractive when the dividend yield is high and unattractive when it is low provides the investor an objective measure of whether a stock's price is high, low, or somewhere in between. Because the relationship between price and yield is the centerpiece of the dividend-value strategy, it makes sense to flesh out the related concepts in detail.

There are two components that comprise the return on a stock market investment. Not surprisingly, the one most investors focus on is capital or price appreciation; everyone wants to sell a stock for a profit. The other component is the dividend, which represents an immediate return on investment. When combined into one measure, the two components become what is known as the total return.

I think it is fairly safe to say that every time an investor buys a share of stock he does so with the absolute certainty that he will sell it later at a profit. Over time, after the inevitable loss or losses, the illusion of certainty is replaced with the wisdom that is gained only through experience; namely, in the stock market, nothing is certain. What isn't illusory, though, is the dividend. Once received the dividend is yours to keep, a tangible return on investment that the market can't snatch away from you as it can a paper profit.

Dividend Truth

A dividend is the portion of a company's earnings that is distributed to its owners, the shareholders. The dividend is most often quoted in terms of the dollar amount each share receives (dividends per share). It can also be quoted in terms of a percent of the current market price, referred to as dividend yield. Dividends are most often paid in cash or additional shares of stock, though they could be paid in scrip, company products, or property. The board of directors decides on the form and amount; ordinarily, dividends are paid quarterly.

Table 3.1 Dividend Yield

Company	Price	Dividend	Dividend Yield
Trinity Corp.	$44	$1.60	3.63%
Keegan, Inc.	$76	$1.80	2.36%
Jillian, Ltd.	$18	$1.28	7.11%
Evan Industries	$69	$2.72	3.94%
Christian & Co.	$25	$1.64	6.56%

Now that you understand what a dividend is and how to calculate the return in terms of yield, let's look closer at the relationship between price, yield, and value. Let's take two stocks, one priced at $10 a share that pays a $.50 dividend and one priced at $20 that pays a $1 dividend.

Beyond the fact that $20 is twice that of $10 and $1 is twice that of $.50, they have equal value in terms of dividend yield; both pay 5.0 percent dividends. Because stock prices and dividends rarely fall into such easy-to-calculate round numbers as in the previous example, let's look at some more examples of how the dividend yield is calculated. Remember, yield is calculated on the price paid for the stock, so unless there is a change in the dividend, the yield on purchase remains constant no matter what the stock's current price is. Table 3.1 shows further information on dividend yield. The company names in this example are fictitious.

Whether dividends or capital appreciation is your favored component of return, you still need a means by which to define and identify the value for any stock under investment consideration.

Measures of Value

Traditionally there are three fundamental measurements of value: price-to-earnings ratio (P/E), price-to-book ratio (PB), and dividend yield. What is immediately apparent with the two ratios *is that they are centered on price. Price, without substantive context, is meaningless.* Of the three measures, the dividend yield is the only one related to an actual return on investment—the dividend payment. So beyond the value of the income to the investor, dividends provide tangible evidence that the company is *actually* making money, which is something that an earnings statement or book values cannot prove.

Dividend Truth

The three fundamental measures of value are:

1. Dividend yield
2. Price/earnings ratio
3. Price/book-value ratio

Quality of Earnings

Earnings are the lifeblood of every company and the sole reason the company exists—to generate a profit. With earnings, however, what is real and what is reported can be two entirely different things. That is, a corporate earnings statement can be a labyrinth to navigate through, with its seemingly endless collection of footnotes, exceptions, and variables. In simple terms, earnings can be sliced and diced to the point where they are often unintelligible. Why is this? To be fair, a company's earnings can be impacted by myriad events ranging from the simple to very complex. A change in company leadership, for example, can lead to asset sales or a string of acquisitions. All these things must be duly noted; however, a recurring pattern of revisions and restatements might be indicative of less than forthright reporting. That earnings can be manipulated is not in question; it happens frequently to varying degrees for varying reasons. To some this may appear cynical, but when you get down to the bottom line, earnings are often what a financial officer says they are.

Rising Dividends Boost Share Price

With the preceding text as a frame of reference, we see why dividend-yield trends are a more predictive indicator for stock price appreciation/depreciation. When a dividend is increased, the price of a stock (which generally represents current value) typically rises to reflect the increased value of the investment. Conversely, when a dividend is lowered, the stock price typically declines to reflect reduced investment value and expectations for further reductions in earnings, not to mention the loss of anticipated income to the investor. The only variable in this equation is the amount of time for the market to realize the increase/decrease in value and adjust the price accordingly.

Why Dividends Are So Important

"The proof is in the pudding boy," was one of my grandfather's many folksy colloquialisms to make a point or teach a lesson. When applied to dividends, it underscores the point that they are tangible proof of a return on investment. When a company has a long-term track record for consistent and rising dividend payments, there is simply no better indicator about the state of the company's financial health. Dividends are real money; the check either clears or it doesn't. Dividends prove the company is making money; you can't pay what you don't have. So instead of trying to determine profitability by studying a company's earnings, study its dividend history. At the end of the day dividends are the surest confirmation of a company's profitability, since dividends can arise only from the reality of earnings.

Now let's take this a step further. If you stop and think about it, there is really only one reason a company's management and board of directors votes for a dividend increase—higher earnings or the reasonable expectation for higher earnings. Once again, the only variable is the amount of time it takes for the market to realize the increased value to the stock because of the dividend increase to push the price higher. This is where the virtue of patience is paramount.

Even if an investor doesn't require immediate income from his stocks, he can still appreciate that dividends provide a floor of safety under the price of a stock. From experience, we know that savvy market observers pay close attention to dividend yield, and when the price of a stock falls to a level that creates an attractive return, investment capital will flow into the stock and halt the decline. A stock that pays no dividend has no such downside protection for its price.

Total Return Revisited

Although this concept was addressed earlier in Chapter 2, it is central to the dividend-value strategy and the underlying justification for investing in the stock market. The primary advantage of a stock investment is the potential for total return:

Dividend yield + capital gains = total return

From the Dividend-Yield Theory comes another factor to add to that equation: dividend growth.

Dividend yield + dividend growth + capital gains = real total return

The idea of real total return is, has been, and always will be the underlying reason why investors are willing to risk their capital in common stocks. It has been the fundamental attraction of stock market investments since they began.

Although the bond market can offer a fixed return and, depending on the trend in interest rates, some potential for capital gains, the growth of dividend income is only available in the stock market. As detailed earlier, dividend growth is the catalyst for and most accurate predicator of rising stock prices.

Over the course of the past 44 years there are untold examples of stocks that realized rates of real total return that would have been virtually impossible to obtain in any other investment vehicle with a commensurate degree of risk. These stocks had been held for several years, during which time there were consistent dividend increases, which precipitated consistent price increases. Here's an example to illustrate the point.

One of the world's most widely recognized brand names is that of McDonald's (MCD), which virtually created the quick-service restaurant industry and today operates and franchises about 32,000 restaurants in 118 countries.

Despite its history and status as *the* American icon company, McDonald's struggled during the late 1990s and early 2000s. Derided in some analytical corners as a relic of the past and a dying industry, McDonald's in many ways epitomized the shift in consumer attitudes away from the old-school brick-and mortar model to the new school of hip-slick-and-cool, as represented by Starbucks.

In 2003, McDonald's management decided it would not go quietly into the night and initiated a corporate strategy to put the luster back into the Golden Arches. Part of the strategy was a commitment to shareholders to increase the value of their investment through a combination of share buybacks and dividend increases; were they ever serious! In 2002 McDonald's (MCD) dividend was $0.06 per quarter or $0.24 per year. By the end of 2003 the dividend had been increased by 60 percent to $0.10 a quarter or $0.40 per year. The dividend has been consistently raised each year since, and through August 2009, the dividend was $.50 per quarter or $2.00 per year.

The first incremental dividend increase in 2003 put MCD into our undervalued area and on our radar screen. Our initial purchases were made at $15 per share and again at $19 per share. At the time of this writing, the stock is trading at $57, just shy of a 300 percent capital gain. More importantly, though, our initial dividend has increased by almost 1,000 percent and our yield on purchase is approximately 10 percent.

Some readers are undoubtedly wondering why we haven't sold this stock to harvest the gains. As will be explained more thoroughly in later chapters, MCD still represents good historic value due to the frequency and size of dividend increases. Figure 3.1 shows a graphic display of this fundamental value in the accompanying chart. As you can see, the stock still has considerable upside potential.

With the potential for real total returns, such as those illustrated by the example of McDonald's, you begin to see how a stock that is held long enough for the concept to work can outpace the twin evils of taxes and inflation.

Dividend Truth

The reasoning behind real total return is a long-term investment concept that will not appeal to short-term traders. It deals with averages—an average dividend yield, average dividend growth, and average annual price appreciation.

To be fair, we cannot be sure that dividends will rise in each and every year. We cannot be sure when and to what extent stock prices will rise. Indeed, since October 2007 the markets have been undergoing the corrective process known as a bear market. However, if stocks are purchased at historically undervalued price levels, and if those stocks have a long, uninterrupted history of dividend payments

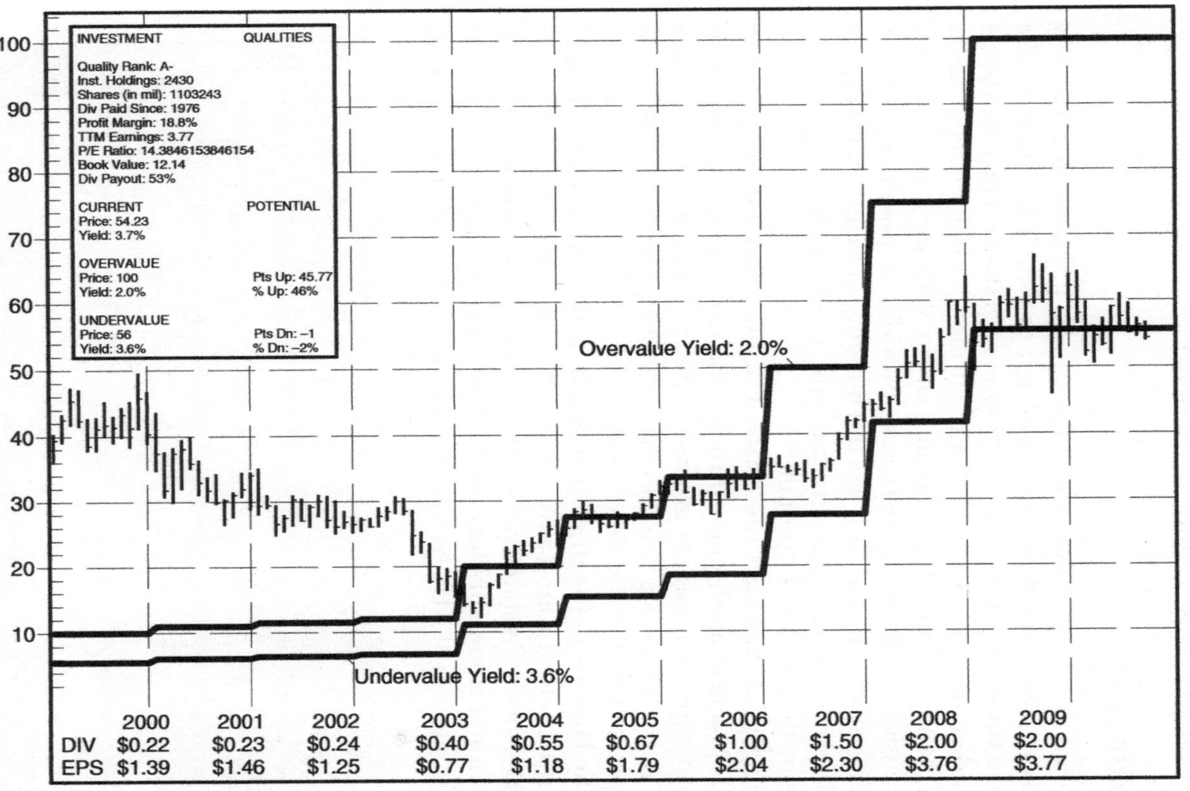

Figure 3.1 McDonald's (MCD)

Source: *Value Trend Analysis.*

and of frequent dividend increases, then over a period of years the real total return on that investment is likely to outperform the total return on any other kind of investment.

Quality Tells

Although the dividend-value strategy can be implemented with any company paying dividends long enough to establish a pattern, the chances for success are greater with blue-chip stocks. Forty-four years of market research show that the dividend-value strategy, when implemented through high-quality stocks with long track records for consistent dividend increases, provides a powerful tool for building wealth. In the end, it is the building of wealth, both capital and income to meet the present and future cash needs of the investor, that is most important.

Figure 3.2 illustrates the concept of the Dividend-Yield Theory and its practical application through the dividend-value strategy in generic terms. The simple premise is that a decision to buy or sell a stock at a certain price is tied to the underlying value of its dividends as expressed by the dividend yield.

The Holy Grail for all stock investors is to buy low and sell high. Unfortunately, for most investors, high and low are typically references for price. As stated previously, though, price without substantive context is meaningless. In 2003 McDonald's was undervalued at $15, but also at $19, *because its dividend yield represented historically*

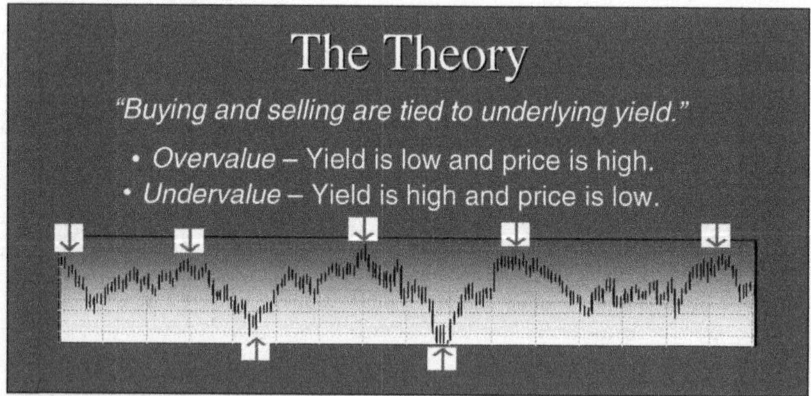

Figure 3.2 The Dividend-Yield Theory
Source: *Investment Quality Trends.*

good value. The same was true in 2004 at $40 and again in 2009 at $57. So without a way to measure value, high and low are nothing but nebulous concepts.

From our perspective, this is fairly simple stuff; the theory and strategy are pretty basic to investing. Maybe it's too basic, because the simplicity often confuses investors who seem determined to find a more complicated method for growth of capital and income and, ultimately, financial security. For over 44 years though, when the concept is applied to high-quality dividend trends, it can help the investor to:

- Minimize downside risk in the stock market
- Maximize upside potential for capital gains
- Maximize growth of dividend income, which allows investors to keep pace with inflation

Dividend Truth

As a general rule, a stock is *overvalued* when it has a relatively high price and a low dividend yield. It is *undervalued* when it has a relatively low price and a high dividend yield.

The Natural Order

The Tax Reform Act of 2003 dramatically lowered the rate of federal income tax levied against dividends received from qualifying companies. For those who believe dividends are a waste of corporate capital, the commonly heard refrain since passage of the Act is "watch what happens to dividend-paying stocks when Congress returns the tax rate to pre-Act levels."

The fact of the matter is that Congress is continually tinkering with the tax code. Depending on the administration and your philosophical side of the aisle, these adjustments can be perceived as positive, negative, or neutral. However, some fail to remember that the markets are dynamic, constantly adjusting to economic fluctuation, legislation, taxation, and innovation; in short, the markets adjust.

Detractors also forget that investors have flocked to dividends since investment records have been kept, so the philosophy that the dividend yield of a quality company can reveal volumes about a stock's future performance is not dependent on a certain tax environment or a particular market cycle. It is a basic principle, one that serves as a consistent guide through even the most frustrating market phases.

"The underlying principles of sound investment should not alter from decade to decade," writes Benjamin Graham in his classic work, *The Intelligent Investor,* "but the application of these principles must be adapted to significant changes in the financial mechanisms and climate."

Dividend Truth

To get the most benefit from the dividend-yield philosophy and adapt it to any stock market "mechanisms and climate" requires the mastering of several illuminating concepts. An investor must

- Confirm the value of a stock
- Identify quality
- Grasp the significance of cycles

Dividends *Still* Don't Lie

A lot of water has passed beneath the bridge since Geraldine Weiss first wrote *Dividends Don't Lie* in 1988. Investment theories have come and gone, various trading techniques and alternative investment vehicles have enjoyed a brief moment in the investment sun only to be abandoned when proven imperfect or ineffective, and investors have flocked to and fled from myriad fads, phenomena, and false hope.

Through it all, one thing has remained constant—the dividend. Dividends are *still* the most reliable component of investment return because dividends are *still* real money. Balance sheets and earnings statements can weave visions of grandeur but they don't put money in your pocket. When a company pays a dividend, it can't be revised or restated. Once a dividend leaves the company bank, it is irretrievable. No number of adjustments, schemes, or tricks can be used to fudge a dividend payment; it's either paid or it isn't. In short, dividends tell a truth that no company report can.

It turns out "creative accounting"
is a creative term for "white collar crime."

Source: *Reprinted with permission.*

In the wake of the Enron and World-Com scandals at the start of the decade and the more recent meltdowns in the banking and credit industries, corporate management and boards of directors are under greater scrutiny than in any previous period in financial market history. As such, ever-greater care and deliberation is being given to the declaration and payment of dividends.

Even without this heightened scrutiny, the management and directors of quality corporations know far better than anyone else the financial condition of their company and the likely direction that future earnings will take. Given the apparent ramifications of pending legislation alongside those existing in Sarbanes-Oxley, competent, well-managed blue chip companies with long track records of excellence and performance are not going to pay or increase a dividend unless the payout is fiscally justified and sound. For these reasons, a trend of consistently rising dividends is more indicative of a company's health and well being than any other measure. For the investor seeking a reliable return on investment from a predictable stream of dividends, there is an added bonus: A trend of rising dividends is also a reliable predictor for future capital growth.

At this juncture, you should have a solid grasp on the concepts that dividends and dividend yields are a component of return, a measure of value, and a predictor of growth. Going forward we explain how to apply these concepts to the process of building a portfolio, managing the portfolio through various market cycles, and anticipating future share price and market directions.

CHAPTER 4

Quality and Blue Chip Stocks

The sweetness of low price is soon forgotten; but the bitterness of poor quality is long remembered.

—Anonymous

A value-based approach to investing such as the dividend-value strategy is a powerful arrow to have in your investment quiver. When properly implemented through high-quality companies that represent historically good value, an investor is well-armed to out-duel the competition.

The terms *quality* and *value* are repeated frequently throughout this book because they are the twin pillars on which the foundation of the dividend-value strategy rests. In previous chapters we have discussed the importance of value in a generic way; in later chapters the discussion will become much more specific.

Before we get into the finer aspects of value identification, however, it is important to introduce and understand the concept of quality and its underlying importance. As stated previously, the dividend-value strategy can be implemented with any company that has paid dividends long enough to establish a repetitive pattern. For optimum investment results, however, it is best implemented through high-quality, blue chip stocks.

More than 40 years of research shows that the dividend-value strategy, when implemented through high-quality stocks with long track records of excellence and performance, provides a powerful tool for building wealth. At the end of the day, it is the building of wealth, both of capital and income, to meet the present and future cash needs of the investor that is most important.

Quality and the Stock Market

The extract that follows first appeared in *The Dividend Connection,* Geraldine's second book written with her son, Gregory Weiss. It is so well written there is simply no way to improve upon it.

> In the real estate market, quality is determined by three measures: location, location, location. Three measures can also be applied to quality in the stock market: performance, performance, performance.
>
> 1. *Financial performance is the first measure of quality.* This includes the company's record of earnings, dividends, debt-to-equity ratio, dividend payout ratio, book value, and cash flow.
> 2. *Production performance is the second measure of quality.* We look for a company that manufactures useful products or services and actively pursues research and development of new products or services. The company must also demonstrate an ability to market its products or services successfully.
> 3. *Investment performance, as reflected in long-term capital gains and dividend growth, is the third measure of quality.* The most important objective of an investor is a rewarding total return. A well-managed company with a strong financial performance will generate a total return that will outperform any other investment vehicle.
>
> These three measures of quality do not stand alone. They are intertwined in the fabric of the company and its shareholders' goals. All of our research has shown that there is as much or more profit potential in high-quality stocks than there is in stocks of inferior or unproven quality—and with far less risk.
>
> Our method of investing in the stock market focuses exclusively on blue chip stock selection. It involves limiting investment selections to blue chip stocks and purchasing or selling those stocks based on their individual profiles of undervalue or overvalue.

What Is a Blue Chip Stock?

As best as we can tell, there are at least 15,000 publicly traded companies in the U.S. financial markets alone. I doubt seriously that anyone would fault me for suggesting that not all of them represent blue chip stocks, let alone companies that are worthy of investment consideration.

There is a certain irony in the fact that, in a book in which we focus on value-based investing as a business as opposed to mere gambling or speculation, the objects of our affection, blue chip stocks, get their name from the highest denomination of betting chips in a poker game. Be that as it may, the term *blue chip* is nonetheless reserved for only the highest quality stocks. The reason for this is simple. Blue chip companies have a reputation for dependability as well as offering the best potential for increasing shareholder value through dividend growth and capital gains.

Although many blue chip companies are household names, an equal number, if not more, are not. There are also many stocks that are household names but are far from being blue chips. As you can see, it is important to have a mechanism or filter if you prefer to eliminate the pretenders from the contenders, so to speak.

Since 1966 we have used six criteria, which we call the Criteria for Select Blue Chips (our designation for the highest-quality blue chip stocks), as a starting place for our investment considerations. When a stock has passed this filter for its qualitative characteristics, we then analyze it further to determine its historically repetitive areas of *undervalued* and *overvalued* dividend yield.

Dividend Truth

These are the six criteria:

1. The dividend has increased five times in the past 12 years.
2. S&P Quality ranks the stock in the "A" category.
3. There are at least 5,000,000 shares outstanding.
4. There are at least 80 institutional investors.
5. The company has at least 25 years of uninterrupted dividends.
6. Earnings have improved in at least seven of the last 12 years.

At first glance these six criteria appear relatively simple, which they are; no rocket science here. When combined into one fundamental filter however, *it effectively eliminates approximately 98 percent of the domestic publicly traded universe of stocks.* To put that into further perspective, of the roughly 15,000 publicly traded companies in the U.S. markets, only 350 companies meet this criteria, and of those 350 we can establish clear-cut dividend-yield profiles for only 273 companies as shown in Figure 4.1.

Company	Symbol	Company	Symbol
Abbott Labs	ABT	Bank of New York Mellon	BK
ABM Industries	ABM	Bank of America	BAC
AFLAC	AFL	Bard, CR	BCR
AGL Resources	AGL	Barnes Group	B
Air Products & Chemicals	APD	BB&T Corp	BBT
Alberto-Culver	ACV	Becton, Dickinson	BDX
Alexander & Baldwin	ALEX	Bemis Company	BMS
Altria Group	MO	Black & Decker	BDK
American States Water	AWR	Block, H&R	HRB
Ameren	AEE	Bob Evans Farms	BOBE
American Express	AXP	Boeing	BA
Ameron International	AMN	Brady Corp.	BRC
Ametek	AME	Bristol-Myers Squibb	BMY
AON Corp.	AOC	Brown-Forman	BF.B
Apache Corp.	APA	Burlington Northern	BNI
Apogee Enterprises	APOG	California Water Service	CWT
Applied Industrial Technologies	AIT	Campbell Soup	CPB
		Cardinal Health	CAH
Aqua America	WTR	Carlisle Companies	CSL
Archer-Daniels-Midland	ADM	Cass Information Systems	CASS
Associated Banc-Corp	ASBC	Caterpillar	CAT
AT&T Inc.	T	CenturyTel Inc.	CTL
Atmos Energy	ATO	Chevron Corp	CVX
Automatic Data Processing	ADP	Chubb Corp	CB
Avery Dennison	AVY	Church & Dwight	CHD
Avon Products	AVP	Cincinnati Financial	CINF
Badger Meter, Inc.	BMI	Cintas Corp	CTAS
Baldor Electric	BEZ	Citigroup Inc.	C
BancorpSouth	BXS	Clarcor	CLC
Bank of Hawaii	BOH	Cleco Corp	CNL
Bank of Montreal	BMO	Clorox	CLX

Company	Symbol	Company	Symbol
Coca-Cola	KO	Franklin Resources	BEN
Colgate-Palmolive	CL	Frisch's Restaurants	FRS
Comerica	CMA	First Midwest Bancorp	FMBI
Commerce Bancshares	CBSH	Fulton Financial	FULT
Commercial Metals	CMC	Gallagher, Arthur J.	AJG
Community Trust Bancorp	CTBI	Gannett	GCI
Consolidated Edison	ED	Gap Inc.	GPS
Conagra Inc.	CAG	GATX Corp.	GMT
Connecticut Water Service	CTWS	General Dynamics	GD
ConocoPhillips	COP	General Electric	GE
Consolidated Water	CWCO	General Mills	GIS
Cooper Industries	CBE	Genuine Parts	GPC
Curtiss-Wright	CW	Gorman Rupp	GRC
CVS Caremark Corp	CVS	Graco Inc.	GGG
Deere & Co.	DE	Grainger, WW	GWW
Diebold Inc.	DBD	Granite Construction	GVA
Disney-Walt	DIS	Greif, Inc.	GEF
Dominion Resources	D	Hancock Holdings	HBHC
Donaldson Company	DCI	Harris Corp.	HRS
Dover Corp.	DOV	Harsco Corp.	HSC
DPL Inc.	DPL	Hasbro Inc.	HAS
Eaton Corp.	ETN	Heinz, H J	HNZ
Eaton Vance	EV	Henry, (Jack) & Associates	JKHY
Ecolab Inc.	ECL	Hershey Foods	HSY
Emerson Electric	EMR	Hewlett-Packard	HPQ
Enbridge Inc.	ENB	HNI Corp.	HNI
Energen Corp.	EGN	Home Depot, The	HD
Ennis Inc.	EBF	Hormel Foods	HRL
Equifax Inc.	EFX	Hubbell Inc Class B	HUB.B
Equitable (EQT) Corp.	EQT	Huntington Bancshares	HBAN
Exelon Corp.	EXC	International Business Machines	IBM
Exxon Mobil	XOM		
Family Dollar Stores	FDO	Illinois Tool Works	ITW
Federal REIT	FRT	Imperial Oil Ltd.	IMO
Fifth Third Bank	FITB	Independent Bank Corp	IBCP
First Merchants Corp.	FRME	Ingersoll-Rand Plc	IR
FirstEnergy Corp.	FE	Integrys Energy	TEG
Florida Public Utilities	FPU	International Flavors & Fragrances	IFF
FPL Group	FPL		

Figure 4.1 Select Blue-Chip Companies A-Z

Company	Symbol	Company	Symbol
Johnson & Johnson	JNJ	Northrop Grumman Corp.	NOC
Johnson Controls	JCI	NSTAR	NST
Kaydon Corp.	KDN	Occidental Petroleum	OXY
Kellogg	K	OGE Energy	OGE
Kimberly-Clark	KMB	Old National Bancorp	ONB
LaClede Group	LG	Omnicom Group	OMC
Legg Mason	LM	ONEOK, Inc.	OKE
Limited Brands	LTD	Otter Tail Power	OTTR
Lincoln Electric Holdings	LECO	Overseas Shipholding Group	OSG
Lincoln National	LNC		
Lockheed Martin	LMT	Owens & Minor	OMI
Lowe's Companies	LOW	Paccar Industries	PCAR
Lufkin Industries	LUFK	Parker-Hannifin	PH
M&T Bank	MTB	Pentair Inc.	PNR
Marriott International	MAR	Peoples Bancorp	PEBO
Marsh & McLennan Companies	MMC	PepsiCo	PEP
		Pfizer Inc.	PFE
Marshall & Ilsley	MI	Philip Morris International Inc.	PM
McCormick	MKC		
McDonald's	MCD	Piedmont Natural Gas	PNY
McGraw Hill	MHP	Pitney Bowes	PBI
MDU Resources	MDU	PNC Financial Group	PNC
Medtronic Inc.	MDT	Polaris Industries	PII
Merck & Company	MRK	PPG Industries Inc.	PPG
Meredith Corp.	MDP	Procter & Gamble	PG
MGE Energy	MGEE	Protective Life	PL
Middlesex Water Co.	MSEX	Public Service Enterprise Group	PEG
3 M Company	MMM		
Mine Safety Appliances	MSA	Pulte Homes Inc.	PHM
Molson Coors Brewing	TAP	Questar Corp.	STR
MTS Systems	MTSC	Raven Industries	RAVN
Northwest Natural Gas	NWN	Raymond James Financial	RJF
National Fuel Gas	NFG	Regal Beloit	RBC
New Jersey Resources	NJR	Reliance Steel & Aluminum	RS
Nike Inc Cl B	NKE		
Noble Energy Inc.	NBL	RLI Corp.	RLI
Nordson Corp.	NDSN	Rockwell Automation	ROK
Nordstrom	JWN	Rollins Inc.	ROL
Norfolk Southern Corp.	NSC	Roper Industries	ROP
Northern Trust	NTRS	Royal Bank of Canada	RY

Figure 4.1 Select Blue-Chip Companies A-Z

Company	Symbol	Company	Symbol
Ruddick Corp.	RDK	Torchmark Corp.	TMK
Schering-Plough	SGP	Toro Co.	TTC
Schlumberger Ltd.	SLB	Travelers Companies, The	TRV
Selective Insurance Group	SIGI	TrustCo Bank Corp. NY	TRST
Sempra Energy	SRE	Trustmark Corp.	TRMK
Sensient Technology	SXT	UGI Corp.	UGI
Sherwin Williams	SHW	Union Pacific Corp.	UNP
Sigma-Aldrich	SIAL	United Technologies	UTX
Smith, A. O.	AOS	Universal Corp.	UVV
Smucker, JM	SJM	Valley National Bank	VLY
Snap-On Inc.	SNA	Valmont Industries	VMI
Sonoco Products	SON	Valspar Corp.	VAL
South Jersey Industries	SJI	VF Corp.	VFC
Southern Company	SO	Vulcan Materials	VMC
Southwest Bancorp	OKSB	Walgreen Co.	WAG
Stanley Works, The	SWK	Wal-Mart Stores	WMT
State Street Corp	STT	Washington Post	WPO
Stepan Company	SCL	Washington Federal	WFSL
Sterling Bancorp	STL	Washington REIT	WRE
Sunoco Inc.	SUN	Watsco Inc.	WSO
SunTrust Banks	STI	Weingarten Realty	WRI
Supervalu Inc.	SVU	Wells Fargo & Company	WFC
Susquehanna Bancshares	SUSQ	Westamerica Bancorporation	WABC
Synovus Financial	SNV	Weyco Group	WEYS
Sysco Corp.	SYY	WGL Holdings	WGL
T. Rowe Price	TROW	Whirlpool	WHR
Target Corp.	TGT	Wilmington Trust	WL
TCF Financial	TCB	Wisconsin Energy Corp	WEC
Teleflex Inc.	TFX	Zions Bancorp	ZION
TJX Companies	TJX		

Figure 4.1 Select Blue-Chip Companies A-Z

The Criteria for Select Blue Chips

Most stock analysis is conducted through two central disciplines: fundamental and technical. Fundamental analysis has two main subsets: the quantitative and the qualitative. *Quantitative* generally refers to numbers, things that can be measured—earnings, dividends, cash flow, payout, debt, and so forth. *Qualitative* generally refers to intangibles—characteristics that can't necessarily be measured but nonetheless are important; for example, name recognition such as a company's brand, management expertise, commitment to research and development, industry cycles, and so forth.

Technical analysis is considered by many to be the polar opposite of fundamental analysis. Whereas fundamental analysis involves analyzing the economic characteristics of a company in order to estimate its value, technicians are primarily interested in price movements because the fundamentals, they believe, have been fully factored into the price. Another definition would be the study of supply and demand in a stock or market to determine what direction, or trend, will continue in the future.

Generally, but not always, analysts tend to favor one discipline over the other. For many practitioners, there is simply no way for the two disciplines to co-exist.

Our approach is based on a combination of the two disciplines, what we call a fundamental approach to technical analysis. The Criteria for Select Blue Chips is how we identify fundamental quality, or what stocks to buy. Our Profiles of Value, the study and identification of the historically repetitive patterns of undervalue and overvalue areas of dividend yield, is how we identify value, or when to buy, sell, or hold.

In later chapters we will discuss undervalue and overvalue in much greater detail. Before we can begin to focus on the *when,* however, we first have to identify the *what.* That is the primary purpose of the Criteria for Select Blue Chips—to identify corporate excellence, or quality.

Dividend Increases and Earnings Improvement

Criteria 1 and 6 earlier both reference 12 years: dividend increases in five of the last 12 years, and earnings improvement in seven of the last 12 years. One of the most frequent questions I am asked is what is so special about 12 years?

The average business/economic cycle lasts approximately four years. Over the course of 12 years, then, the economy and markets will go through three complete cycles. During that period, a company will experience the inevitable economic surprise, be it on a macro level, which affects all companies, or on a micro level, which is specific to that company, industry, or sector. There is an equally high probability for major legislative and/or tax changes that will require a period of adjustment. In short, adversity is part of the cost of doing business. As such, a consistent track record for earnings growth is not only difficult to achieve, but also to sustain over significant periods of time.

For a company to meet both of these criteria, their earnings and dividends must show consistent improvement. Steady and improving earnings and dividend performance over the course of 12 years is not luck; it is evidence of strong and capable management.

The list of Select Blue Chips that have achieved consistent earnings and dividend growth is quite extensive. Only those from the Undervalued category in the mid-September, 2009, are listed below in Figure 4.2.

Company	Symbol
Abbott Laboratories	ABT
AFLAC	AFL
Altria Group	MO
Archer-Daniels-Midland	ADM
Automatic Data Processing	ADP
Bank of Hawaii	BOH
Bank of Montreal	BMO
Becton, Dickinson	BDX
Boeing	BA
Cardinal Health	CAH
Caterpillar	CAT
CenturyTel	CTL
Chevron	CVX
Cincinnati Financial	CINF
Cintas Corp	CTAS
Clorox	CLX
Coca-Cola	KO
Colgate-Palmolive	CL
Community Trust Bancorp	CTBI
ConocoPhillips	COP
CVS Caremark Corp.	CVS
Eaton Vance	EV
Exelon Corp.	EXC
Gallagher, Arthur J.	AJG
Greif, Inc.	GEF
Harris Corp.	HRS
Hasbro Inc.	HAS
Henry, Jack	JKHY
HNI Corp.	HNI
Home Depot, The	HD
International Business Machines	IBM
Johnson & Johnson	JNJ
Kimberly-Clark	KMB
Lockheed Martin	LMT
M&T Bank	MTB
McDonald's	MCD
Meredith Corp.	MDP
Mine Safety Appliances	MSA
Nike, Inc Class B	NKE
Noble Energy Inc.	NBL
Overseas Shipholding Group	OSG
PepsiCo Inc.	PEP
Philip Morris International	PM
Polaris Industries	PII
Procter & Gamble	PG
Raymond James Financial	RJF
Sigma-Aldrich	SIAL
Sysco Corp.	SYY
Target Corp.	TGT
Teleflex Inc.	TFX
TJX Companies	TJX
Trustmark Corp.	TRMK
United Technologies	UTX
Valspar Corp.	VAL
VF Corp.	VFC
Walgreen Company	WAG
Wal-Mart Stores	WMT
Weyco Group	WEYS

Figure 4.2 Blue Chips with 12-Year Average Annual Dividend Growth of At Least 10 Percent

The most reliable measure of good management is long-term performance, a proven ability to grow the net earnings of its company and maintain a rising trend of increased dividends. You work hard to save the capital you put to work in the markets. Don't entrust it to just any company; put it to work with the best. The proof, once again, is in the pudding.

S&P Quality Ranking in the "A" Category

Standard & Poor's has provided Earnings and Dividend Rankings, commonly referred to as Quality Rankings, on common stocks since 1956.

Dividend Truth

According to Standard & Poor's:

> The Quality Rankings System attempts to capture the growth and stability of earnings and dividends record in a single symbol. In assessing Quality Rankings, Standard & Poor's recognizes that earnings and dividend performance is the end result of the interplay of various factors such as products and industry position, corporate resources, and financial policy. Over the long run, the record of earnings and dividend performance has a considerable bearing on the relative quality of stocks. The rankings, however, do not profess to reflect all of the factors, tangible or intangible, that bear on stock quality.
>
> The rankings are generated by a computerized system and are based on per-share earnings and dividend records of the most recent 10 years—a period long enough to measure significant secular growth, capture indications of basic change in trend as they develop, encompass the full peak-to-peak range of the business cycle, and include a bull and a bear market. Basic scores are computed for earnings and dividends, and then adjusted as indicated by a set of predetermined modifiers for change in the rate of growth, stability within long-term trends, and cyclicality. Adjusted scores for earnings and dividends are then combined to yield a final ranking.

The Standard & Poor's Earnings and Dividend Rankings for Common Stocks are as follows:

A+ Highest	B+ Average	C Lowest
A High	B Below average	D In reorganization
A– Above average	C Lower	NR*

*A ranking of NR signifies no ranking or insufficient data because the stock in not amenable to the ranking process.

For inclusion in the universe of Select Blue Chips, a company must initially have at minimum an A– Quality Ranking. The company may remain in the roster if its Quality Ranking declines to a B+, but will be removed from the listing if it is downgraded further.

At Least Five Million Shares Outstanding

There is an extensive body of research on the impact that market capitalization, or cap size, exerts on the returns of stocks. As a result of this research, the mutual fund complex has designed and offers a multitude of funds that invest solely in one capitalization segment of the market. These funds are easily identifiable as the term *Cap* will be part of the fund name. By example: Mega Cap, Large-Cap, Mid-Cap, Small-Cap, Micro-Cap, and so forth.

Also common today, particularly among financial consultants, is to provide their clients who invest in individual stocks the ever-ubiquitous pie chart, to show what percentage of their holdings fall into the various capitalization segments.

For many, this type of analysis is sacrosanct. So be it; it is not within the purview of this book to engage in that debate. For our purposes of identifying quality, we aren't overly concerned with market capitalization. What we do care desperately about though is liquidity.

With enough common shares outstanding, a stock is assured of liquidity; we never want to be in the position of having to make an appointment to buy or sell a stock. Institutional investors, whose importance to our method is outlined in the next section, prefer to invest in companies that are liquid so they can establish large investment positions without disturbing the price of the stock. Equally important is that when the time comes to sell, they want to know that there will be sufficient numbers of buyers. Few experiences are as frustrating as trying to buy or sell a large position in a thinly traded stock. For institutional investors who frequently deal in large sums of capital, an orderly entrance and exit are extremely important. Lastly, liquidity helps to guard against share price manipulation.

At Least 80 Institutional Investors

When we use the term *institutional investor,* we are referring to the vast number of mutual funds, Exchange Traded Funds (ETFs), hedge funds, banks, insurance companies, pension fund and retirement companies, major brokerages, and money managers. On any given trading day, these groups account for the vast majority of trading activity. As such, their collective buying and selling decisions will exert an enormous impact on the trend of stock prices. In other words, institutions are the 800-pound gorillas of Wall Street.

Whether they choose to acknowledge it or not, institutional investors can exhibit some fairly predictable behavior. This is due, in no small part, to the fact that it is a closely linked community. This is to say that they associate with, listen to, and behave like other institutional investors. As value investors, we can use this propensity for like-minded behavior to our advantage.

It is not uncommon when using the dividend-value strategy to be early to the table, which means that we often take positions in high-quality companies that offer excellent historic value long before other investors. Eventually one or two institutional analysts will stumble upon one of our companies, write up a buy recommendation, and distribute it to its traders or sales force.

Nothing in the institutional community remains secret very long, so when the word gets out, the full force that is institutional buying power kicks in. Strong institutional buying eventually hits the radar screens of our favorite investor type, the momentum investor. In simple terms, a momentum investor attempts to capture capital gains by buying a stock with a discernible uptrend in price, or to short a stock with a discernible downtrend in price. The underlying belief is that, once a trend has been established, it is likely to continue in that direction than to move against the trend.

There is nothing intrinsically wrong with this idea. In fact, we engage in some momentum investing ourselves. There is nothing more attractive than a high-quality company with an undervalue price, a high-yield and upward momentum in its dividend trend.

Okay, we're not really momentum investors, but I think you get the point.

To bring this point to conclusion, between institutional interest and momentum investing, stocks that we purchased at excellent historic value will often reach their historic upside potential, at which point we lock in our profits and search for another high-quality undervalued opportunity.

Of the six Criteria for Select Blue Chips, the number of institutional sponsors is the least rigid, which is to say there is nothing magical about the number 80. What is important is evidence of widespread interest in a stock, and that it has attracted a broad and diverse institutional following. In terms of price stability, we prefer to find that 80 or more institutions hold 50 percent of the common shares outstanding, rather than one or several institutions holding the same amount; with diversity comes an element of safety. Most full-service brokers and investor databases can provide information on the number of institutional investors and their percentage of holdings in any individual stock.

At Least 25 Years of Uninterrupted Dividends

Of the six criteria that comprise the Criteria for Select Blue Chips, this is the one that separates the big dogs in the tall grass from the pups in the weeds. We are often asked if there is really a meaningful difference between a company that has paid uninterrupted dividends for 25 years and one with 10, 15, or 20. The short answer is absolutely.

In a sufficient number of instances, our research indicates there is a greater likelihood for price volatility and less reliability in the trends of earnings and dividends for companies with shorter track records of uninterrupted dividend payments.

Although we lack a single empirical measurement that explains this phenomenon, our best guess, based on our experience, is that the market, which posseses all the wisdom from its collective participants, has determined that companies that have achieved this milestone have earned elite status and investors simply treat them differently.

What we do know is that over a 25-year period a company *will* go through many business and economic cycles, *will* experience the exhilaration of bull markets and the despondence of bear markets, *will* see their products or services enjoy periods of wide popularity and periods of less; the list can go on and on.

In the final analysis I believe it all boils down to one factor, namely, competence. If a company can weather the myriad challenges it will inevitably face over such a period of time and maintain a strong record of earnings growth and maintain a rising dividend trend, that is competence. If a company can keep its products and services at the forefront of consumer interest, or reinvent itself if necessary, that is competence. If a company can consistently attract, train, and retain the next generation of management that will continue a tradition of excellence—that is competence.

You work hard to save the investment capital you put to work in the financial markets. All things being equal, who are you most comfortable associating with that capital? For us the answer is easy: the most competent companies we can find.

With the rare exception, the majority of the current 273 companies in the *Investment Quality Trends* roster of Select Blue Chips have paid uninterrupted dividends for 25 years.

The Importance of Dividends

At this juncture the importance of cash dividends should be crystal clear. When a dividend is increased, the stock price will inevitably rise to reflect the increase in value. Conversely, when a dividend is reduced, the stock price will inevitably decline to reflect the decrease in value.

Dividends are an indicator of value and a predictor of future growth, which attracts new investors to the company and provides a tangible reward for accepting investment risk. Value-conscious investors can depend on cash dividends to either provide a reliable stream of income to meet their current cash needs or as capital to reinvest to keep pace with inflation and improve their standard of living. A company that pays cash dividends year after year and increases those dividends regularly is well managed.

An ongoing dividend stream is the most reliable evidence a company is generating sufficient earnings to cover expenses, pay the interest on its debt, grow the company, and reward its owners. When a dividend is increased, the stock owner knows without reading a balance sheet or an annual report that their company is performing.

There Is No Profitable Substitute for Quality

In this chapter we have explored the importance of quality as it pertains to the dividend-value strategy. Although the strategy can be implemented through any stock that has paid dividends long enough to establish a discernible pattern for repetitive areas of undervalue and overvalue, four-plus decades of research has proven that for the best investments results, investors should confine their investment considerations to only the highest-quality, blue chip stocks.

High quality, blue chip stocks are the first to rise in a bull market and the last stocks to fall when the market declines. In good times, blue chip companies outperform both their lesser competitors and the economy. In bad times, they resist adversity best. Time and time again, experience has shown, there is no profitable substitute for quality.

Although quality is one of the twin pillars of the dividend-value strategy, it isn't the final word; *value* is. In the following chapters, we discuss the importance of identifying value to build a winning portfolio.

CHAPTER 5

Value and Blue Chip Stocks

Nowadays people know the price of everything and the value of nothing.

—Oscar Wilde

Recognizing quality is an essential component of the dividend-value strategy, but quality and value are entirely different measurements. The Select Blue Chips listed within the pages of *Investment Quality Trends* are all high-quality companies, but not all of them represent current good value. That is, even the highest-quality stock can be overpriced. Accordingly, once investors have established the qualitative bona fides for a blue chip stock, the measures of good value should be applied to maximize both the safety of capital and the potential for real total return.

Finding Good Value

If I had to choose just one factor as the key to investment success, it would be the ability to recognize and appreciate good value, which leads to two important questions: How is value measured in the stock market, and how does an investor know when the price of a stock represents good value?

There are three fundamental tools that investors use to establish value in the stock market: dividend yield, price-earnings ratio (P/E), and price-book value ratio (P/B), as shown in Figure 5.1.

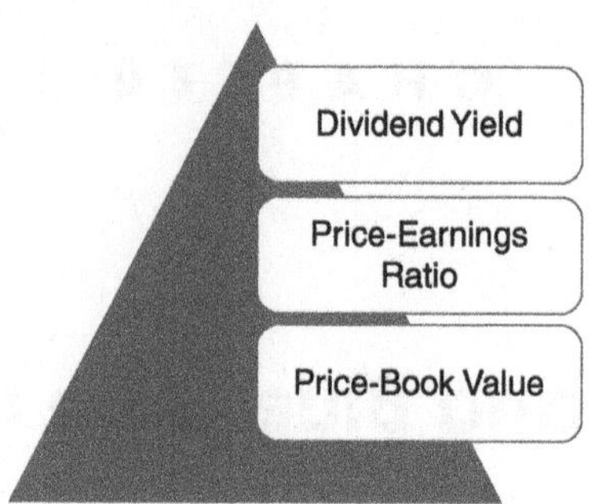

Figure 5.1 Three Fundamental Investor Tools

Of the three measures, the *primary* measure of value in the stock market is the receipt of dividends, which is expressed as dividend yield. Dividend yield cuts to the chase; when all else is stripped from the bone it is the dividend yield that reveals the true value of a company's stock.

This is not to suggest that price-to-earnings (P/E) ratios or price-to-book-value (PB) ratios are unimportant. As *primary* measures of value, both ratios are less than perfect; however, as *confirmation measures* for the value the dividend represents, both can be quite useful.

Price-Earnings Ratio

The price-earnings or P/E ratio is probably the first analytical tool most investors learn about because it is the most commonly used measure of value. In brief, the ratio expresses the stock's price in relation to the company's trailing 12-month earnings. The ratio is calculated by dividing the earnings per share into the price of the stock. The resulting figure produces a ratio of the price to the earnings.

By example, if a company's trailing 12-month earnings are $1.95 per share and the current stock price is $24 per share, by dividing $1.95 into $24, the result is 12.30, which we round down to 12. When expressed as a ratio we would say the P/E is 12 to 1. Depending on current economic and market conditions, 12 to 1 could be high, low, or somewhere in the middle.

When earnings, stock prices, and interest rates are depressed, as they typically are in a bear market, it is not uncommon for P/E ratios to fall into the single digits. Conversely, when earnings, stock prices, and interest rates are robust, as they typically are during periods of expansion, it is not uncommon for P/E ratios to rise well into the teens and twenties.

In general, depending on the overall growth rate within any stock industry group, any ratio below 15 to 1 is believed to represent fair value. In like fashion, a P/E ratio above 20 to 1 suggests that the stock price may be overvalued. However, stocks have their own personalities, and a high P/E ratio for one stock may be an acceptable ratio, depending on the company's growth characteristics. The market will also often grant higher valuations to a particular stock or industry that captures its fancy. Our personal preference as a firm is a P/E ratio that is closer to 10 to 1.

As you can tell, there is a certain amount of subjectivity when it comes to P/E ratios, another reason why identifying the repetitive extremes of *undervalue* and *overvalue* dividend yield is so important.

Price-Book Value Ratio

In accounting terms, book value is all of a company's tangible assets (what you can see and touch), minus debt, minus preferred stock, and minus intangible assets (such as patents and goodwill). For normal people, book value is what is left if the company were to go out of business, liquidate all of its assets, and pay off all its debts. This figure is then divided by the total common shares outstanding to determine the book value per share.

The P/B ratio compares the market's valuation of a company (price per share) to the value indicated on its financial statements (book value per share). By example, if a company's stock price is $20 per share and the most recent book value is $10 per share, by dividing $20 by $10 the result is 2. When expressed as a ratio we would say the P/B is 2 to 1.

When the P/B ratio is one (1 to 1), it means the market value is in sync with what the company is reporting on its financial statement. When the ratio is greater than one, it means the market is willing to pay a premium above what the company reports on its financial statements. When the ratio is less than one, it can mean one of two things: The market is nervous about the value of the company and is unwilling to pay full price, or investors have incorrectly valued the stock.

For some analysts, to question the validity of book values is to commit heresy. For the truly objective analyst, however, it is difficult to overlook the obvious deficiencies in book values for making accurate valuations. For one, how assets and liabilities are valued leaves room for creative interpretation, as we have discovered recently with financial companies. Another is that some companies, such as those in the technology and service sectors, have hidden (intangible) assets such as intellectual property that are of great value, but are not reflected in the book value. Lastly, most accounting procedures fail to account for the effects of inflation on asset prices. Book value figures, therefore, can just as easily be understated as overstated.

Even the great Benjamin Graham, whose work I credit for much of my academic/intellectual development, and whose favorite measure for value identification was book values, cautioned investors that a stock does not necessarily represent good value simply because it can be purchased at or close to book value. In his book *The Intelligent Investor,* Graham advises investors to be cognizant, too, of the price the market is placing on shares, to know how many dollars are on hand for each dollar of short term debt, and to know that the dividend is well protected.

As is the case with earnings and the P/E ratio, book values and the P/B ratio cannot be dismissed. They are important measures of value *as they can confirm the message of the dividend-yield trend.*

Dividend Yield

We believe that the most important measure of investment value is the dividend yield. We believe this to be true because of three factors:

1. Dividends are the result of earnings.
2. A rising dividend trend is a predictor of growth.
3. Repetitive dividend-yield extremes establish reliable areas for *undervalue* and *overvalue* prices.

Enlightened investors have learned there is generally one catalyst—higher earnings or management's reasoned expectations for higher earnings—that justifies a dividend increase. Think about it. No management, particularly that of a blue chip company, wants to suffer the public embarrassment of a bad call. Before the decision to raise a dividend is made, then, management has to believe the prospects for improved earnings, now as well into the future, must be strong. No manager with a lick of sense will raise the dividend if there is any doubt about future earnings.

Throughout this book, you will read the terms *undervalue* and *overvalue.* In our lexicon, these are historically repetitive extremes of low-price/high-yield and high-price/low-yield, which we call Profiles of Value. There is no one Profile of Value that can be applied to every stock. Each stock has it unique Profile of Value that must be analyzed and evaluated individually.

Dividend Truth

Measures of good value include the following:

Rule 1. A dividend yield that is historically high for that particular stock, and has repeatedly signaled the bottom of a major declining trend in the price of that stock.

Rule 2. A P/E ratio that is historically low for that particular stock, and is below the multiple for the Dow Jones Industrial Average. The only exception to this rule would be growth stocks with consistent records of rising earnings that are advancing faster than the market average and, therefore, can command higher-than-average P/E ratios.

Rule 3. A strong financial position with a ratio of current assets to current liabilities of at least two to one, and a debt-to-equity ratio of no more than 50 percent debt to equity.

Rule 4. A price that is no higher than one-third above the book value of the company—and the closer to book value, the better. Again, this fourth rule can be broken in the case of companies with proven, superior, long-term growth characteristics.

The Bluest of the Blue Chips

Even among blue chips, some stocks are more blue chip than others. These are stocks that have both an A+ quality ranking and the *Investment Quality Trends* "G" designation. A stock is awarded the "G" designation when the company achieves average annual dividend growth of 10 percent or greater over the past 12 years.

Company	Symbol
Archer-Daniels-Midland	ADM
Automatic Data Processing	ADP
Caterpillar, Inc.	CAT
Cintas, Corp.	CTAS
Colgate-Palmolive	CL
CVS Caremark Corp.	CVS
Jack Henry & Associates	JKHY
Nike, Inc. Class B	NKE
PepsiCo, Inc.	PEP
Philip Morris International	PM
Sigma-Aldrich	SIAL
Sysco Corp.	SYY
Target Corp.	TGT
TJX Companies	TJX
United Technologies	UTX
Walgreen Company	WAG
Wal-Mart Stores, Inc.	WMT

Figure 5.2 Royal Blue Chips—Highest Investment Quality (A+)

Companies that meet this threshold and offer current good value (Undervalued) are shown in Figure 5.2.

The Faded Blues

The Select Blue Chips listed in *Investment Quality Trends* are an elite representation of the highest-quality publicly traded companies in America. Achieving Select Blue Chip status is not a one-time event, however; the designation must be continuously earned.

For varying reasons, more than 100 stocks have been deleted from our blue-chip-stock list over the last 44 years. Many were deleted because they were acquired by another company, some because they eliminated their dividend. On occasion, a Select Blue Chip can run into temporary or cyclical difficulties and their S&P Quality Ranking may be downgraded to "B," which signifies below- average quality. Even if they meet the five remaining criteria, we feel compelled to delete the stock from our blue chip roster and transfer it to our list of faded blues.

Figure 5.3 shows our list of approximately 75 stocks that are faded blues. They will be eligible for blue chip reinstatement if their quality rankings return to "B+"(above average) or cure other criteria deficiencies.

Back to Basics

It has been said that an investor can find whatever he is looking for in the stock market. If questioned, most investors will tell you they want to make money. Although all investors *like* to make money, some are really interested in the excitement or being entertained. Others, believe it or not, use the stock market to work out deep-rooted psychological issues. Some simply want to commiserate with their friends or neighbors about how the stock market stuck it to them again and there is no way the little guy can beat the big boys at their game.

Investing is a business, and most businesses that are successful are the result of the owner's willingness to do things that others don't want to do or won't do. Accordingly, identifying high-quality stocks that represent historical good value and giving them time to reach their full potential may not appeal to the investor looking for fireworks and immediate gratification. However, patience, in the stock market, is indeed a virtue.

In 1974, Geraldine conducted an interview with Benjamin Graham, which was later published in what at the time was the *San Diego Union.* In that interview Graham offered an interesting perspective on the value of patience:

> It's hard enough to find good values. When a stock rises slowly, intrinsic value can keep pace with the gradual increase in the price of the stock. However, when the price escalates quickly, faster than the fundamental development of the company, then the stock must be sold and a new investment decision made. Every new investment decision bears the risk of being a mistake.

Although the approach outlined in this book may not be entertaining or exciting enough for some, for the serious investor whose

These 75 stocks at one time were listed in I.Q. Trends as select blue chips. They were deleted from our service when their Quality Rankings declined to below average or if they failed to meet the minimum criteria for select blue chips. If their ranking returns to B+ or they cure their deficiences, they will be eligible for reinstatement. Meanwhile, for the benefit of investors who may have purchased these stocks when they were true blue, we present the following statistical review. Although their investment quality has been tarnished, the yields at Undervalue and Overvalue for these stocks still are valid.

STOCK		Price	Dividend	Yield	Pts Dn	% Down	Undervalue LoPr/	HiYld	Pts Up	% Up	Overvalue HiPr/	LoYld	S&P	52 wk Lo	52 wk Hi	Bk Val	12–mo Earn	P/E	Pay out	Div in Dgr	Tic
Alcoa	O	12	0.12	1.0%	8	67%	4	3.0%	–3	–24%	9	1.3%	B	5	30	13	*–2.21*	–6	–5%	X	AA
Amcol Int'l	R	22	0.72	3.3%	4	19%	18	4.0%	50	226%	72	1.0%	B	11	38	11	*0.39*	57	185%	X	ACO
Amer Elec Pwr	R	31	1.64	5.3%	13	42%	18	9.2%	24	76%	55	3.0%	B	24	42	27	*2.85*	11	58%		AEP
Amer Nat'l Insur	D	84	3.08	3.7%	37	44%	47	6.5%	35	41%	118	2.6%	B	34	110	123	*–9.14*	–9	–34%	X	ANAT
Barrick Gold	U	40	0.40	1.0%	0	0%	40	1.0%	93	233%	133	0.3%	B	17	41	19	*0.74*	54	54%		ABX
Baxter Int'l	R	57	1.04	1.8%	22	39%	35	3.0%	47	84%	104	1.0%	A–	45	70	11	**3.43**	17	30%		BAX
Belo Corp.	U	3	0.30	9.1%	–12	–357%	15	2.0%	27	815%	30	1.0%	C	0	8	2	*–4.41*	–1	–7%	X	BLC
Black Hills Corp.	U	24	1.42	5.8%	–4	–16%	28	5.0%	32	133%	57	2.5%	B	15	39	28	**3.05**	8	47%		BKH
Centerpoint	D	12	0.76	6.3%	4	30%	8	9.0%	18	152%	30	2.5%	B	8	16	6	*1.09*	11	70%		CNP
CH Energy Grp	R	45	2.16	4.8%	18	40%	27	8.0%	27	61%	72	3.0%	B+	33	53	33	**2.26**	20	96%		CHG
Cigna Corp.	O	30	0.04	0.1%	29	98%	1	7.0%	–27	–90%	3	1.3%	B	8	43	16	**2.22**	13	2%		CI
Cohu Inc.	R	12	0.24	2.0%	6	46%	7	3.6%	36	292%	48	0.5%	B–	7	18	11	*–1.56*	–8	–15%	X	COHU
Constellation Enrgy	R	31	0.96	3.1%	14	45%	17	5.5%	9	27%	40	2.4%	B	13	68	18	*–9.22*	–3	–10%	X	CEG
Cooper Tire	U	14	0.42	2.9%	0	2%	14	3.0%	6	40%	20	2.1%	B–	3	17	4	*–3.96*	–4	–11%	X	CTB
Deluxe Corp.	U	16	1.00	6.4%	–4	–27%	20	5.0%	51	325%	67	1.5%	B	6	18	1	*1.61*	10	62%		DLX
Dillard's A	U	12	0.16	1.4%	1	8%	11	1.5%	20	177%	32	0.5%	B	3	15	30	**–3.05**	–4	–5%	X	DDS
Dow Chemical	R	21	0.60	2.8%	10	49%	11	5.5%	19	88%	40	1.5%	B	6	40	14	*–1.67*	–13	–36%	X	DOW
DTE Energy	R	35	2.12	6.1%	8	24%	27	8.0%	29	84%	64	3.3%	B	23	44	38	**3.47**	10	61%		DTE
Duke Energy	R	16	**0.96**	6.2%	2	12%	14	7.0%	16	106%	32	3.0%	B	12	19	16	*0.91*	17	105%	X	DUK
DuPont	R	32	1.64	5.2%	4	14%	27	6.0%	59	187%	91	1.8%	B	16	48	8	*0.70*	45	234%	X	DD

Eastman Kodak	U	5	0.50	9.5%	–5	–89%	10	5.0%	33	627%	38	1.3%	B–	2	17	0	*–5.02*	–1	–10%	X	EK
FirstMerit Corp	R	18	*0.64*	3.6%	6	34%	12	5.5%	14	81%	32	2.0%	B	12	31	12	*1.19*	15	54%		FMER
Fuller (HB)	D	20	0.27	1.3%	11	52%	10	2.8%	7	34%	27	1.0%	B	10	28	12	*0.06*	336	450%	X	FUL
Goodrich Corp	O	56	1.00	1.8%	45	80%	11	8.8%	–14	–26%	42	2.4%	B+	25	58	21	*5.45*	10	18%		GR
Haliburton	O	25	0.36	1.5%	16	66%	8	4.3%	–1	–2%	24	1.5%	B	13	42	9	*1.22*	20	30%		HAL
Hawaiian Electric	U	17	1.24	7.3%	1	8%	16	8.0%	24	144%	41	3.0%	B+	12	30	15	*0.99*	17	125%	X	HE
Honeywell	R	37	1.21	3.3%	7	19%	30	4.0%	44	117%	81	1.5%	B+	23	50	11	*3.07*	12	39%		HON
Intl Paper	O	22	0.10	0.4%	20	88%	3	3.8%	–18	–81%	4	2.3%	B	4	31	11	**–2.96**	–8	–3%	X	IP
Keycorp	O	6	*0.04*	0.6%	6	91%	1	7.4%	–5	–79%	1	3.0%	B–	4	17	10	**–2.98**	–2	–1%	X	KEY
Kimball Intl	R	6	0.20	3.1%	1	23%	5	4.0%	7	106%	13	1.5%	B–	4	13	10	**0.46**	14	43%		KBALB
Lancaster Colony	D	50	1.14	2.3%	27	55%	23	5.0%	26	51%	76	1.5%	B	26	53	14	**3.18**	16	36%		LANC
Lance	O	26	0.64	2.5%	16	62%	10	6.5%	0	0%	26	2.5%	B	17	26	8	**0.95**	27	67%		LNCE
Lawson Prod	O	17	0.12	0.7%	12	72%	5	2.5%	–2	–11%	15	0.8%	B	10	38	16	**–0.76**	–22	–16%	X	LAWS
La–Z–Boy	O	9	0.08	0.9%	7	80%	2	4.5%	–4	–50%	4	1.8%	B–	1	12	6	**–2.15**	–4	–4%	X	LZB
Leggett&Platt	U	18	**1.04**	5.6%	–2	–12%	21	5.0%	47	252%	65	1.6%	B	10	25	11	*0.23*	80	452%	X	LEG
Lilly, Eli	U	33	1.96	5.9%	–32	–98%	65	3.0%	163	494%	196	1.0%	B	27	48	7	**–1.48**	–22	–132%	X	LLY
Liz Claiborne	U	4	0.23	5.6%	–4	–99%	8	2.8%	29	698%	33	0.7%	A–	1	20	4	*–11.41*	0	–2%	X	LIZ
LSI Industries	U	7	0.20	2.8%	0	7%	7	3.0%	10	133%	17	1.2%	B	3	10	6	**–0.62**	–12	–32%	X	LYTS
Lubrizol Corp	O	66	1.24	1.9%	41	62%	25	5.0%	–9	–14%	56	2.2%	B	24	65	25	**–0.32**	–205	–388%	X	LZ
Marcus Corp.	U	12	0.34	2.8%	1	7%	11	3.0%	19	152%	31	1.1%	B	6	20	11	*0.58*	21	59%		MCS
Masco Corp.	R	13	0.30	2.3%	2	15%	11	2.7%	4	27%	17	1.8%	B	4	22	8	*–1.42*	–9	–21%	X	MAS
McKesson	R	56	0.48	0.9%	12	22%	44	1.1%	40	71%	96	0.5%	B+	28	60	24	**3.17**	18	15%		MCK
Mercury General Corp.	U	36	2.32	6.4%	–15	–42%	52	4.5%	56	155%	93	2.5%	B	22	62	30	**–1.79**	–20	–130%	X	MCY
Morgan/Chase	O	42	0.20	0.5%	39	92%	3	6.0%	–34	–81%	8	2.5%	B	15	51	37	*0.90*	47	22%		JPM
Nicor	R	36	1.86	5.2%	8	21%	28	6.6%	19	53%	55	3.4%	B	28	52	22	*2.55*	14	73%		GAS
Nucor	U	44	1.40	3.2%	–26	–58%	70	2.0%	96	217%	140	1.0%	B	25	53	24	*1.64*	27	85%		NUE
Old Republic Int'l	U	11	0.68	5.9%	–6	–48%	17	4.0%	29	248%	40	1.7%	B	7	17	16	**–1.05**	–11	–65%	X	ORI
Omnicare	O	23	0.09	0.4%	19	81%	5	2.0%	–15	–65%	8	1.1%	B+	19	33	31	**1.34**	17	7%		OCR
Pall Corp.	D	30	0.58	1.9%	11	36%	19	3.0%	28	92%	58	1.0%	B+	18	40	9	*1.63*	19	36%		PLL
Penney, JC	O	30	0.80	2.6%	17	56%	13	6.0%	–3	–9%	28	2.9%	B	14	44	19	*1.59*	19	50%		JCP

Figure 5.3 DJIA 1896–2008

Pep Boys	R	9	0.12	1.3%	7	71%	3	4.5%	3	29%	12	1.0%	C	3	11	8	**–0.46**	–20	–26%	X	PBY
Perkinelmer	R	18	0.28	1.5%	9	48%	9	3.0%	10	55%	28	1.0%	B	11	29	13	*0.98*	18	29%		PKI
Pinnacle West	U	32	2.10	6.5%	–10	–30%	42	5.0%	48	150%	81	2.6%	B	22	38	32	*0.24*	135	875%	X	PNW
Progress Energy	R	39	2.48	6.3%	8	21%	31	8.0%	43	111%	83	3.0%	B	31	46	33	*2.87*	14	86%		PGN
Regions Financial	O	6	0.04	0.7%	5	88%	1	6.0%	–4	–72%	2	2.6%	B	2	20	13	*–8.63*	–1	0%	X	RF
Robbins–Myers	D	24	0.16	0.7%	16	66%	8	2.0%	8	35%	32	0.5%	B–	13	42	15	*2.17*	11	7%		RBN
RPM Inc	U	16	0.80	4.9%	0	2%	16	5.0%	13	81%	30	2.7%	B	9	22	9	**0.94**	17	85%		RPM
Sara Lee Corp.	D	9	0.44	4.7%	3	33%	6	7.0%	13	135%	22	2.0%	B	7	14	3	**0.52**	18	85%		SLE
Schulman	R	20	0.60	3.0%	5	24%	15	4.0%	40	203%	60	1.0%	B	11	24	15	**0.37**	54	162%	X	SHLM
Skyline Corp.	R	23	0.72	3.2%	5	20%	18	4.0%	13	60%	36	2.0%	B–	15	31	17	*–1.84*	–12	–39%	X	SKY
Standard Regist	R	5	0.20	4.3%	2	34%	3	6.5%	5	116%	10	2.0%	B–	3	12	2	*–0.17*	–27	–118%	X	SR
Standex Int'l	O	18	*0.20*	1.1%	14	75%	4	4.5%	–8	–45%	10	2.0%	B–	8	30	14	*–0.44*	–41	–45%	X	SXI
Superior Inds	U	14	0.64	4.5%	–23	–163%	38	1.7%	114	794%	128	0.5%	B–	8	20	15	*–4.19*	–3	–15%	X	SUP
Tasty Baking	D	7	0.20	2.9%	4	58%	3	7.0%	1	21%	8	2.4%	B–	3	8	4	**–0.47**	–15	–43%	X	TSTY
Tele & Data Sys	U	28	0.43	1.5%	–3	–10%	31	1.4%	80	284%	108	0.4%	B	21	41	35	*0.65*	43	66%		TDS
Texas Instruments	R	25	0.44	1.8%	8	32%	17	2.6%	30	121%	55	0.8%	B	13	25	7	*0.73*	34	60%		TXN
Textron Inc.	O	17	0.08	0.5%	16	94%	1	7.5%	–14	–81%	3	2.5%	B	4	41	11	*0.10*	171	80%		TXT
Timken	O	21	0.36	1.7%	16	76%	5	7.0%	–11	–51%	10	3.5%	B	10	31	16	*0.33*	64	109%	X	TKR
Tootsie Roll	D	24	0.32	1.4%	17	73%	6	5.0%	30	126%	53	0.6%	B	19	34	11	**0.77**	31	42%		TR
Verizon	U	31	1.84	6.0%	0	0%	31	6.0%	18	58%	48	3.8%	B	23	36	15	*2.12*	14	87%		VZ
Wausau Mos	R	10	0.34	3.5%	1	13%	9	4.0%	24	247%	34	1.0%	C	4	12	4	**–0.06**	–163	–567%	X	WPP
Weis Markets	U	32	1.16	3.6%	–1	–2%	33	3.5%	64	198%	97	1.2%	B	23	40	25	**2.11**	15	55%		WMK
Weyerhauser	O	37	*0.20*	0.5%	34	91%	3	6.0%	–28	–77%	9	2.3%	B–	19	66	20	*–6.16*	–6	–3%	X	WY
Worthington Ind	R	14	*0.40*	3.0%	7	51%	7	6.0%	10	74%	24	1.7%	B	7	22	9	*–1.37*	–10	–29%	X	WOR
Wyeth	D	48	1.20	2.5%	24	50%	24	5.0%	12	25%	60	2.0%	B	28	48	16	**3.38**	14	36%		WYE

Figure 5.3 DJIA 1896–2008 (*Continued*)

goal is developing wealth to meet his current and future cash needs, the dividend-value strategy has delivered time and again over the course of the last 40-plus years. For the enlightened investor, the growth of wealth is sufficient award to make patience well worth the effort.

Now that you know how to identify quality and value, we can turn our attention to understanding how cycles and trends impact both stocks and the stock market.

PART II

BARGAINS STILL COME IN CYCLES

CHAPTER 6

Value and the Stock Market

To know values is to know the meaning of the market.
—Charles Dow

Long-time radio commentator Paul Harvey is credited with saying, "In times like these, it helps to recall that there have always been times like these." Although a little on the folksy side, Mr. Harvey does a pretty good job of hitting the nail on the head. Business, the economy, and the markets move in cycles, not in straight lines.

Investor sentiment is subject to cycles as well. When all is well in the financial world, no amount of bad news can drag the markets down. When sentiment falls, no amount of good news can move the markets higher. Intellectually, experienced investors should understand this. Emotional extremes are part of the natural order and thus are necessary, but they are also short-lived.

Cycles have a rhythm and a pattern, much like the seasons: Winter follows fall and spring follows winter, and so forth. In similar fashion, recessions follow boom times and bull markets lead into bear markets. Through it all, the world keeps spinning on its axis.

According to the Dividend-Yield Theory, just as dividend-yield extremes represent historically repetitive areas of *undervalue* and *overvalue* in individual stocks, so, too, are there dividend-yield extremes that represent historically repetitive areas of undervalue and overvalue in the stock market.

Indeed, both the Dow Jones Industrial and Utility Averages have long established Profiles of Value, which can provide investors with invaluable information about the level of value that is present or absent in these widely followed proxies for the broad markets at any given time.

Investors who understand these cyclical patterns of dividend yield and know how to measure whether the cycle is in the early stage and offers good current value, or if the cycle is in the later stages where most of the value has been realized, have a greater probability for maximizing their real total return and minimizing their potential downside risk.

Maximizing return and minimizing risk are key for the investor whose primary investment goal is to build a pool of capital and growing income stream from that capital sufficient to fund their or someone else's cash needs.

Dividend-Yield Cycles

Volumes of books can be written about cycles because they can be observed in infinite ways. Time and space prohibit a lengthy recitation of the myriad examples, but most readers will be familiar with cyclical patterns we observe without a second thought: in agriculture, the weather, the seasons, history, politics, sports, and, of course, in human life. Some cycles are hard-wired by nature. Others are the result of the collective thoughts and actions of billions of people.

One of the central postulates of the Dividend-Yield Theory is that there is a cyclical aspect to dividend-yield patterns. Indeed, decades of stock market research has produced strong evidence that high-quality stocks with long histories of dividends and rising dividend trends generally fluctuate between repetitive extremes of high dividend yield and low dividend yield. The nexus for these fluctuations is the cyclical ebb and flow of the stock market, which is the result of market participants anticipating or reacting to news and information from the worlds of economics and politics.

Fundamental to the dividend-value strategy is that these recurring themes of yield can be used to establish envelopes of *undervalued* (low) and *overvalued* (high) price levels.

These lows and highs, which represent the bottoms and tops of cycles, are identified by simply charting the dividend yield over a sufficient period of time for the dividend-yield pattern to emerge. By calculating the repetitive dividend-yield areas where a stock or index turns down, or reverses a slide and turns up, the future behavior of that stock or index can be anticipated.

Once a dividend-yield pattern is established, the pattern tends to remain constant unless an exogenous event compels market participants to establish new parameters of undervalue and overvalue of dividend yield.

When a dividend is raised, undervalue and overvalue price limits will automatically adjust higher to maintain the historically established yield percentages. In general, the stock price will adjust accordingly to reflect the increased value as the result of the dividend increase.

The dividend-yield cycles are established by the market, which can be explained by the most basic of economic principles of the supply-and-demand theory as taught in Economics 101. When a high-quality, dividend-paying stock declines in price to the point where the dividend-yield is historically high, experienced investors with substantial amounts of capital earmarked for opportunities that represent good value begin to accumulate a position. This accumulative buying halts the decline, stabilizes the price, and begins to reverse the trend. When a price reversal in a stock becomes apparent, other investors initiate purchases and the price begins to rise.

Once a rising trend has been established and appears to have legs, less disciplined investors will begin to take positions in the stock. Almost simultaneously, investors who purchased the stock at undervalued prices become increasingly inclined to secure their profits by selling. By the time the price reaches its historic level of overvalue, the yield is no longer attractive enough to compel sufficient numbers of new buyers to take positions in the stock.

As soon as the early buyers become sellers and new buying interest evaporates, the price will begin to decline. Once a declining price trend becomes evident, the remaining stockholders will move to salvage what they can of any profits and their original principal. This wave of selling will continue until a historically high dividend yield again attracts enough new investors to halt the decline. There, at undervalue, the long-term investment cycle appears all over again.

To summarize this point before we move ahead: It can be observed that dividend-paying stocks fluctuate over time within a range of low dividend yield—establishing a peak of overvalue—and high dividend yield—establishing a valley of undervalue. The peaks and valleys identify areas in which stocks should be bought or sold.

Undervalue and Overvalue Cycles

Each stock has a unique profile of undervalue and overvalue; that is, distinctive high- and low-yield characteristics, as shown in Figure 6.1. Because no two profiles are identical, each stock must be studied on an individual basis, so in addition to producing income, dividend yield can also be used as a tool to identify value in the stock market.

Dividend Truth

Investors who buy shares when they are at the undervalued stage of the cycle and sell when they reach their historic overvalued level accomplish three objectives:

1. Minimize downside risk in the stock market.
2. Maximize upside potential for capital gains.
3. Maximize growth of dividend income by buying maximum dividends at the lowest price possible.

Depending on the primary trend of the market and economy, the average length of time for a stock to rise from undervalue to overvalue has fluctuated between three years and five and three-quarters years. Some stocks cycle at a faster pace. Other stocks, especially those with frequent dividend increases, have a long upward climb and may be held longer before a sale at overvalue is necessary. In general, the amount of time required to cycle down from overvalue, through the declining trend and back to undervalue, is two years.

Bull and Bear Market Cycles

There are moments in every market cycle when investors question whether it is a bull market, a bear market, or a sideways trading range. A 200-point drop could just as easily be a correction in a bull

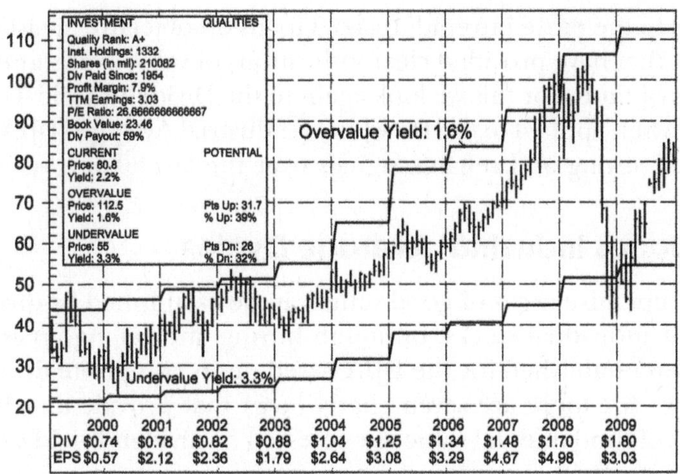

Figure 6.1 Air Products & Chemicals, Inc. (APD)
Source: *Copyright © Value Trend Analysis.*

market, the first break in a bear market, or the low point of the range in a sideways market. In hindsight we all have 20-20 vision, which provides little comfort at the moment clarity is most critical.

Although no one likes uncertainty, this is particularly true for investors. Benjamin Graham has said, "Individuals who cannot master their emotions are ill-suited to profit from the investment process." This is especially poignant during periods of extreme market volatility when emotions are running high, because investors will often make decisions that can undermine their ability to build long-term wealth.

Throughout investment history, pearls of wisdom about the proper course of action for investors during times of market uncertainty have come from figures such as John D. Rockefeller and his now famous exhortation to "buy when the blood is running in the streets." Even the Oracle of Omaha, Warren Buffett, has weighed in with, "Be fearful when others are greedy. Be greedy when others are fearful."

The quotes from Rockefeller and Buffett may represent sound contrarian philosophy and appear simple enough, but what qualified as "blood in the streets" to John D. and "fearful and greedy" to Brother Buffett may be subject to interpretation.

When your goal is to maximize real total return and minimize risk, it may prove more prudent to leave subjective measures of analysis to the more intrepid. Instead focus on objective measures of analysis that have provided clear indications of value over significant periods of time. For this we look again to the Dividend-Yield Theory, which, when applied to the Dow Jones Industrial Average (DJIA), has provided strong and reliable signals over the last 80-plus years.

Dow Jones Industrial Average Cycles

Just as repetitive areas of good value can be established by dividend yield for individual stocks, optimum buying and selling areas have also been established for the DJIA based on its composite dividend. In Figure 6.2 there are seven charts (a–g) that provide a technical portrait of fundamental value as expressed by dividend yield extending back to 1949.

For readers who are not proficient in using charts, here are some useful tips to help you understand the information that is displayed: The vertical axis on the far left edge of the chart displays price; the horizontal axis along the bottom of the chart displays time. Because this is a monthly chart, each of the vertical lines within the chart area represents one month. The top of the line is the high price for the period, the bottom of the line is the low price for the period, and the hash mark to the right is the closing price of the period.

As discussed previously, every stock has a unique profile of undervalue and overvalue dividend yield. In the case of the DJIA, there are four distinct areas: one that represents overvalue and three that represent undervalue. Unique to the *Investment Quality Trends* charts are horizontal lines that represent the price levels at which specific areas of dividend yield are reached. When the dividend is increased, the line will move up to display the price for that specific level of dividend yield. When the dividend is decreased, the line will move down to reflect the price for that specific level of dividend yield.

What these charts illustrate is that four specific areas of dividend yield have a repetitive pattern: 3.0 percent at overvalue; 4.0 percent, 5.0 percent, and 6.0 percent at undervalue. Historically, the DJIA has offered good value whenever the dividend yield has risen to 6.0 percent, as it did in 1949–1953, 1974, and in 1978–1982. Strong price support also has been evidenced at the 4.0 percent yield level, which halted and reversed declines in 1960, 1962, 1966, 1971, and, most notably, on October 19, 1987.

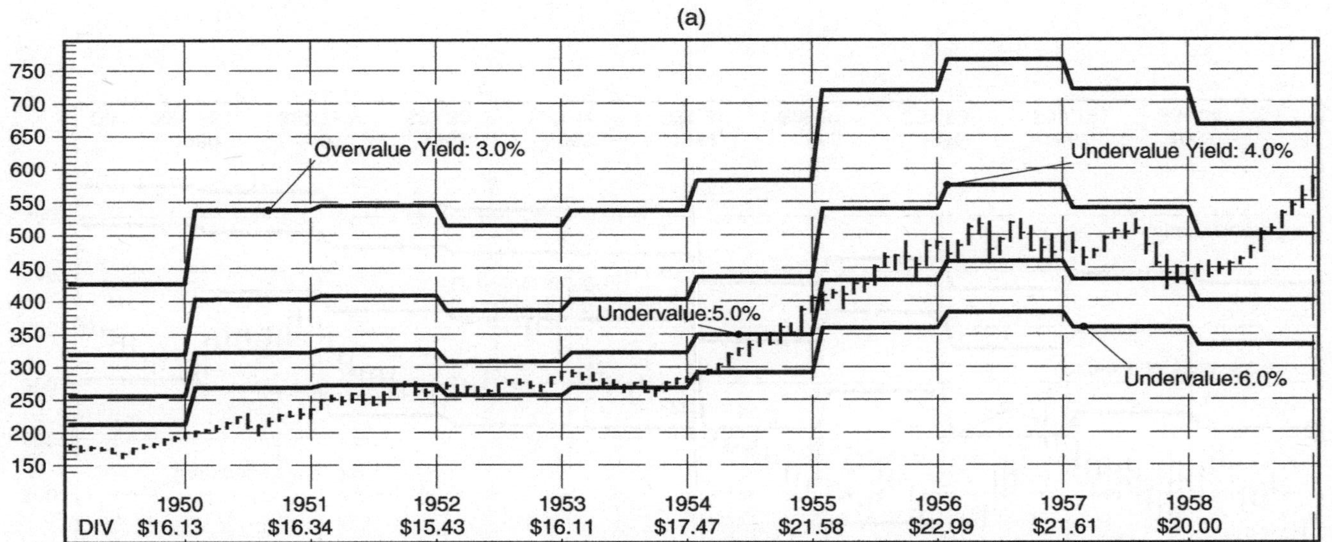

Figure 6.2 Undervalue and Overvalue Levels for the DJIA

Source: *Value Trend Analysis.*

(b)

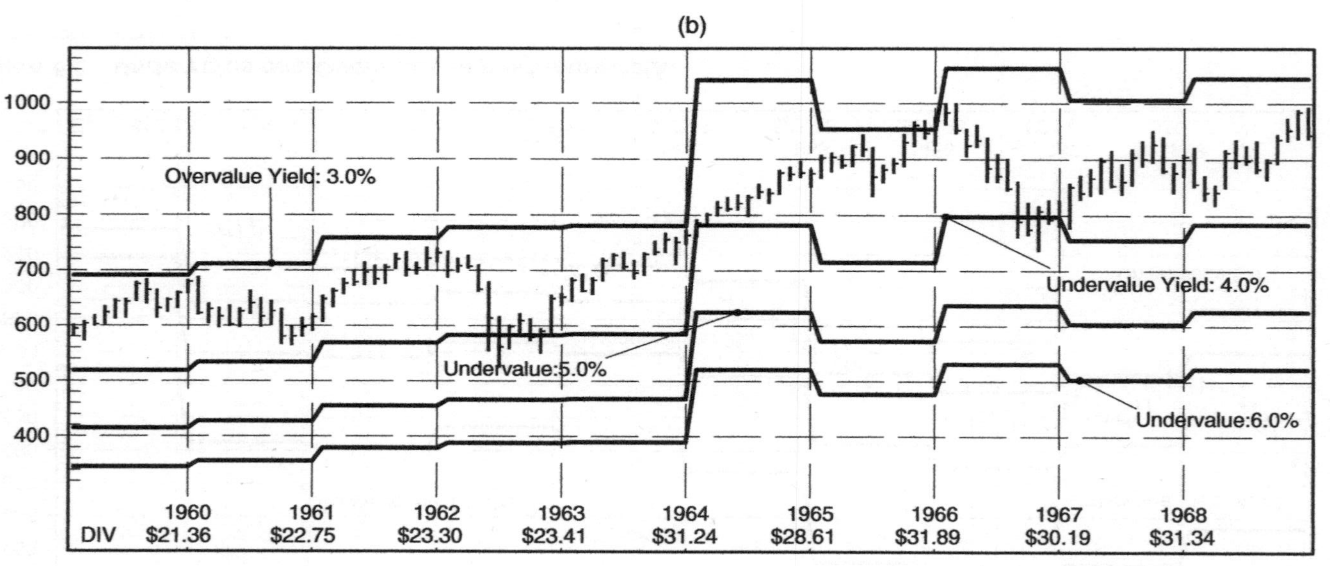
1000
900
800
700
600
500
400
Overvalue Yield: 3.0%
Undervalue Yield: 4.0%
Undervalue:5.0%
Undervalue:6.0%
DIV
1960 $21.36
1961 $22.75
1962 $23.30
1963 $23.41
1964 $31.24
1965 $28.61
1966 $31.89
1967 $30.19
1968 $31.34

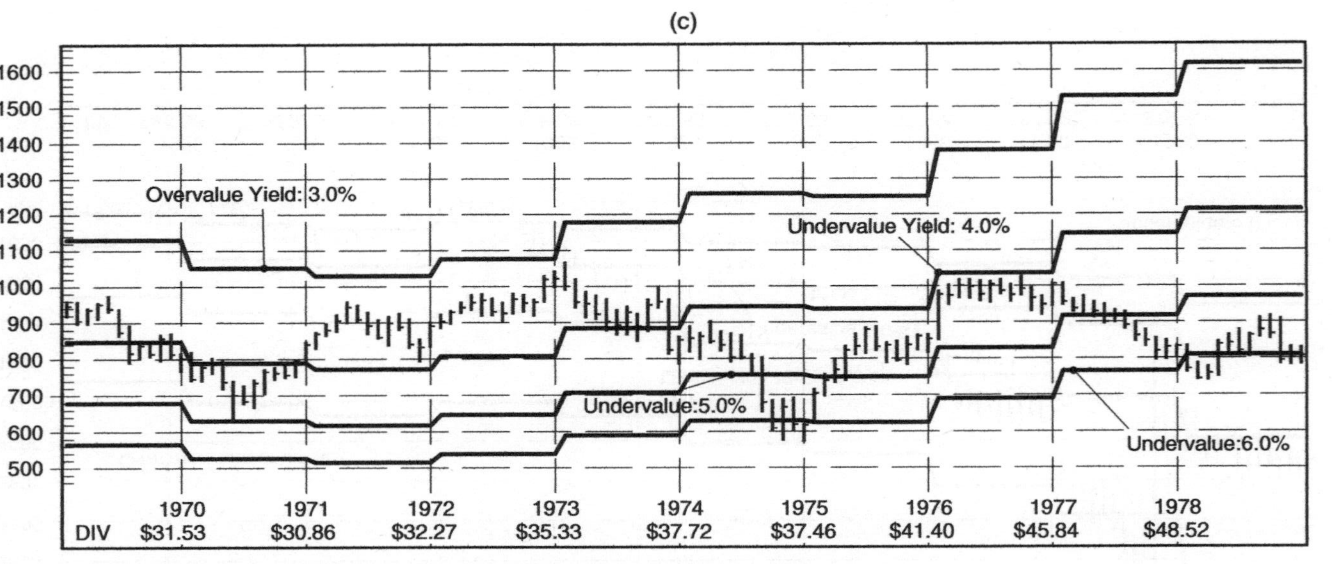

Figure 6.2 Undervalue and Overvalue Levels for the DJIA (*Continued*)

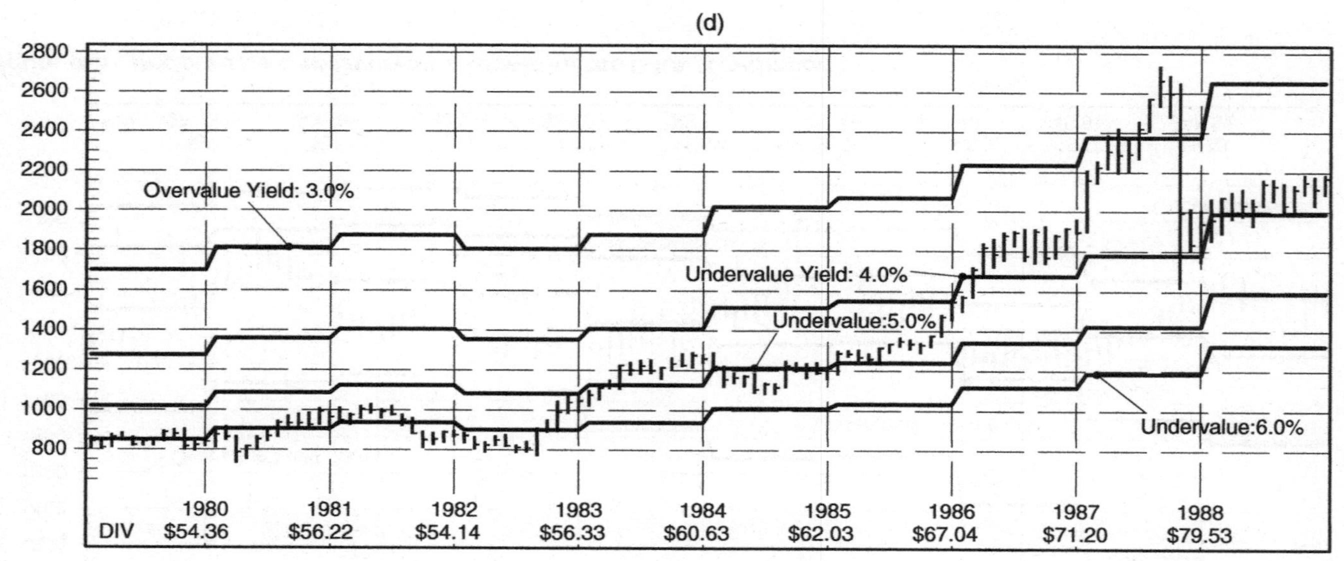
(d)
Overvalue Yield: 3.0%
Undervalue Yield: 4.0%
Undervalue:5.0%
Undervalue:6.0%
2800
2600
2400
2200
2000
1800
1600
1400
1200
1000
800
DIV
1980 $54.36
1981 $56.22
1982 $54.14
1983 $56.33
1984 $60.63
1985 $62.03
1986 $67.04
1987 $71.20
1988 $79.53

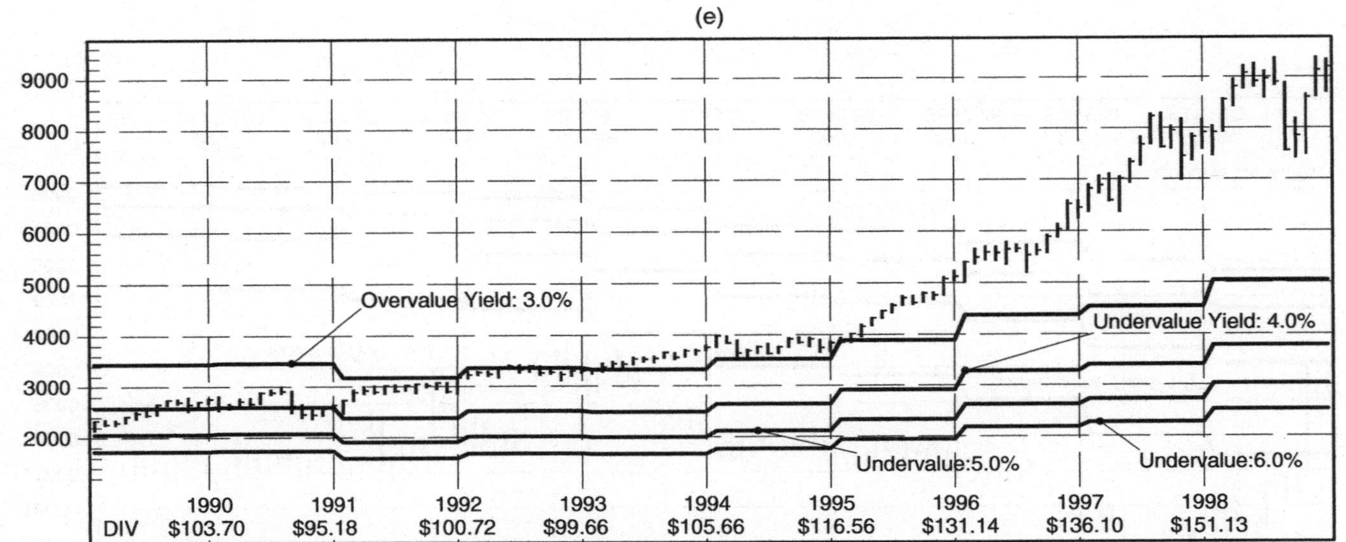

Figure 6.2 Undervalue and Overvalue Levels for the DJIA (*Continued*)

(f)

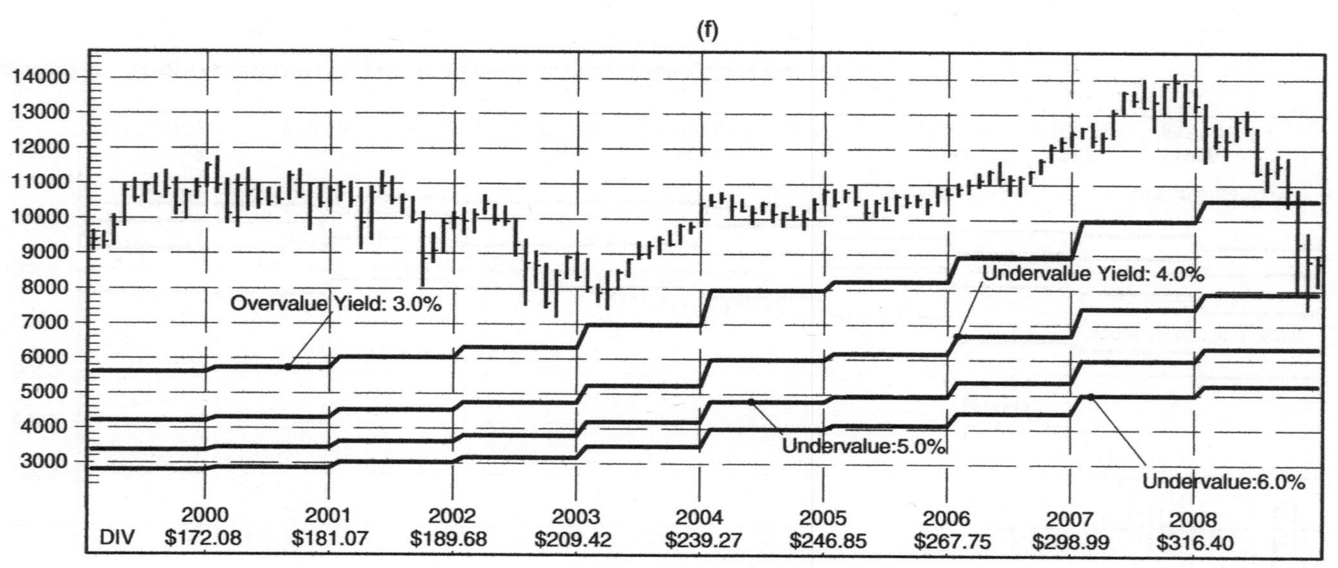

14000
13000
12000
11000
10000
9000
8000
7000
6000
5000
4000
3000
Overvalue Yield: 3.0%
Undervalue Yield: 4.0%
Undervalue:5.0%
Undervalue:6.0%
DIV
2000 $172.08
2001 $181.07
2002 $189.68
2003 $209.42
2004 $239.27
2005 $246.85
2006 $267.75
2007 $298.99
2008 $316.40

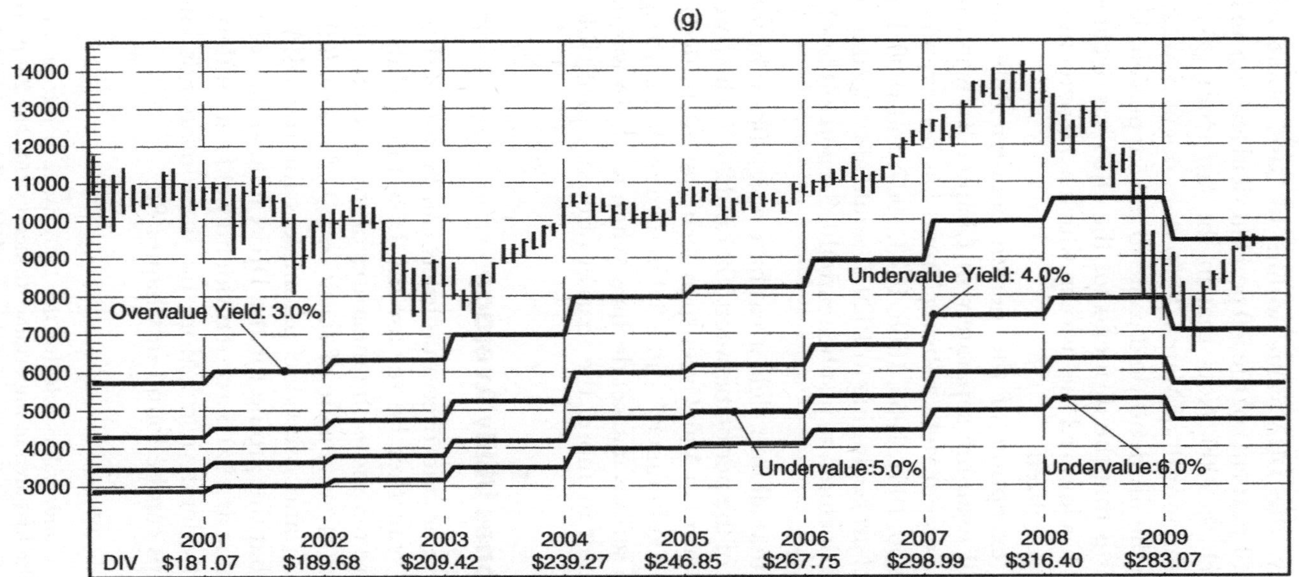

Figure 6.2 Undervalue and Overvalue Levels for the DJIA (*Continued*)

A 5.0 percent yield halted and reversed a major decline in 1970. More recently, the DJIA came within 10 basis points (10 one-hundredths of 1 percent) of the 5.0 percent yield level on an intraday basis on March 9, 2009. Note that in the last chart (g), the line representing the month of March, 2009 does not accurately display just how close the dividend yield came to the 5.0 percent level. The reason for this is that the dividend for the DJIA has declined since March, which has lowered the price at which a 5.0 percent dividend yield would be realized.

With the exception of the period between 1995 and 2007 (which we will examine separately in Chapter 8), when the Dow reaches a 3.0 percent yield a Rising Trend has been reversed. This occurred in 1950, 1961, 1966, 1968, 1973, 1987, and 1990. If we were to produce a chart beginning in 1929, it would also illustrate that the dividend yield declined to just beneath the 3.0 percent level prior to the Great Crash.

So we see that all four yield areas have a significant history. With the exception of the period between 1995 and 2007, which we believe former Fed Chairman Alan Greenspan accurately identified as a time of "Irrational Exuberance," did a 3.0 percent yield fail to signal the approach of a serious market decline. When the DJIA was priced to yield 6.0 percent or more, the market offered a profitable buying opportunity.

The Dow Jones Utility Average

Just as undervalue and overvalue levels can be established for the DJIA, so, too, can they be set for the Dow Jones Utility Average (DJUA). Figure 6.3 shows the measures of the market, a feature on the front cover of every issue of *Investment Quality Trends* that tracks the undervalue and overvalue parameters for the DJIA and the DJUA. Note that the profile for the DJUA follows that of the DJIA closely: overvalue at a 3.0 percent dividend yield and undervalue at a 6.0 percent dividend yield.* More on these dividends and these industry groups can be found in Chapter 8.

* The 4.0 percent undervalue yield for the DJIA listed in the measures of the market reflects the first area of undervalue dividend yield. The 2.0 percent dividend yield referenced for overvalue for the DJIA will be explained in greater detail in Chapter 8.

	Current			Potential to Overvalue				Potential to Undervalue			
Dow Jones Industrial Average	Price	Annual Dividend	Dividend Yield	Points Up	% Up	High Price	Low Yield	Points Down	% Down	Low Price	High Yield
	9544	$286.88	3.01%	4800	50%	14344	2.00%	2372	25%	7172	4.00%
	Current			Potential to Overvalue				Potential to Undervalue			
Dow Jones Utility Average	Price	Annual Dividend	Dividend Yield	Points Up	% Up	High Price	Low Yield	Points Down	% Down	Low Price	High Yield
	377	$16.67	4.42%	179	49%	556	3.00%	99	26%	278	6.00%

Figure 6.3 Measures of the Market (First-September 2009)

Source: *Investment Quality Trends.*

Value Cycles

Since the dawn of stock-market analysis, investors have searched for the one indicator that is perfect in its predictive capabilities. Although it is titillating to entertain such a notion, if such an indicator were to exist, it would eventually destroy the markets because all risk would be removed for practitioners and they would eventually own everything.

Even when investors are successful at identifying the primary trend of the market, there are stocks that rise during bear markets as well as stocks that decline during bull markets. All things being equal, I would rather know the direction of the primary trend at not, but market indicators can only tell you what the current temperature of the market is, not where to find good current value. The truth of the matter is there is the stock market and there is the market of stocks, which are two entirely different things.

We have reached that understanding after having observed our market of stocks, the Select Blue Chips, over the course of the last 40-plus years. As a result of these observations, we have developed another cyclical indicator, which measures what is always most important—values.

Our universe of Select Blue Chips is grouped into four distinct categories: Undervalued, Rising Trends, Overvalued, and, Declining Trends as shown in Figure 6.4.

The Undervalued category consists of stocks that represent historically repetitive extremes of low-price and high dividend-yield.

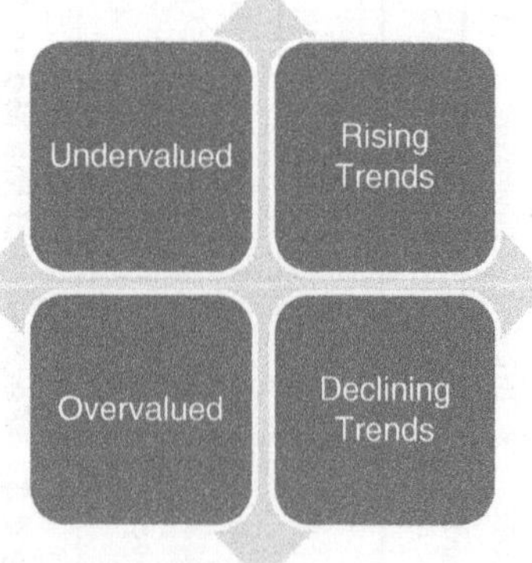

Figure 6.4 Select Blue Chip Categories

Category	Stocks	Percent
Undervalued stocks	84	30.8%
Overvalued stocks	61	22.3%
Rising Trends	90	33.0%
Declining Trends	38	13.9%
	273	100%

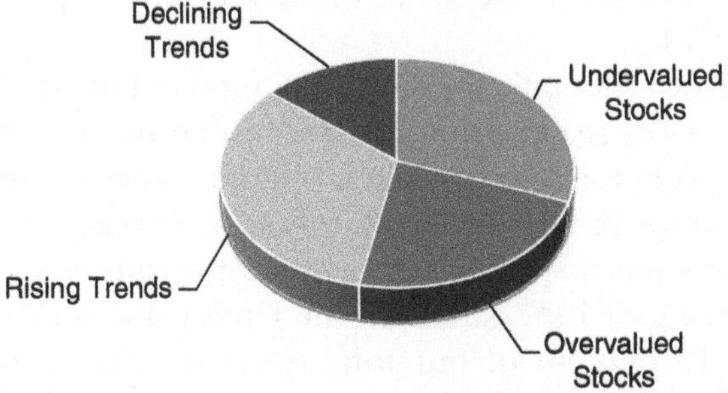

Figure 6.5 The Trend Verifier Chart (First-September 2009)

The Rising-Trend category consists of stocks whose stock price have risen at least 10 percent from its Undervalued base. The Overvalued category consists of stocks that have reached historically repetitive extremes of high price and low dividend yield. The Declining-Trend category consists of stocks whose stock price has declined at least 10 percent from its overvalued peak.

Twice each month, we calculate how many stocks are in each category and what percent that number is of the total. For over 40 years, we have tracked each category in the *Investment Quality Trends* "Blue-Chip Trend Verifier" as shown in Figure 6.5.

By tracking the movements between categories and comparing those movements against the highs and lows on the DJIA, we have established that whenever the percentage of stocks in the Undervalued category rises between 70 percent and 80 percent of the total, it has been coincident with a low cycle in the DJIA and many good buying opportunities. In contrast, when the percentage of stocks in the Undervalued category declines to 17 percent or less, it has been coincident with a high cycle in the DJIA, which indicates the market is Overvalued and susceptible to a major market decline.

By example, in early 1973 the DJIA eclipsed the high price established in 1966 and 1969, which many investors believed signaled the beginning of a new bull market. What many failed to take into consideration however, was that the new high was reached at the 3.0

percent dividend-yield level, which you now know represents the historically repetitive area of overvalue dividend-yield. At the same time the "Blue-Chip Trend Verifier" in the first January 1973 edition indicated there were just 17 percent of the Select Blue Chips in the Undervalued category. Shortly thereafter, the rally failed and the market declined until the bear market bottom was recorded in December 1974.

Now contrast the statistics just mentioned to January 1975. In the First-January 1975 issue, the measures of the market indicate that the dividend yield for the DJIA was 6.1 percent and the percentage of Select Blue Chips in the Undervalued category reached 80 percent. Obviously, this was a spectacular buying opportunity.

In the spring of 1987, stocks in the Undervalued category represented only 12 percent of our total universe. The dividend yield? You guessed it. Not only did it reach the 3.0 percent, overvalue area but shot through it to boot. At that juncture it was obvious the market was extremely overvalued on an historical basis. This situation was corrected thoroughly on October 19, when the DJIA registered its largest percentage drop ever in a single day.

A more contemporary example can be found in January 2000, when the DJIA peaked just below the 12,000 level. In the First-January 2000 issue, we find that only 13 percent of our Select Blue Chips were in the Undervalued category. The market slide that ensued did not end until October, 2002. Interestingly, even though the market decline was halted, in the First-November 2002 issue we find that only 16 percent of our stocks were in the Undervalued category, a clear indication that the bear market was far from over and a harbinger of what was to come five years later.

Value *Still* Prevails

In Chapter 8, we address cycles, indicators, and value in the market further because there are some important issues between 1995 and 2007 that must be addressed. At this juncture, however, we have learned the value of being able to identify both dividend-yield cycles and undervalue/overvalue cycles.

Knowing these cycles exist and having the means to measure them will be a tremendous help in achieving your long-term investment goals. A word of caution before we close, however; don't lose sight of the forest because of the trees. That is, don't get so caught up in following the stock market that you lose focus of the market of stocks.

CHAPTER 7

Finding Undervalued and Overvalued Stocks

The real voyage of discovery consists not in seeking new landscapes, but in having new eyes.

—Marcel Proust

One need not be a market wizard to understand that for every stock there are optimum times to buy and sell. For the investor whose primary objective is to maximize capital gains and to capture as much dividend income and growth possible, it is imperative to establish the repetitive areas of *undervalue* and *overvalue.*

Although capital gains can be achieved in stocks that are not purchased at undervalued levels, the potential for upside is reduced and the downside risks are increased. In a rising market, an investor may get away with this practice for a time, but one too many trips to that well and investment capital can disappear in a hurry. That is to say, there is a higher probability for consistent growth of capital and income when the investor maintains a buying and selling discipline based on the understanding of values.

In our experience, the most reliable way to identify stocks that offer good values is to limit investment considerations to only the highest-quality stocks and then establish the repetitive patterns of dividend yield, which reveals the areas of undervalue and overvalue. For some, this process, which you know now as the dividend-value strategy, can be viewed as overly mechanical or perhaps even rigid, but there is a method to the madness. Even seasoned investors can be seduced by the energy and momentum of a fast-moving market and be tempted to follow the crowd.

Those are the instances when most investors make mistakes that can inflict long-lasting damage to a portfolio. With the calm objectivity that comes from an adherence to quality and value, however, investors can avoid the pitfalls that derail others from reaching their ultimate objective, building a pool of wealth from which to secure current and future cash needs.

Finding and buying a stock that is undervalued requires patience and fortitude. For the investor who can master these virtues, the rewards are well worth the time and effort. In this chapter, we focus on how to identify the four categories of value: Undervalued, the Rising Trend, Overvalued, and the Declining Trend. Although it is important to recognize and understand the rising and declining trends, the majority of this chapter is directed toward undervalue and overvalue. In later chapters, we discuss how to incorporate our understanding of these four categories of value into the dividend-value portfolio.

Dividend Truth

Technical: Charting repetitive extremes of dividend yield
Fundamental: The identification of blue chip stocks, as defined by the Criteria for Select Blue Chips

A Sophisticated Approach

As mentioned in previous chapters, most stock market analysis is conducted through either fundamental or technical analysis. The dividend-value strategy is a marriage between the two disciplines. Although the process of identifying historic parameters of value by charting the highs and lows of dividend yield is clearly technical, our insistence that explorations for value be limited to only those stocks worthy of Select Blue Chip status is rooted in the most basic of fundamentals, the dividend, which represents a spendable return on investment capital.

Each stock has its own profile of undervalue and overvalue dividend yield, which means each stock must be studied individually. Any investor can establish the dividend-yield profile of any stock that has paid a dividend over sufficient time to establish a pattern. To identify these patterns you must first compute the dividend yield over a decade or longer (15 to 25 years is optimum) and then chart the channels on a grid.

At *Investment Quality Trends,* we have a fairly sophisticated algorithm that identifies the low-price/high-yield areas and the high-price/low-yield areas. In the "old days" this process required mastery of a slide rule; for a period we rented time on the old Computer Data computers that were programmed by punch cards. Geraldine has often said that the greatest invention of all time was the hand-held calculator, which dramatically shortened the process. Today, we have the luxury of a computer workstation.

To explain this process in detail, we will use the chart found in Figure 7.1. As with most stock charts, the price is found on the left (vertical) axis, and time is displayed along the bottom (horizontal) axis. The first step is to identify all the high-price extremes and the low-price extremes. In this example, we would note the highs in 1999, 2002, and 2007. For the lows we would note 2000 and 2008. The

Figure 7.1 Finding Undervalue/Overvalue

second step is to find the high price for each high-price year and the low price for each low-price year. These prices would be $49.25, $53.52, and $105.02 for the years 1999, 2002, and 2007, respectively. The data points for the low price areas in this example are $23 in 2000 and $50.71 in 2008. The third step is to find the dividend paid for each year of data points and then to calculate the dividend yield for each point. These would be 1.42 percent, 1.53 percent, and 1.41 percent for the highs and 3.21 percent and 3.47 percent for the lows.

Beginning with the high-price data points we add the three dividend yields together and then divide by three, finding an average of 1.45 percent. Unfortunately, due to space limitations in presenting the charts, what you don't see in this example is that this stock in 1987 and 1992 recorded low yields of 1.60 percent. Since there is a divergence between 1.45 percent and 1.60 percent, we would like to find a confirmation of the low yields recorded in 1987 and 1992. By adding a fourth yield from the 2005 high price, which is 1.89 percent, then dividing by four, we find an average of 1.56 percent, which we will round up to 1.60 percent and, therefore, confirm that the 1.60 percent dividend yield is the repetitive low.

Now, turning to the low-price/high-yield data points, we note that there are three minor lows (2001, 2003, and 2005) between the major lows in 2000 and 2008. When we calculate the dividend yields for these periods we find a major divergence. Hence, we discard these three and focus on the two extremes in 2000 and 2008. By adding these two yields together and then dividing by 2 we find an average of 3.34 percent, which we will round down to 3.30 percent. Once again, by looking back to 1987, 1988/1989, and to 1990, we find additional instances where the 3.30 percent dividend yield has marked a halt in declining prices and the stock reversed course, confirming that this is the high-yield undervalue area for this stock.

Undervalued Stocks

Using the simplest definition, undervalue is a relatively high dividend yield that in the past has coincided with the bottom of a major price decline. The term can apply to an individual stock, a group of stocks, or the overall market. When these repetitive areas of high-dividend yield are plotted on a stock chart, it becomes visually apparent that the stock has a tendency toward halting and reversing a decline in the same relative area of dividend yield each cycle. By averaging these relative areas of high yield, a boundary for the bottom can be established.

To further illustrate this point, let's consider the example of a company we will call Widgets "R" Us. In 1999, the stock recorded a 2.5 percent yield, which represented the top price for that cycle. In 2003, 2005, and 2007, the stock recorded low yields of 2.5 percent, 2.3 percent, and 2.7 percent, respectively. In 2002 a decline in the stock was halted and reversed at a 5.0 percent dividend yield, in 2004 at a 4.8 percent yield, and again in 2004 at a 5.2 percent dividend yield.

When we average these respective areas of high and low yield, it suggests that Widgets "R" Us has a tendency to halt and reverse a declining trend in the 5.0 percent dividend-yield area and a rising trend at the 2.5 percent dividend-yield area. Note that dividend yield is calculated from both price and dividend; as such the price of the stock at each of those turning points can vary depending on the dollar amount of the dividend.

Now let's take a look at a real-world example by examining the chart of The Stanley Works (SWK) in Figure 7.2. As noted on the chart, The Stanley Works (SWK) offers good historic value when the dividend yield is at 5.0 percent. The stock reaches its historic level of overvalue when the price rises and the dividend yield declines to 2.0 percent.

In October of 2000, The Stanley Works (SWK) declined to a price of $18.80. Based on the annual dividend of $0.94, the dividend yield was 5.0 percent and the stock was historically undervalued, which is displayed in the following equation:

Dividend Price Yield

$$\$0.94/\$18.80 = 5.0 \text{ percent}$$

A 5.0 percent dividend yield also identified historic good value in 2003, 2008, and 2009.

If there were one high yield that identified an undervalued price for every stock, it would make life ever so much simpler. Unfortunately, that just isn't the case. Because each stock has a unique profile of value, based on its repetitive extremes of high and low dividend yield, undervalue is not simply a very low price; rather, it

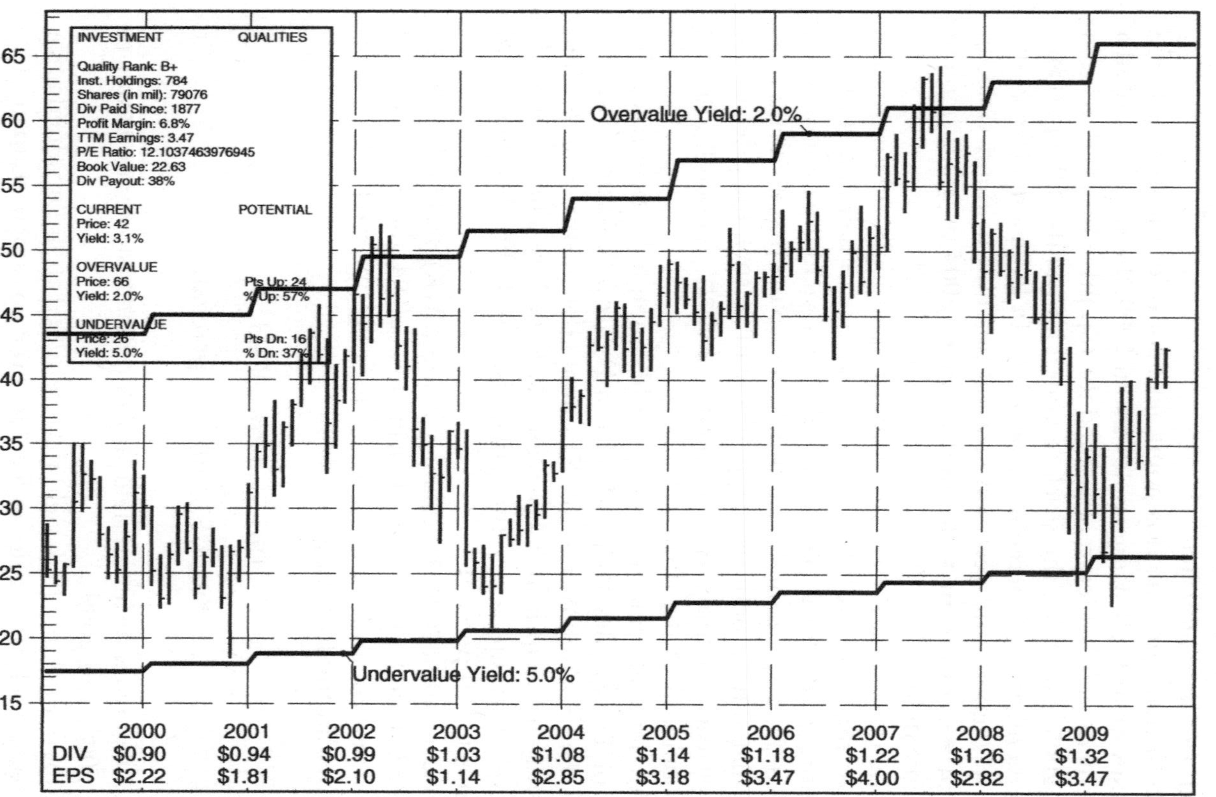

Figure 7.2 The Stanley Works (SWK)

Source: *Value Trend Analysis.*

represents a relatively high yield in relation to a currently low price. This is what makes an undervalued stock a bargain—high-quality at good value at a low price.

To take full advantage of the dividend-yield strategy, you will have to put in some work, which at the very least means keeping track of the undervalue and overvalue boundaries on the stocks under investment consideration. Once a purchase is made, you must continue to monitor the stock as it winds its way through its cycle. When dividends are increased, the yields at undervalue and overvalue must be recalculated to avoid selling your position too soon or to add to the position if a short-lived dip in price provides another undervalued opportunity.

Dividend Rule

Some stocks are undervalued when their yields are 4 percent, 5 percent, or 6 percent. Others may be equally undervalued on the basis of their historic profiles of dividend yield when their yields are 1 percent, 2 percent, or 3 percent. The point is that each stock has established its own profile of value, its own individual parameters of dividend yield, and each stock must be evaluated individually.

As we did with The Stanley Works (SWK) example, we have identified the Profiles of Value for 272 additional Select Blue Chips. Based on the current dividend yield, each of these stocks are categorized as Undervalued, in Rising Trends, Overvalued, or in Declining Trends. Beyond the respective category of value, the data tables display current prices, dividends, yields, trailing 12-month earnings, book values, and other fundamental information. The Undervalued category as of the mid-September issue of *Investment Quality Trends* can be observed in Figure 7.3. In later chapters, we show how to filter through these data tables when making investment considerations.

Are the Numbers Chiseled in Stone?

An undervalued stock should never be purchased before considering other factors, particularly when the market is at or close to the top of

Stock			Price	Dividend	Yield	Pts Dn	% Down	Undervalue LoPr/	HIYld	Pts Up	% Up	Overvalue HiPr/	LoYld	S&P	52-wk Lo	52-wk Hi	Bk Val	12-mo Earn	P/E	Pay out	Div in Dgr	Debt	BC	Tic
Abbott Labs	G	U	47	1.60	3.38%	−6	−13%	53	3.00%	67	141%	114	1.40%	A−	41	60	13	3.43	14	47%		45%	6	ABT
AFLAC	G	U	42	1.12	2.68%	−14	−34%	56	2.00%	145	347%	187	0.60%	A	11	68	14	2.50	17	45%		20%	6	AFL
Alberto-Culer		U	27	0.30	1.10%	−3	−10%	30	1.00%	33	119%	60	0.50%	A−	19	29	12	2.37	12	13%		0%	6	ACV
Altria	G	U	18	**1.36**	7.56%	−9	−51%	27	5.00%	27	152%	45	3.00%	A	14	21	2	1.52	12	89%		260%	6	MO
Applied Inds. Tech		U	22	0.60	2.79%	−1	−3%	22	2.70%	28	132%	50	1.20%	A−	14	30	12	0.99	22	61%		5%	5	AIT
Archer Daniels	G	U	29	0.56	1.95%	1	2%	28	2.00%	27	95%	56	1.00%	A+	14	32	21	2.65	11	21%		46%	6	ADM
AT&T Inc.		U	27	1.64	6.18%	−3	−12%	30	5.50%	55	209%	82	2.00%	B+	21	32	17	2.02	13	81%		57%	4	T
Automatic Data	G	U	38	1.32	3.44%	−31	−81%	69	1.90%	150	391%	189	0.70%	A+	31	46	11	2.64	15	50%		1%	6	ADP
Bancorpsouth		U	23	0.88	3.79%	0	0%	23	3.80%	8	35%	31	2.80%	A−	16	32	15	1.30	18	68%		NA	6	BXS
Bank of Hawaii	G	U	40	1.80	4.56%	−5	−14%	45	4.00%	32	82%	72	2.50%	A	25	70	18	3.21	12	56%		NA	6	BOH
Bank of Montreal	G	U	48	2.62	5.43%	−8	−16%	56	4.70%	53	109%	101	2.60%	B+	19	52	29	2.79	17	94%		NA	4	BMO
Becton Dickinsn	G	U	71	1.32	1.87%	5	7%	66	2.00%	94	133%	165	0.80%	A	58	85	22	4.82	15	27%		20%	6	BDX
Bemis Company		U	27	0.90	3.36%	−3	−12%	30	3.00%	23	86%	50	1.80%	A−	17	30	15	1.61	17	56%		44%	6	BMS
Bob Bans Farms		U	28	0.64	2.29%	−1	−4%	29	2.20%	30	103%	58	1.10%	B+	13	33	20	−0.09	−310	−711%	X	22%	5	BOBE
Boeing	G	U	51	1.68	3.30%	−9	−18%	60	2.80%	78	1.54%	129	1.30%	B+	29	63	0	3.11	16	54%		84%	5	BA
Bristol Mjers Sq		U	22	1.24	5.54%	−2	−11%	25	5.00%	40	177%	62	2.00%	B+	16	24	7	2.74	8	45%		56%	5	BMY
Cardinal Health	G	U	27	0.70	2.63%	−17	−64%	44	1.60%	113	426%	140	0.50%	A	25	53	24	3.19	8	22%		47%	6	CAH
Caterpillar	G	U	49	1.68	3.44%	−1	−1%	49	3.40%	56	115%	105	1.60%	A+	22	75	12	2.90	17	58%		186%	6	CAT
Central Pac Fin'l		U	2	*0.25*	11.16%	−6	−272%	8	3.00%	14	644%	17	1.50%	A−	2	22	17	−1.03	−2	−24%	X	NA	5	CPF
CerturyTel Inc	G	U	31	2.80	8.89%	−59	−187%	90	3.10%	669	2124%	700	0.40%	A−	20	40	31	3.22	10	87%		85%	6	CTL
Chevron Corp.	G	U	71	2.72	3.83%	−7	−9%	78	3.50%	65	91%	136	2.00%	A−	56	90	44	8.13	9	33%		8%	6	CVX

Cincinn Finl	G	U	26	1.58	6.09%	−14	−52%	40	4.00%	53	205%	79	2.00%	A	17	35	26	2.62	10	60%		NA	6	CINF
Cintes Corp.	G	U	29	0.47	1.63%	−18	−63%	47	1.00%	65	226%	94	0.50%	A	18	34	15	1.48	19	32%		42%	6	CTAS
Clorox	G	U	58	200	3.46%	−14	−24%	71	2.80%	96	166%	154	1.30%	A	46	65	−1	3.81	15	52%		NA	6	CLX
Coca-Cola	G	U	52	1.64	3.14%	−3	−5%	55	3.00%	153	293%	205	0.80%	A	37	56	10	2.70	19	61%		12%	6	KO
Colgate-Palmolive	G	U	75	1.76	2.35%	2	2%	73	2.40%	85	113%	160	1.10%	A+	54	80	5	3.91	19	45%		165%	6	CL
Community Trst Bncrp	G	U	26	1.20	4.69%	−2	−9%	28	4.30%	21	80%	46	2.60%	A	23	46	21	1.21	21	99%		NA	5	CTBI
Conoce Phillips	G	U	47	1.88	4.04%	−3	−6%	49	3.80%	52	112%	99	1.90%	B+	34	80	40	−16.38	−3	−11%	X	24%	4	COP
CVS Caremark Corp.	G	U	37	0.30	0.82%	−1	−3%	38	0.80%	38	105%	75	0.40%	A+	23	39	25	2.25	16	13%		26%	5	CVS
BatonCorp		U	58	200	3.46%	−9	−15%	67	3.00%	42	73%	100	2.00%	A−	30	72	40	2.74	21	73%		43%	6	ETN
Eaton Vance	G	U	29	0.62	2.11%	−12	−41%	41	1.50%	48	164%	78	0.80%	A−	12	44	3	0.97	30	64%		271%	6	EV
Ennis Inc.		U	15	0.62	4.27%	1	7%	13	4.60%	20	137%	34	1.80%	B+	7	18	11	−1.44	−10	−43%.	X	22%	5	EBF
Exelon Corp.	G	U	49	210	4.26%	4	7%	46	4.60%	51	103%	100	2.10%	B+	38	69	18	4.20	12	50%		134%	5	EXC
First Merch		U	7	0.32	4.91%.	−1	−9%	7	4.50%	4	64%	11	3.00%	A−	7	27	17	-1.11	−6	−29%	X	NA	5	FRME
Gallagher Arthr	G	U	24	1.28	5.30%	−8	−32%	32	4.00%	40	165%	64	2.00%	A−	15	30	8	1.16	21	110%	X	57%	5	AJG
Greif, Inc.	G	U	53	1.52	2.84%	−7	−14%	61	2.50%	63	119%	117	1.30%	B+	26	73	22	*1.93*	28	79%		71%	5	GEF
Harris Corp.	G	U	36	**0.88**	2.42%	−27	−73%	63	1.40%	89	246%	126	0.70%	B+	26	55	14	0.28	130	314%	X	38%	4	HRS
Hasbro lnc.	G	U	29	0.80	2.78%	−2	−7%	31	2.60%	71	248%	100	0.80%	A−	21	42	10	1.92	15	42%		54%	6	HAS
Heinz		U	40	1.68	4.21%	3	6%	37	4.50%	36	91%	76	2.20%	B+	31	53	5	2.85	14	59%		251%	4	HNZ
Henry (Jack)	G	U	24	0.34	1.39%	−10	−39%	34	1.00%	89	363%	113	0.30%	A+	14	24	7	1.22	20	28%		1%.	5	JKHY
HNI Corp.	G	U	23	0.86	3.82%	−12	−53%	34	2.50%	44	194%	66	1.30%	A−	8	34	9	0.33	68	261%	X	78%	5	HNI
Home Depot	G	U	28	0.90	3.27%	−7	−26%	35	2.60%	54	197%	82	1.10%	A	17	30	11	1.38	20	65%		64%	S	HD
IBM	G	U	119	220	1.85%	−3	−3%	122	1.80%	126	106%	244	0.90%	A	70	124	12	9.37	13	23%		76%	6	IBM
Integrys Energy		U	35	2.72	7.77%	−1	−4%	36	7.50%	24	69%	59	4.60%	A−	19	54	.37	−2.33	−15.	−117%	X	67%	5	TEG
Johnson & Johnson	G	U	60	1.96	3.25%	4	7%	56	3.50%	49	80%	109	1.80%	A+	46	73	17	4.55	13	43%		19%	6	JNJ

Figure 7.3 Undervalued Category

Stock			Price	Dividend	Yield	Pts Dn	% Down	Undervalue LoPr/	HIYld	Pts Up	% Up	Overvalue HiPr/	LoYld	S&P	52-wk Lo	52-wk Hi	Bk Val	12-mo Eam	P/E	Pay out	Div in Dgr	Debt	BC	Tic
Kaydon Corp.		U	34	0.72	2.13%	−2	−6%	36	2.00%	38	113%	72	1.00%	A−	21	59	20	1.48	23	49%		41%	5	KDN
Kelly Services		U	13	0.54	4.16%	−1	−4%	14	4.00%	23	177%	36	1.50%	B+	6.	20	17	−5.24	−2	−10%	X	13%	4	KELYA
Kimberly-Cark	G	U	58	2.40	4.14%	−9	−15%	67	3.60%	83	143%	141	1.70%	A	43	66	11	3.95	15	61%		107%	6	KMB
Limited Brands		U	16	0.60	3.79%	−11	−72%	27	2.20%	104	657%	120	0.50%	B+	6	22	6	0.30	53	200%	X	135%	4	LTD
Lockheed Martin	G	U	76	2.28	3.02%	−24	−31%	99	2.30%	87	115%	163	1.40%	B+	57	118	7	7.51	10	30%		41%.	5	LMT
M&T Bank	G	U	59	2.80	4.72%	−11	−18%	70	4.00%	156	263%	215	1.30%	A−	29	109	57	2.58	23	109%	X	NA	6	MTB
McDonalds	G	U	54	2.00	3.69%	−1	−2%	56	3.60%	46	84%	100	2.00%	A−	46	65	12	3.77	14	53%		71%	6	MCD
Merck & Co.		U	33	1.52	4.62%	−11	−32%	43	3.50%	68	208%	101	1.50%	B+	20	34	10	2.70	12	56%		19%	4	MRK
Meredith Corp.	G	U	28	0.90	3.19%	−41	−145%	69	1.30%	122	432%	150	0.60%	A−	11	31	14	−2.38	−12	−38%	X	39%	6	MDP
Mn Mn Mg		U	75	2.04	2.74%	7	9%	68	3.00%	45	61%	120	1.70%	A+	41	75	15	4.05	18	50%		32%	8	MMM
Mne Safety Appl.	G	U	27	0.96	3.51%	−6	−21%	33	2.90%	53	192%	80	1.20%	B+	16	42	11	1.51	18	64%		21%	5	MSA
Nike lnc CL B	G	U	55	1.00	1.82%	−1	−1%	56	1.80%	112	204%	167	0.60%	A+	38	68	18	3.03	18	33%		6%	6	NKE
Noble Energy Inc.	G	U	67	0.72	1.08%	−1.3	−20%	80	0.90%	113	169%	180	0.40%	B+	31	69	35	5.79	12	12%		39%.	5	NBL
Notfotk Southen		U	49	1.36	2.77%	4	8%	45	3.00%	48	98%	97	1.40%	A−	27	73	27	3.72	13	37%		64%	5	NSC
NorthropGrumm		U	49	1.72	3.49%	−8	−16%	57	3.00%	65	133%	115	1.50%	A−	34	71	38	−3.79	−13	−45%	X	22%	5	NOC
Overseas Shiptotefing	G	U	38	1.75	4.65%	3	7%	35	5.00%	65	173%	103	1.70%	B+	20	71	71	8.35	5	21%		83%	5	OSG
PepsiCo	G	U	59	1.80	3.07%	−23	−39%	82	2.20%	91	156%	150	1.20%	A+	44	75	9	3.23	18	56%		36%	6	PEP
Pfizer		U	16	0.64	3.91%	0	2%	16	4.00%	33	201%	49	1.30%	B+	12	19	9	1.12	15	57%		11%	4	PFE
Philip Morris Intl Inc.	G	U	48	216	4.53%	4	9%	43	5.00%	24	51%	72	3.00%	A+	32	55	3	3.25	15	67%		45%	6	PM
Pitney Bowes		U	23	1.44	6.14%	−5	−23%	29	5.00%	73	309%	96	1.50%.	B+	.18	40	0	1.90	12	76%		800%	4	FBI
Polaris lnds	G	U	38	1.56	4.09%	−14	−36%	52	3.00%	66	173%	104	1.50%	A−	15	54	5	3.04	13	51%		189%	5	Pll

PPG Industries Inc.		U	58	2.12	3.66%	5	8%	53	4.00%	24	41%	82	2.60%	B+	28	70	19	1.35	43	157%	X	74%	4	PPG
Procter Gamble	G	U	55	1.76	3.18%	−15	−27%	70	2.50%	105	189%	160	1.10%	A+	44	74	21	4.26	13	41%		34%	6	PG
Raymond James Fncl	G	U	23	0.44	1.90%	−1	−6%	24	1.80%	26	112%	49	0.90%	A−	11	38	16	1.34	17	33%		12%	5	RJF
Selective Ins Grp		U	16	0.52	3.16%	−1	−5%	17	3.00%	18	111%	35	1.50%	A−	10	30	18	−0.05	−329	−1040%	X	27%	5	SIGI
Sigma-Aldrich	G	U	52	0.58	1.12%	3	6%	48	1.20%	64	125%	116	0.50%	A+	31	57	13	2.67	19	22%		12%	6	SIAL
Sterling Bancorp		U	8	0.36	4.69%	−1	−17%	9	4.00%	8	104%	16	2.30%	A−	6	19	7	0.58	13	62%		NA	5	STL
Sysco Corp.	G	U	26	0.96	3.71%	−22	−85%	48	2.00%	111	430%	137	0.70%	A+	19	35	6	1.77	15	54%		62%	6	SYY
Target Corp.	G	U	47	0.68	1.43%	−21	−43%	68	1.00%.	89	187%	136	0.50%	A+	25	60	19	2.77	17	25%		105%	6	TGT
Teleflex Inc.	G	U	47	1.36	2.87%	−24	−51%	72	1.90%	104	219%	151	0.90%	A−	37	68	37	7.12	7	19%		106%	6	TFX
TJX Companies	G	U	37	0.48	1.30%	0	0%	37	1.30%	59	160%	96	0.50%	A+	18	37	7	2.22	17	22%		40%	6	TJX
Trustmark Corp.	G	U	19	0.92	4.83%	−7	−38%	26	3.50%	27	141%	46	2.00%	B+	14	34	17	1.47	13	63%		NA	4	TRMK
United Technol	G	U	62	1.54	2.50%	−8	−14%	70	2.20%	67	108%	128	1.20%	A+	37	67	18	4.40	14	35%		37%	6	UTX
Valley Nat'l Bnk		U	12	0.76	6.60%	1	6%	11	7.00%	14	120%	25	3.00%	A−	8	24	8	0.43	27	177%	X	NA	6	VLY
Valspar Corp.	G	U	27	0.60	2.19%	2	9%	25	2.40%	27	99%	55	1.10%	B+	14	28	15	1.35	20	44%		55%	5	VAL
VF Corp.	G	U	72	2.36	3.26%	7	9%	66	3.60%	59	81%	131	1.80%	A	38	84	33	4.74	15	50%		31%	6	VFC
Walgreen Co.	G	U	34	0.55	1.61%	−5	−15%	39	1.40%	103	302%	138.	0.40%	A+	21	37	14	2.03	17	27%		1%	6	WAG
Wal-Mart Stores	G	U	50	1.09	2.16%	−4	−8%	55	2.00%	59	116%	109	1.00%	A−	46	64	17	3.41	15	32%		57%	6	WMT
Weyco Group	G	U	22	0.60	2.70%	−5	−23%	27	2.20%	32	145%	55	1.1.0%	A−	20	42	14	1.08	21	56%		1%	6	WEYS

Figure 7.3 Undervalued Category (*Continued*)

its cycle. Upon further investigation, you may discover serious fundamental problems within the company that have forced the price to drop to undervalued levels. A high level of debt or an excessively high payout ratio may indicate the dividend is in danger. In general, however, if the stock is a blue chip and its dividend is well protected by earnings, a purchase at undervalued levels is definitely worthy of consideration.

When a high-quality stock such as SWK has declined to its undervalued area, the likelihood for a deeper decline in price is greatly reduced, but is by no means eliminated. Although the repetitive points of undervalue and overvalue are established over long periods of time, the prices designating undervalue and overvalue levels are not chiseled in stone.

Remember, the markets are a reflection of the thoughts, opinions, and emotions of millions of investors, who can display a wide range of behaviors at any given moment. Yes, Virginia, the markets are sometimes even irrational. As such, investors can drive prices above or below undervalue and overvalue areas by a few points or even to ridiculous extremes. Depending on how investors react to news and information, no power on earth can limit price movements between specific boundaries. If nothing else has been learned over the course of the present bear market, when sufficiently exercised, investors have the ability to move prices beyond logical norms and to speculative extremes.

As a case in point, observe the chart of UTX in Figure 7.4. Note that UTX offers good historic value when the dividend-yield is 2.2 percent and reaches its historic level of overvalue when the price rises and the yield declines to 1.2 percent. When the market reopened after the September 11, 2001 attacks, UTX declined along with broad market to just above $20 per share.

Based on the then-current dividend of $0.45, the dividend yield reached 2.2 percent and the stock offered good historic value. The following bar, which represents the month of October, illustrates that investors were motivated sufficiently to accumulate UTX, and the price rose until April, 2002 to within 10 percent of its historic level of overvalue. At this juncture, the broad market turned down to test the September 2001 lows, and UTX followed suit until October 2002, within 10 percent of the undervalue yield of 2.2 percent. Almost on cue, the stock reversed to the upside and entered a rising

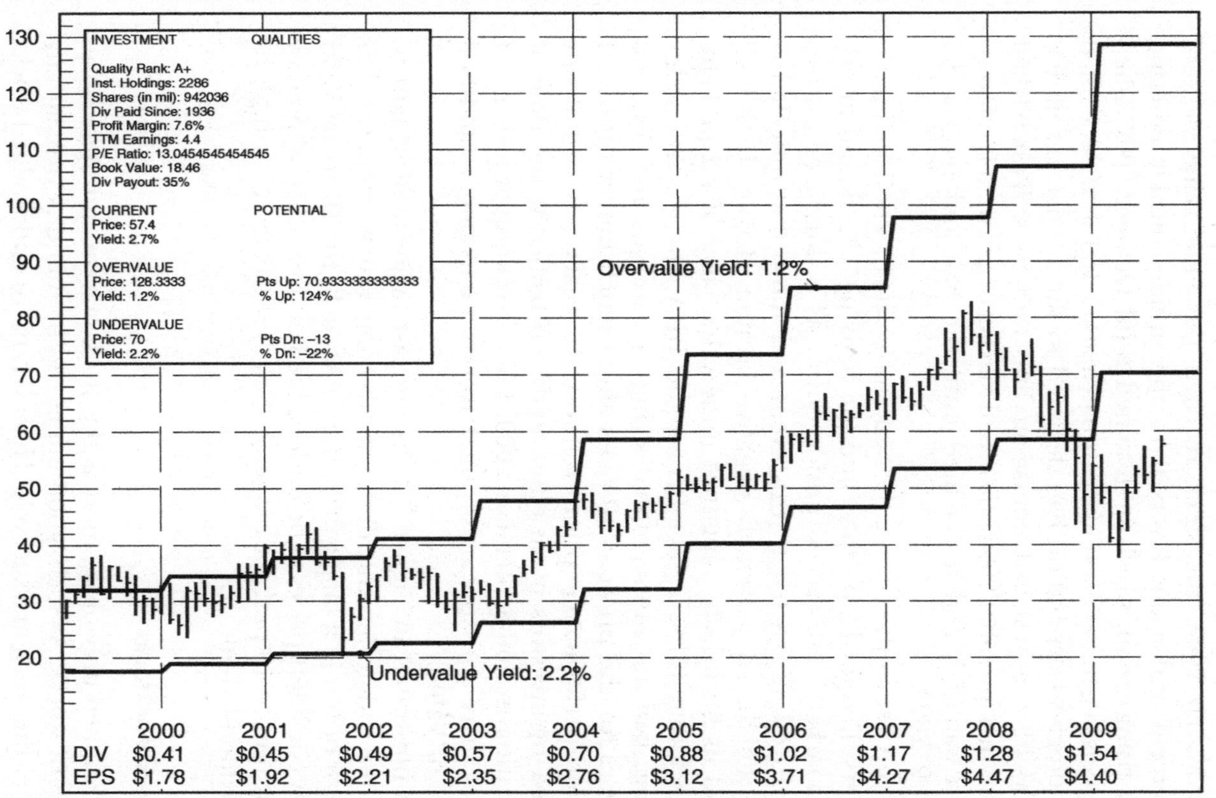

Figure 7.4 United Technologies Corporation (UTX)

Source: *Value Trend Analysis.*

trend, which was aborted in February 2003 when the markets tested the October 2002 lows.

In March 2003, the stock reached the undervalue yield of 2.2 percent and again reversed to the upside, quickly entering into a rising trend, which it sustained until October 2007, when the wheels began to fall off in the broad market. In July 2008, United Technologies Corporation had declined to the 2.2 percent undervalue yield and reversed course in line with its well-established pattern. In September 2008, the broad market began what is referred to as a waterfall, and it declined until the halt and reversal on March 9, 2009.

If you remember, it was in September 2008, when Lehmann Brothers filed for bankruptcy and the banking, credit, and investment markets were turned upside down. As is illustrated on this chart, investors reacted to this event and those that quickly followed suit in an extremely negative fashion, driving UTX well beyond its historically repetitive undervalue yield of 2.2 percent. The fact that UTX, a member of the DJIA with an A+ quality ranking, had an uninterrupted string of earnings and dividend increases for the previous 10 years and a much longer history of superior performance prior to those 10 years was completely ignored by investors in an emotion-driven panic. At the time of this writing in mid-September 2009, UTX is trading at just shy of $63 per share and appears on track to resume its long-established Profile of Value.

As illustrated in Figure 7.4, in the vast majority of instances, overvalue and undervalue designations come within ten percent of the high or low in a major price move. As such, the Dividend-Yield Theory considers prices to be undervalued or overvalued when they are within the 10 percent range of their historic levels of high or low dividend yield.

The Market of Stocks

As mentioned previously, there is the stock market and there is the market of stocks. As such, good values can be found at virtually any phase of the stock market cycle. However, more undervalued stocks can be found at the end of a bear market or during a major correction in a bull market. Because the selection of undervalued stocks is likely to be large, it is a time that investors have an exceptional opportunity to diversify their holdings.

By example, in the mid-March 2009 issue of *Investment Quality Trends,* 177 or 65 percent of our 273 Select Blue Chips represented historic good values and were in the Undervalued category. An extraordinary number, too many to list, were trading at or below book values. Also extraordinary, as was illustrated in the UTX example, were the number of stocks investors had driven beyond long-established extremes of high dividend yield.

Although the Dividend-Yield Theory has accurately defined the repetitive levels of undervalue time and again over four decades, it cannot determine precisely when a stock purchased at undervalue will begin to rise in price. Nonetheless, it is clear that these stocks are bargains, and that high-quality stocks that have consistently proved their worth over the years will eventually garner investor attention.

As all experienced investors know, timing is almost impossible to nail down on a consistent basis. Even so, when the timing of an acquisition is not exactly in synch with that of the broad market trend, undervalued stocks have a propensity for maintaining their value and price, which can even be seen in a bear market. As my partner Mike frequently says, "With undervalued stocks it is a when and not an if." If there is one thing knowledgeable investors cannot ignore for very long, it is a high-quality company that offers exceptional, historic value. Although all economic and business cycles eventually come to an end and the markets will respond with a period of contraction, the conditions that initiated the decline will improve, and animal spirits will gravitate toward undervalued stocks to realize excellent long-term capital gains.

The Overvalued Phase

Using the simplest definition, overvalue is a relatively low dividend-yield that in the past has coincided with the top of a major rising price trend. The term can apply to an individual stock, a group of stocks, or the overall market. When these repetitive areas of low-dividend yield are plotted on a stock chart, it becomes visually apparent that the stock has a tendency toward halting and reversing a rising trend in the same relative area of dividend-yield each cycle.

By averaging these relative areas of low-yield, a boundary for the top can be established.

The process for identifying the historically repetitive areas of overvalue is identical to that for the historically repetitive areas of undervalue detailed earlier in this chapter. For a refresher, refer back to Figure 7.1 and the accompanying text.

For an example of overvalue, refer back to the undervalued stocks section and review the examples for the fictitious Widgets "R" Us and the real-world example of The Stanley Works (SWK). The mechanics for identifying Undervalue and overvalue are the same; the only difference is with overvalue you are looking for tops rather than bottoms.

When a stock approaches the undervalue area it is a signal to investors that historic good value is in the offing. Conversely, when a stock approaches the overvalue area, it is a signal to investors that much of the historic value has been realized over the course of the rising trend. This is not to say that that an overvalued stock cannot continue to rise; our charts are replete with dozens of examples that prove otherwise. What is fundamental to the overvalue area, however, is any further upside potential is far outweighed by the downside risk. The only caveat to this is if an overvalued company increases its dividend, the price at overvalue will also rise, creating further upside potential for the continuation of the rising trend.

Any experienced investor with an ounce of self-honesty will admit to have engaged in speculative roulette at some point in his investment experience; anyone who has felt the energy and excitement of a rampaging stock or market knows exactly what I am referring to. Once euphoria sets in, however, it is much like unwanted company; hard to get rid of. Although everyone enjoys feeling on top of the world, for investors it can present a major problem because investment euphoria often masks the fact that the top of a cycle has been reached. For the investor with eyes to see, the overvalued area is the time to ring the bell and plant the flag, meaning that it's time to harvest well-deserved profits.

The overvalue area also tends to coincide with the time that less sophisticated investors succumb to the allure of the large sums of money being made all around them, which all too often leads them to buy at the top. This phenomenon is most prevalent in the hot stock of the times, which perpetuates even more buying, which pushes stock prices beyond all measures of fundamental value. At some point, though, comes the inevitable correction; trees cannot grow to the sky.

When the broad market is overvalued, the risk level for all stocks is ratcheted higher. However, investment decisions should still be based on the specific values for individual stocks. Remember, each stock has its own distinctive level of overvalue. So, even when a bull market is in its latter stages, not all stocks are overvalued. For the ones that are overvalued, not all stocks are overvalued to the same extent.

For these reasons, it is important to plot each stock's dividend yield on a chart and make note of the yield area where the stock historically reverses course. In so doing, it is possible to identify the dividend yield at which it is overvalued. When a stock's price is pushed to the upper channel line on the dividend-yield charts shown in this book, the yield is reaching a level at which the investor is overpaying for the dividend to be received. This is the textbook portrait for the historically repetitive area of overvalue. See Figure 7.5 for a list of Overvalued stocks as of mid-September 2009.

No One Gets Bonus Points for Being a Hero

Of my grandfather's many lessons, the one most constantly reinforced was "the gain is made on the buy, son." Although most of my grandfather's folksy quips of wisdom are immediately understood, whenever I share this one it almost always is met with a blank stare of confusion. "How do you establish a gain on the buy? You don't know what you've made until you sell!"

In the accounting sense, this, of course, is correct. What my grandfather was teaching me though was a values-based mindset; when you buy right, the gains are almost assured. In *IQ Trends* speak we would say that when you focus on quality and value there is a higher probability that gains will follow. In either case, the point should be easy to understand: The maximum potential for capital appreciation and the highest dividend yields are secured when a stock is purchased at historically good value.

So what is buying right? According to the Dividend-Yield Theory, stocks trade between two channels of dividend-yield extremes: An area of low price/high yield (undervalue), and an area of high price/low yield (overvalue). Therefore, purchases should be limited to shares that offer historically repetitive high dividend yields and low prices (undervalue), which offers the maximum upside potential and minimum downside risk. That is buying right.

Overvalue: (Selling Area)

Each stock has reached its own distinctive high price with low dividend yield. Unless dividends are raised, it may be anticipated that overpriced stocks will decline toward undervalue. It is important to recognize the potential downside risk, which exists at the overvalue level. Selling here preserves profits and capital.

Stock			Price	Dividend	Yield	Pts Dn	% Down	Under-value LoPr/HIYld		Pts Up	% Up	Over-value HIPr/LoYld		S&P	52-wk Lo	52-wk HI	Bk Val	12-mo Earn	P/E	Pay out	Div in Dgr	Debt	BC	Tlc
ABM Industries		O	21	0.52	2.52%	10	50%	10	5.00%	2	10%	23	2.30%	A-	12	24	13	0.98	21	53%		49%	5	ABM
Amer. States Wr		O	36	1.00	2.77%	16	45%	20	5.00%	−8	−21%	29	3.50%	B+	27	41	19	1.35	27	74%		88%	5	AWR
Ametek		O	35	0.24	0.69%	31	90%	4	6.70%	−11	−31%	24	1.00%	A	25	50	13	2.10	17	11%		52%	5	AME
AON Corp.		O	42	0.60	1.43%	34	80%	8	7.30%	−24	−57%	18	3.30%	B+	33	50	21	1.87	22	32%		31%	4	AOC
Assoc Bank Corp.		O	10	0.20	1.94%	6	56%	5	4.40%	0	−8%	10	2.00%	A-	9	32	18	0.49	21	41%		NA	5	ASBC
Bank of NY		O	29	0.36	1.24%	19	65%	10	3.50%	1	3%	30	1.20%	B+	15	40	23	0.72	40	50%		NA	4	BK
Bank America		O	17	0.04	0.24%	16	95%	1	5.00%	−15	−86%	2	1.70%	B+	3	40	23	0.60	28	7%		NA	5	BAC
Bard CR		O	81	0.68	0.84%	54	67%	27	2.50%	4	5%	85	0.80%	A	69	102	21	4.77	17	14%		8%	6	BCR
Bames Group		O	17	0.32	1.89%	8	46%	9	3.50%	−2	−10%	15	2.10%	B+	8	25	12	0.80	21	40%		63%	5	B
Black & Decker		O	47	0.48	1.01%	35	75%	12	4.00%	1	1%	48	1.00%	B+	20	70	19	2.91	16	16%		97%	4	BDK
Calif. Wat Svc		O	37	1.18	3.19%	20	54%	17	7.00%	−8	−20%	30	4.00%	B+	28	48	20	2.11	18	56%		75%	4	CWT
Church & Dwight	G	O	56	0.56	1.01%	32	58%	23	2.40%	−12	−22%	43	1.30%	A+	45	66	21	3.01	18	19%		61%	6	CHD
Citigroup Inc.		O	5	0.04	0.88%	3	68%	1	2.80%	−1	−12%	4	1.00%	B+	1	24	14	−3.65	−1	−1%	X	NA	4	C
Clarcor		O	33	0.36	1.11%	24	72%	9	4.00%	−15	−45%	18	2.00%	A	23	43	13	1.56	21	23%		18%	6	CLC
Cleco Corp.		O	25	0.90	3.63%	13	52%	12	7.50%	1	4%	26	3.50%	B+	17	28	18	1.40	18	64%		84%	5	CNL
Comerica		O	28	0.20	0.72%	25	91%	3	8.00%	−21	−76%	7	3.00%	B+	12	42	33	−0.06	−460	−333%	X	NA	4	CMA
Ecolab Inc.	G	O	46	0.56	1.22%	31	67%	15	3.70%	1	2%	47	1.20%	A+	29	52	8	1.49	31	38%		42%	6	ECL
Enbridge	G	O	38	1.36	3.59%	17	45%	21	6.50%	−8	−20%	30	4.50%	A	26	41	17	3.47	11	39%		177%	6	ENB
Energen		O	43	0.50	1.15%	31	71%	13	4.00%	−23	−54%	.20	2.50%	A	23	52	28	4.02	11	12%		74%	6	EGN

Equifax Inc.		O	28	0.16	0.58%	25	91%	2	6.60%	−21	−76%	7	2.40%	B+	19	37	12	1.95	14	8%		82%	4.	EFX
Federal REIT		O	62	2.64	4.25%	29	47%	33	8.00%	4	6%	66	4.00%	A-	37	95	18	1.85	34	143%	X	88%	6	FRT
Fifth Third Bank		O	10	0.04	0.41%	9	90%	1	4.20%	−8	−77%	2	1.80%	B+	1	21	13	−2.45	−4	−2%	X	NA	4	FITB
Fst Mdwest Bk		O	10	0.04	0.40%	9	88%	1	3.30%	−8	−83%	2	2.30%	A	6	31	14	0.01	1010	400%	X	NA	6	FMBI
Fulton Financial		O	7	0.12	1.63%	4	59%	3	4.00%	−3	−35%	5	2.50%	A	5	17	9	−0.33	−22	−36%	X	NA	5	FULT
Gorman Rupp		O	26	0.40	1.55%	16	64%	9	4.30%	−9	−35%	17	2.40%	A	15	45	10	1.29	20	31%		1%	6	GRC
Harsco Corp.		O	34	0.80	2.37%	21	63%	13	6.40%	−2	−5%	32	2.50%	A-	17	47	18	1.87	18	43%		60%	5	HSC
Huntington Bnk		O	4	0.04	0.98%	4	86%	1	7.00%	−3	−67%	1	3.00%	B+	1	14	6	−7.86	−1	−1%	X	NA	4	HBAN
Imperial Oil Ltd.		O	38	0.37	0.96%	29	76%	9	4.00%	−22	−58%	16	2.30%	A+	24	48	10	**2.72**	14	14%		1%	6	IMO
Ingersol Rand		O	32	0.28	0.87%	28	86%	5	6.00%	−18	−57%	14	2.00%	A	11	38	21	−9.26	−3	−3%	X	11%	6	IR
Int'l Flav & Frag		O	38	1.00	2.64%	18	47%	20	5.00%	2	6%	40	2.50%	A-	25	45	9	2.55	15	39%		184%	5	IFF
Johnson Controls	G	O	27	0.52	1.92%	19	71%	8	6.70%	−6	−23%	21	2.50%.	A+	8	36	14	−1.05	−26	−50%	X	32%	6	JCL
LaClede Group		O	33	1.54	4.74%	11	32%	22	7.00%	−2	−5%	31	5.00%	B+	29	56	24	2.97	11	52%		74%	5	LG
Legg Mason		O	30	0.12	0.40%	25	84%	5	2.50%	−18	−60%	12	1.00%	A	10	52	33	−13.20	−2	−1%	X	46%	5	LM
Lincoln National		O	26	0.04	0.15%	25	98%	0	8.30%	−25	−95%	1	3.30%	B+	5	60	30	−4.27	−6	−1%	X	42%	4	LNC
Marriott Int'l		O	25	0.02	0.08%	23	92%	2	1.00%	−20	−80%	5	0.40%	A	12	30	4	0.27	92	7%		209%	5	MAR
Marshall & Ilsley		O	7	0.04	0.58%	6	88%	1	5.00%	−5	−73%	2	2.10%	A-	3	30	18	−8.11	−1	0%	X	NA	5	MI
MGE Energy		O	37	1.47	3.98%	19	50%	18	8.00%	−8	−20%	29	5.00%	B+	27	37	21	2.35	16	63%		53%	5	MGEE
N.W Nat'l Gas		O	41	1.58	3.82%	16	39%	25	6.30%	−6	−15%	35	4.50%	A-	37	55	25	2.76	15	57%		81%	6	MWN
Nat'l Fuel Gas		O	46	1.34	2.94%	30	65%	16	8.50%	−8	−18%	37	3.60%	B+	27	50	20	1.45	31	92%		55%	4	NFG
Paccar Industries		O	39	0.36	0.91%	27	70%	12	3.00%	−3	−9%	36	1.00%	B+	20	46	14	1.28	31	28%		68%	4	PCAR
Rarker-Hannifin	G	O	53	1.00	1.90%	33	62%	20	5.00%	−13	−24%	40	2.50%	A-	28	62	27	3.13	17	32%		23%	6	PH
PNC Fin'l Group		O	43	0.40	0.94%	34	80%	8	4.80%	−27	−63%	16	2.50%	B+	16	88	42	1.26	34	32%		NA	4	PNC
Protective Life		O	22	0.48	2.15%	14	64%	8	6.00%	2	7%	24	2.00%	A-	3	37	19	−0.04	−559	−1200%	X	51%	5	PL

Figure 7.5 Overvalued Stocks, mid-September 2009

Stock			Price	Dividend	Yield	Pts Dn	% Down	Undervalue LoPr/	HIYld	Pts Up	% Up	Overvalue HIPr/	LoYld	S&P	52 wk Lo	52 wk HI	BK Val	12-mo Earn	P/E	Pay out	Div in Dgr	Debt	BC	Tlc
Questar Corp.		O	35	0.50	1.42%	27	76%	8	6.00%	−13	−36%	23	2.20%	A	21	48	20	2.67	13	19%		75%	6	STR
Regal Beloit		O	49	0.64	1.32%	37	75%	12	5.30%	−17	−34%	32	2.00%	A-	25	50	30	2.66	18	24%		62%	5	RBC
Roper Indust	G	O	51	0.33	0.65%	28	54%	24	1.40%	−4	−8%	47	0.70%	A	35	70	24	2.80	18	12%		43%	5	ROP
Schering-Pl		O	29	0.26	0.91%	23	80%	6	4.60%	−3	−9%	26	1.00%	B+	12	29	6	1.50	19	17%		79%	4	SGP
Southwest Bancorp		O	13	0.10	0.78%	9	70%	4	2.60%	−4	−29%	9	1.10%	A-	5	24	16	0.72	18	14%		NA	6	OKSB
State Street		O	53	0.04	0.08%	52	97%	1	3.00%	−50	−94%	3	1.30%	A	14.	73	25	−4.91	−11	−1%	X	29%	6	STT
Stepan Co.		O	60	0.88	1.47%	35	59%	24	3.60%	−22	−36%	38	2.30%	B+	23	60	24	4.99	12	18%		59%	5	SCL
Suntrust		O	22	0.04	0.18%	22	97%	1	7.00%	−20	−92%	2	2.30%	A	6	64	36	−3.04	−7	−1%	X	NA	5	STI
Synovus Finan		O	4	0.04	1.05%	2	65%	1	3.00%	0	−12%	3	1.20%	A-	2	13	6	−4.34	−1	−1%	X	NA	6	SNV
TCF Financl		O	14	0.20	1.40%	9	65%	5	4.00%	−4	−30%	10	2.00%	A	9	28	9.	0.69	21	29%		NA	5	TCB
Torchmark		O	44	0.56	1.28%	35	81%	8	6.70%	−9	−20%	35	1.60%	A	16	65	32	4.62	9	12%		19%	6	TMK
TrustCo Bank Crp		O	6	0.25	4.08%	2	32%	4	6.00%	0	2%	6	4.00%	B+	5	14	3	0.37	17	68%		NA	4	TRST
Valmont Inds	G	O	87	0.60	0.69%	57	65%	30	2.00%	−27	−31%	60	1.00%	A-	37	101	27	5.55	16	11%		31%	6	VMI
Washington Fed		O	15	0.20	1.37%	11	77%	3	6.00%	−8	−54%	7	3.00%	B+	10	27	16	−0.09	−162	−222%	X	NA	4	WFSL
Weingarten Realty		O	21	1.00	4.78%	11	54%	10	10.50%	−9	−44%	12	8.50%	A-	8	40	16	1.03	20	97%		221%	5	WRI
Wells Fargo		O	28	0.20	0.72%	23	81%	5	3.70%	−18	−64%	10	2.00%	A-	8	45	18.	0.91	31	22%		NA	6	WFC
Wilmington Trst		O	13	0.04	0.31%	12	94%	1	5.00%	−11	−88%	2	2.50%	A-	7	36	14	−0.63	−21	−6%	X	NA	5	VMI
Zions Bancorp		O	16	0.04	0.24%	16	96%	1	6.00%	−14	−88%	2	2.00%	A-	6	55	33	−12.00	−1	0%	X	NA	5	ZION

Figure 7.5 Overvalued Stocks, mid-September 2009 (*Continued*)

The corollary to buying right is obviously selling right. When a stock or a market reaches its overvalue phase, investors should be planning their exit rather than searching for new acquisitions. Let's be clear about one thing—the market isn't going anywhere. If you've gone to the trouble of sifting through dozens of stocks to find the few that are worthy of your investment capital, bought right, and sat patiently through the rising trend until the historic level of overvalue is reached, you've done your job; now collect your rewards. That is selling right.

Value can always be found in the stock market. As Geraldine has told me many times, "stocks are like streetcars, another will come along soon." It takes courage to purchase a stock at undervalue, it takes wisdom to sell it at overvalue.

The Rising Trend

Once a stock has moved up 10 percent or more off of its undervalued base, it has entered into a rising trend. As undervalue represents the buying area and overvalue represents the selling area, the rising trend can generally be characterized as the hold area. From the *Investment Quality Trends* perspective, a stock remains in a rising trend until it comes within 10 percent of its historically repetitive area of overvalue or falls back to within 10 percent of its undervalued area.

As any veteran market observer knows, stocks rarely move in a straight line from point A to point B. In fact, a stock may enter into a rising trend only to fall back to the undervalue area on a broad market decline. On the other hand, a stock can remain above its undervalue area in a rising trend for an extended period of time, moving sideways until the price breaks out and resumes its upward climb.

When making investment considerations, an investor should always look to stocks that are undervalued first because they represent historically repetitive extremes of low price and high dividend yield. In some cases, however, when a stock is near its undervalued area yet technically in a Rising Trend, there may still be a viable opportunity to make a profitable purchase.

Before making such a purchase decision though, there are two important things to take into consideration. The first is the primary trend of the broad market. Is it in a bull cycle or a bear cycle? In most cases it is best to avoid purchasing rising-trend stocks in a bear market because the overall wave of selling can engulf the stock, which will halt and reverse the upward trend. In this instance the stock can return to its undervalued area, which necessarily results in a loss to the investor.

Secondly, what is the upside potential to overvalue for the stock versus the downside risk back to undervalue for the stock? In this case, when the primary trend is up or in a bull cycle, stocks in a rising trend may still offer an attractive buying opportunity. The salient question at this point is how far into the rising trend the stock has traveled.

When the broad market is at undervalue or early in its rising trend and a stock is within 15 percent of its undervalued area, a purchase could still realize significant gains. This is particularly true if the stock has a long history of dividend increases. As referenced earlier, a dividend increase will lift the prices at undervalue and overvalue, which provides an additional layer of safety to the original investment. Also previously noted, dividend increases are a predictor for future price growth, not to mention the increased income, which can add momentum to the uptrend.

Figure 7.6 shows the chart for Emerson Electric (EMR). In October of 2002, a decline in EMR was halted within 10 percent of its undervalued yield of 4.0 percent, from which it entered into a rising trend. This advance was halted as the broad market moved lower in a test of the 2002 lows before reversing in March 2003 and resuming its upward move. Brief pullbacks in 2004 and 2005 offered additional buying opportunities as rising dividends moved the boundaries for undervalue and overvalue higher.

In 2006, EMR reached overvalue again and began the expected decline. However, the rising trend resumed as further dividend increases provided additional upside potential. In 2007, EMR breached the overvalue level on the strength of its dividend increases, and while it declined with the broad market in early 2008, investors pushed the stock into a rising trend one more time before the weight of the bear market broke its ascent and it declined to its undervalued area of 4.0 percent in 2009.

When the broad market stabilized and reversed course in March 2009, EMR followed suit. As of mid-September 2009, EMR has once again moved into a rising trend.

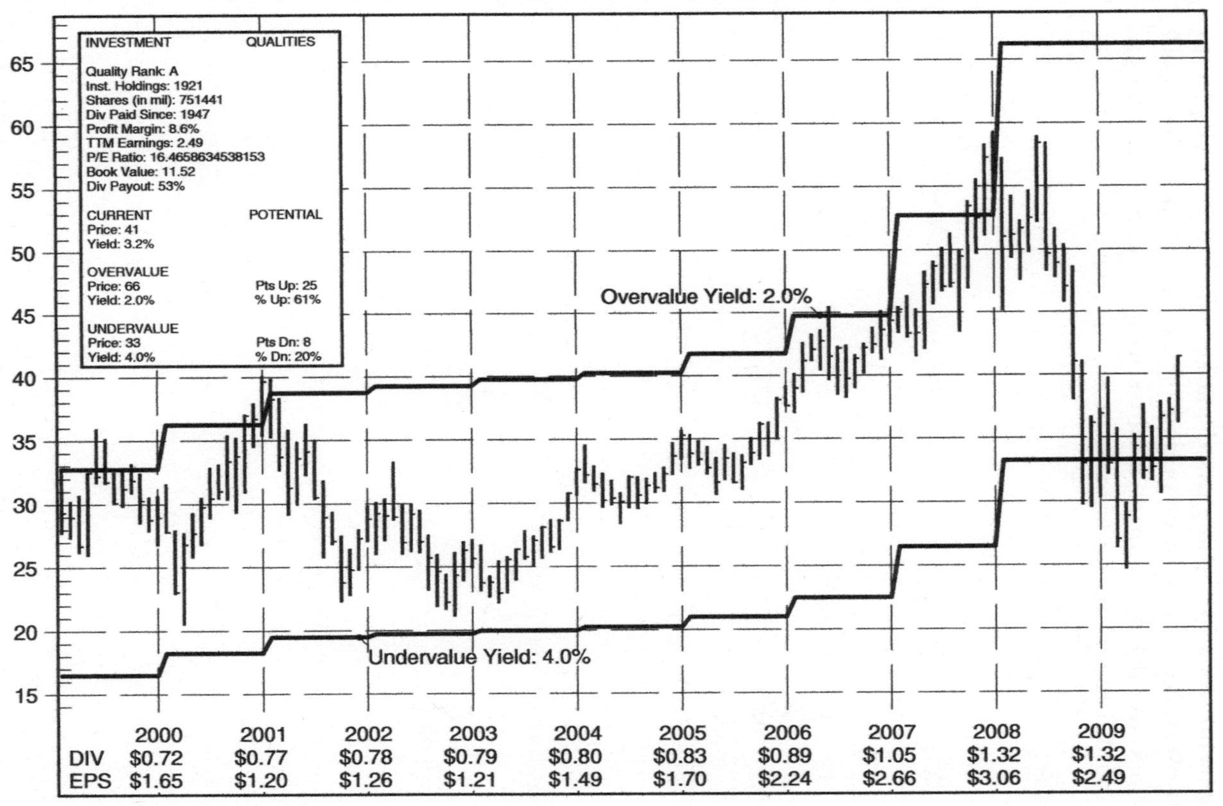

Figure 7.6 Emerson Electric (EMR)

Source: *Value Trend Analysis.*

When the broad market is in a rising trend, stocks that are in a rising trend can provide excellent short-term profit opportunities. A rising-trend stock in a rising-trend market has a greater chance to reach overvalue in a shorter period of time than an undervalued stock because it has a shorter distance to travel and it has the all-important force of market momentum at its back.

CHAPTER 8

Value, Cycles, and the Dow Jones Averages

Order and simplification are the first steps toward mastery of a subject.

—Thomas Mann

In the preceding chapters, I have attempted to lay out in a logical manner the importance of quality, value, cycles, and trends. To narrow our considerations to only the highest quality blue chips we use the Criteria for Select Blue Chips. To identify historically repetitive areas of *undervalue* and *overvalue* of dividend yield we use the Dividend-Yield Theory. By combining the fundamental qualities of the Criteria with the technical attributes of the Dividend-Yield Theory we have the components of the dividend-value strategy.

In addition to identifying the areas of undervalue and overvalue for individual stocks, the cyclical aspect of the Dividend-Yield Theory applies to the broad market, as measured by the Dow Jones Industrial Average (DJIA), in equal manner. By understanding the cyclic nature of value in the Dow, it allows the investor to further hone his buy, sell, and hold decisions. While many stocks will cycle through the phases of value contra to the primary trend of the broad market, it is no secret that it is easier to swim with the tide than against it.

In the next chapter, I combine what has been written through this chapter into a roadmap for building and managing the dividend-value portfolio. Central to that discussion is the primary trend of the Dow, which phase of value is currently in force, and how this information should be included in your buy, sell, and hold considerations.

Because there are so many references to the DJIA throughout this book, there are undoubtedly some critics who will suggest that another index, such as the S&P 500 or perhaps the Dow Jones/ Wilshire 5000, would be more appropriate as a proxy for the overall market. While the S&P and Wilshire are important comparative measurements (the S&P 500 in particular, as it is the most widely recognized benchmark that most equity managers compare performance to), the DJIA has more of the blue chip quality characteristics that we are interested in and is still the most widely recognized of all market indexes.

As understanding the primary trend and current phase of value of the Dow is so important to the dividend-value investor, in Chapter 5 I illustrated the historically repetitive patterns of dividend yield that marked areas of undervalue and overvalue for the DJIA between 1926 and 1995. Also noted in Chapter 5, between 1995 and 2008 there was a divergence in this pattern, which requires an explanation. It is my belief that the DJIA is now in the process of reverting back to the historic pattern prior to 1995. If my assumption is correct, I feel it is incumbent to discuss what this portends for the remainder of the present bear market and how to prepare for the bull market that will eventually follow.

Before we dive into this section however, I want to provide a brief history of Charles Henry Dow, the genesis of the Dow Jones indexes, and Dow's contribution to value investing.

Charles H. Dow and the Dow Jones Averages

Charles Henry Dow was not an investment banker, a money manager, or a stockbroker. He was the son of a poor farmer who died when Charles was six years old. Wanting more than the hard farming life that killed his father, he struck out at the age of 16 to become a newspaper man, although he had no formal education in journalism or even much formal education to speak of.

Be that as it may, Charles managed to find work as a reporter for several newspapers, including the *Springfield Daily Republican* and the *Providence Journal*. He left Providence and moved to New York, where he was employed by the Kiernan News Agency, a company that gathered and disseminated the financial news of the day. Also employed by Kiernan was a fellow by the name of Edward D. Jones, who Dow had known in the newspaper business in Providence.

In 1882, Dow, Jones, and a third man named Charles Bergstresser formed Dow Jones & Company. In 1884 Dow Jones published its first average of U.S. stocks in the *Customer's Afternoon Letter,* the forerunner to the *Wall Street Journal.* In 1886, Dow Jones published its first industrial average consisting of 12 companies that reflected a cross-section of industries.

The Index averaged the stocks of the following companies: American Cotton Oil, American Sugar, American Tobacco, Chicago Gas, Distilling & Cattle Feeding, Laclede Gas, National Lead, North American, Tennessee Coal, Iron and Railroad Company, U.S. Leather, U.S. Rubber, and General Electric. Of these original 12, the lone survivor is General Electric.

According to a book titled *The Dow Jones Averages* that was published by Barron's in the early 1920s (another Dow Jones & Company publication), there are references to various stock averages, comprised of as few as 12 stocks to as many as 60 stocks, that Dow experimented with as far back as 1872. Unfortunately, there is no record for what Dow's thinking was with these various averages, but one could conclude that he was searching for the appropriate mix of stocks that could reveal the primary trend of the market.

In any event, Dow must have found what he was looking for, and by 1897 there were dual Averages, the Industrial and the Railroad, the latter of which became the Transportation Average. In 1929, Dow Jones & Company introduced the Dow Jones Utility Average to track the utilities subset of the market.

Most of Dow's writings are not available, but 16 editorials were published in *The ABC of Stock Speculation* in 1903, a year after Dow's death, by S.A. Nelson. Although the conventional wisdom is that Dow was purely a technician (practitioner of technical analysis), which is obvious to the extent that Dow believed that his Averages, and the individual stocks from which they were comprised, were influenced by the cycles that coincided with bull and bear markets, he was also clearly cognizant of the importance of values.

These discussions of values, along with the works of Benjamin Graham, greatly influenced my predecessor and mentor Geraldine Weiss and me. From these two academic fathers came the underpinnings of the Dividend-Yield Theory and Geraldine's original interpretation, which forms the approach outlined in this book and is promulgated by *Investment Quality Trends.*

If you refer back to the foreword to this book, Geraldine supplies the Dow quote that has graced the pages of our newsletter since inception and is one of our guiding principles: "The legendary Charles Dow has written, '*To know values is to know the meaning of the market. And values, when applied to stocks, are determined in the end by the dividend yield.*'"

Although the majority of Dow's legacy is attributed to the *Wall Street Journal* and the Dow Theory that bears his name, it is clear he understood the importance of values and that dividends are the primary indicator of value.

The Dividend-Yield Theory and the Dow Jones Industrial Average

Just as parameters of value can be established for individual stocks, so, too, can good buying and selling areas be established for the DJIA. From the early days of the stock market, the DJIA fluctuated between dividend-yield extremes of 6.0 percent and 3.0 percent, which represent undervalue and overvalue, respectively (see the charts in Figure 6.2). That profile of value guided the stock market through every bull and bear market from 1929 through 1995.

Prior to the current bear market, the worst bear market of modern times began in 1966 at an overvalue yield of 3.0 percent and was not completed until December, 1974 when the undervalue yield of 6.0 percent was reached. From 1975 to 1982 the market fluctuated between dividend yield extremes of 5.0 percent and 6.0 percent until a new bull market was launched.

The bull market that began at undervalue in 1982 rose to overvalue in 1992, remained there until 1995, and then a remarkable thing happened: For the first time in history the DJIA continued to ascend above its historically repetitive low yield and appeared to have formed a new profile of investment value. From the mid-1990s through September 2008, what formerly was the yield at overvalue (3.0 percent) became the new floor of undervalue and a dividend yield of 1.50 percent became the new selling area of overvalue.

In October 2008, however, the DJIA broke below 10,000 and eventually reached an intraday low price of 6440.08. Based on the composite dividend at that time, the dividend yield on the DJIA rose to 4.90 percent, a decisive violation of the undervalued dividend-yield floor of 3.0 percent.

A Long Blow-Off Top

When the long-term dividend-yield profile of the DJIA was violated in the early to mid-1990s, it came as a great shock. Intuitively, we knew something was amiss but we just couldn't put our finger on it. Because the new pattern persisted, we had to report it, but now that it appears there is a reversion to the mean, it begs an important question. What convinced the global body of investors to change their behavior after 60-plus years of predictability? In the rear view mirror in which all post mortems are conducted, the evidence points to the financial equivalent of the perfect storm.

By the mid-1990s, the ascension of the personal computer, operating systems that the average person could learn, along with associated software applications that increased productivity, launched a modern-day Industrial Revolution. With technology at their fingertips that was previously available to only the wealthiest of companies or individuals, the average person could now access the Internet and the Information Age was born.

News and financial information that once took weeks if not months to be disseminated and synthesized was now available in real time, *to everybody*. Simultaneous to this explosion of information technology and the industries that grew from it, an era of fiscal responsibility (short-lived that it was) descended upon the halls of Congress. The promise of smaller government and balanced budgets lit a fire under the bond market. Interest rates, which had already declined significantly since 1982, continued their downward trajectory.

The Federal Reserve Open Market Committee (the FOMC or more simply, the Fed), which at the time was led by Chairman Alan Greenspan, fell in love with this new-found productivity and for the most part remained accommodative. Oversight and regulation of the financial industry and markets by the Congress and other regulators was virtually nonexistent. Corporate and personal income taxes were generally low, and favorable tax treatment was afforded to capital gains.

In retrospect, it is no wonder investors ignored the message of overvalue that a 3.0 percent dividend yield on the Dow represented.

Who cares about values and the meaning of dividends when the powers that be are aligned with the speculative stars? With the investment winds at their back and a tax code designed to ignore dividends and embrace capital gains, investors said to heck with values and plunged in with both feet; hence the tech and dot-com markets.

We should backtrack for a moment and revisit the environment from which the bull market that began in 1982 was launched. From 1966 through 1974 the market was decimated by a vicious bear cycle. By late 1974 the dividend yield on the Dow was 6.0 percent and our undervalued category was 80 percent of our Select Blue Chip universe. Between 1974 and 1982, the Dow fluctuated between dividend yields of 5 percent and 6 percent and our undervalued category fluctuated only slightly above and below the 80 percent level.

In Figure 8.1 we display our Blue Chip Trend Verifier in bar-graph form to illustrate the incredible level of values during this period.

When the third and final leg down of the bear market began in 1973, the Undervalued category rose to dominance and remained there until the bull market began in 1982. As frustrated capital that had been pent up since the end of the bear in 1974 came rushing in, the Rising-Trends category eclipsed the Undervalued category as stock prices were pushed higher.

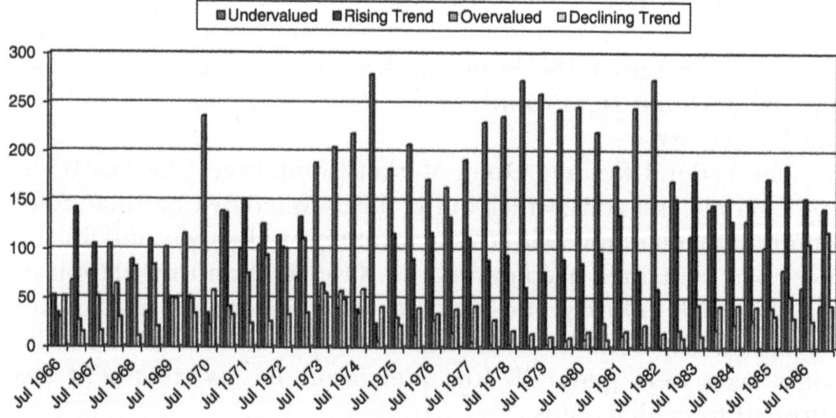

Figure 8.1 Select Blue Chips Percent Change by Category July 1966 to January 1987

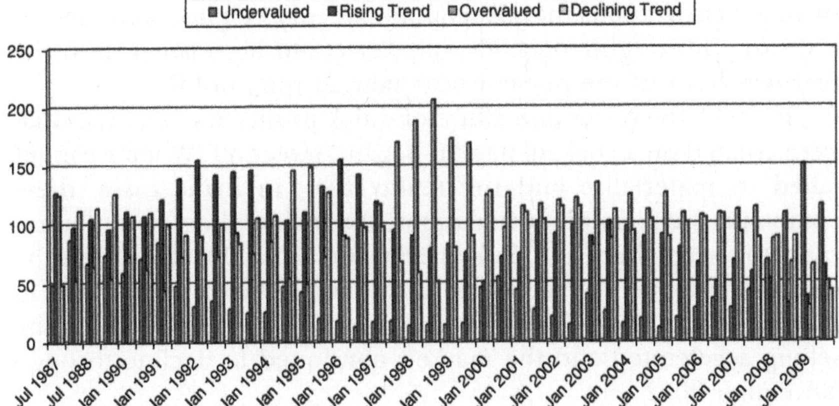

Figure 8.2 Select Blue Chips Percent Change by Category July 1987 to July 2009

Now look at the bar graph in Figure 8.2 that illustrates the period from 1987 through July 2009 to see what happened to all of those historically good values.

On the far left edge of Figure 8.2 is the reading from July 1987. Note that the Rising and Declining Trend categories are about even. The dividend yield on the Dow had breached the 3.0 percent overvalue yield at this point. The next set of bars represents the reading of January 1988. Here we can see that the crash on October 19, 1987 had moved the majority of stocks into declining trends and the dividend yield on the Dow had declined back to 4.0 percent. The readings from July 1988 and January 1989 depict similar levels of value to January 1988. By the January 1990 reading, the rising trends had reasserted their dominance and the dividend yield on the Dow had declined once again to the 3.0 percent overvalue area.

From mid-year 1994 through January 1995 the Declining-Trends category took center stage. There is really only one explanation for this: The majorities of Select Blue Chips had declined below overvalue and were moving toward their respective areas of undervalue. You can almost sense that investors knew intuitively the market was overbought and needed to retrench.

Then the perfect storm, as described earlier, kicked into gear. From mid-year 1995 until mid-year 1997 the rising trends returned to the fore. At that point the dividend yield on the Dow was so low that well diggers would have had trouble finding it. From that point through early 2000, the Overvalue category reigned supreme as investors thoroughly trashed whatever could be trashed until the first leg down of the present bear market took hold.

In 2000, the luster and allure of quick profits in companies that were created on a cocktail napkin began to wear off. When earnings failed to materialize and the reality that, in many cases, these companies were simply speculations, the tech and dot-com illusion came to a screeching halt. By late 2000 and early 2001 it was clear the economy was in recession and the markets began to tumble in earnest. When America was attacked on September 11, 2001, the selling accelerated and the markets continued to decline through November 2002.

In response to recession and the market seizure as a result of 9/11, the Federal Reserve embarked on an unprecedented easing of Fed Fund rates. The only pool of capital readily available was tied up in home equity and the only way to unlock it was to drive interest rates down to Depression-era levels and to hold them there.

In the name of market reform, the Tax Reform Act of 2003 was passed and income tax rates on dividends and capital gains were lowered dramatically to stimulate investor interest. This Act, along with the tech and dot-com bust fresh in their minds, not to mention the Enron, World Com et al. scandals, encouraged investors to rediscover value stocks and dividends. As a result, high-quality dividend-paying blue chip stocks that had been virtually ignored during the decade of the 1990s were once again embraced, and shares appreciated dramatically.

Returning to the graph in Figure 8.2, we see that although investors had fallen in love with dividends again, in 2003 there was an obvious absence of anything that even remotely resembled historically good values. Also, when the first leg down bottomed in 2002 and retested in early 2003, the dividend yield on the Dow *was still below its historically repetitive area of overvalue dividend yield!*

At the risk of being redundant, I need to drive this point home. Since 1966, when the Undervalue category represented 17 percent or less of our select blue-chip universe, it has been coincident with major market tops. When the Undervalue category is between 70 percent and 80 percent of our universe, it has been coincident with major market bottoms. At the market top in 2000, our Undervalue category was 12 percent of our universe. When the first leg down bottomed in late 2002 our Undervalue category still represented only 16 percent of our universe! So after dropping 5,000 points, the Dow was still dramatically overvalued! By mid-year 2005, our undervalued stocks had fallen further to only 4 percent of our universe. Now consider this: With the previous as a backdrop, the market continued to move higher for two more years. At this point the terms *overvalue* and *irrational exuberance* have no meaning; we are talking sheer insanity. Isn't it amazing what massive amounts of liquidity created by rock-bottom interest rates and the illusion of derivatives can create?

Obviously some segment of investors had recognized that the massive leverage and speculation that had been compounding since the end of World War II had finally reached a tipping point. How can I write this? The majority of stocks in the Undervalue category were banks and other financials.

The Walls Come Tumbling Down

When housing prices had reached unsustainable levels and buyers were no longer able to flip at higher prices, it became clear that many of these buyers/borrowers were unable to meet and carry the debt service.

Subsequently the mortgage-backed securities that had been formed from these mortgages became suspect as the value of the underlying properties began to deteriorate. Banks, brokerage firms, and hedge firms that were heavily invested in these securities now had to mark-to-market, and with no reliable metric to value these properties and securities, the entire structure began to fall apart. For all intents and purposes what ensued was one giant margin call as everybody needed liquidity to shore up their balance sheets.

When one receives a margin call there are two options: sell positions or deposit more cash. Unable to sell their mortgage-backed securities, the banks, brokers, and hedge funds had to sell whatever they could—blue chip stocks, oil, gold, commodities, you name it. As the selling became a waterfall, the investing public began to hear about derivatives, synthetic securities with names like collateralized debt obligations (CDOs) and credit default swaps, which actually had been in use since the mid-1990s.

Institutions that at one time were believed to be too big to fail like Bear Sterns were absorbed, and Lehman Brothers declared bankruptcy. Merrill Lynch was acquired by Bank of America. Washington

Mutual, which had raised its dividend over 40 consecutive quarters, was taken over by the FDIC and sold to JP Morgan Chase for next to nothing.

The End Game

My thought is the market pattern that is developing is similar to that of the bear market from 1966 through 1974. This is not to say I expect the bear market to last for eight years, but that I suspect the Dow will go through a similar sequence of three down legs interspersed by two highly profitable counter-trend rallies until the dividend yield on the Dow declines to between 5.0 percent and 6.0 percent, which should set the stage for a new bull market.

For a point of reference, let's look at the chart in Figure 8.3, which illustrates the pattern described earlier in the 1966–1974 bear market.

The bear market began in 1966 when the dividend-yield on the Dow declined to its historically repetitive area of overvalue at 3.0 percent. The first leg down was completed later that year and reversed course when the dividend yield on the Dow reached 4.0 percent. The first counter-trend rally topped out in 1969 just below the 1966 high.

The second leg down commenced shortly thereafter and did not halt and reverse until the dividend yield reached 5.0 percent. The second counter-trend rally topped out in early 1973. Note that this counter-trend rally exceeded the 1966 and 1969 high-price areas. Coincidentally, the dividend yield on the Dow at the 1973 top was 3.0 percent. Many investors believed a new bull market was underway at this point due to the Dow eclipsing the 1966 high price. As you can see, however, the market rolled over into a third leg down, which was completed when the dividend yield on the Dow registered 6.0 percent in December, 1974.

Now let's compare the this with the current bear market as depicted in Figure 8.4.

If my analysis is accurate, the first leg down began in early 2000 and ended in October 2002. If you refer back to the *Investment Quality Trends* chart for the Dow in Figure 6.2 in Chapter 6, note that at the bottom of the first leg down the dividend yield was below the 3.0 percent yield area. The counter-trend rally began in earnest in 2003 as the Greenspan Fed and the Bush administration unleashed

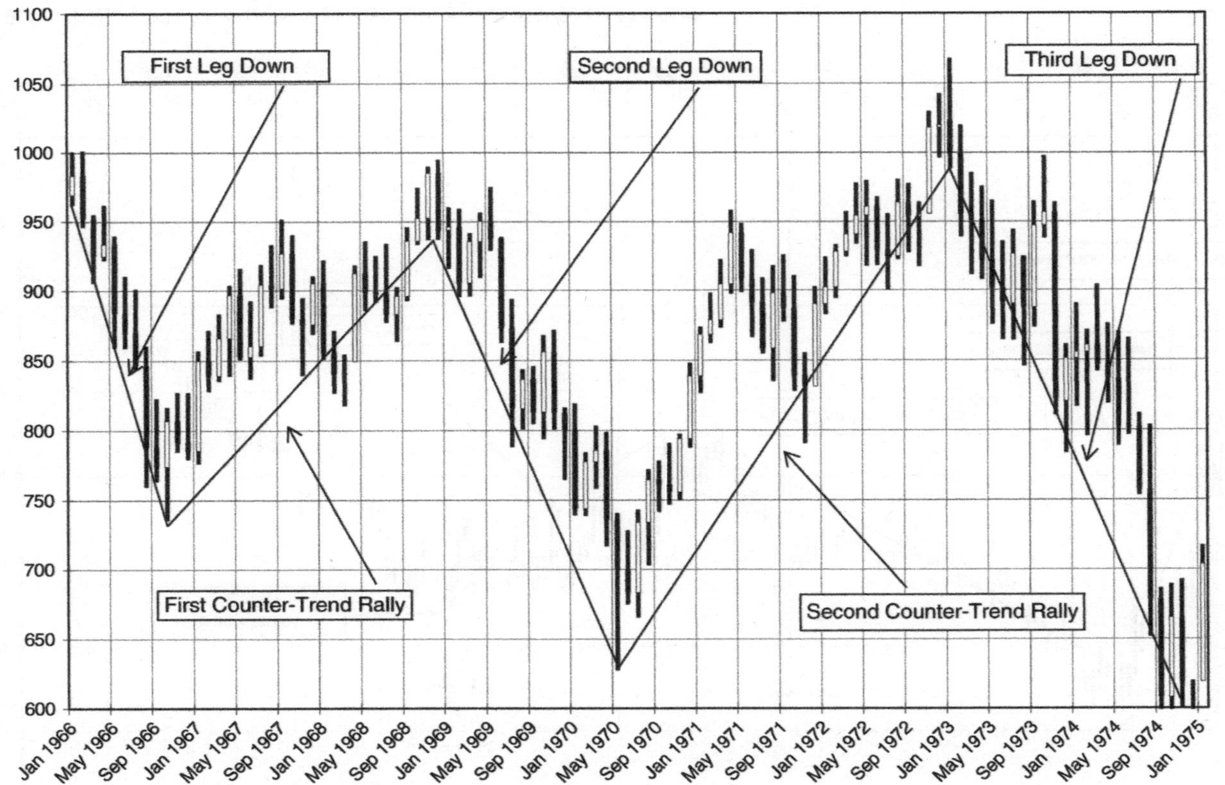

Figure 8.3 DJIA 1966 through 1974 Bear Market

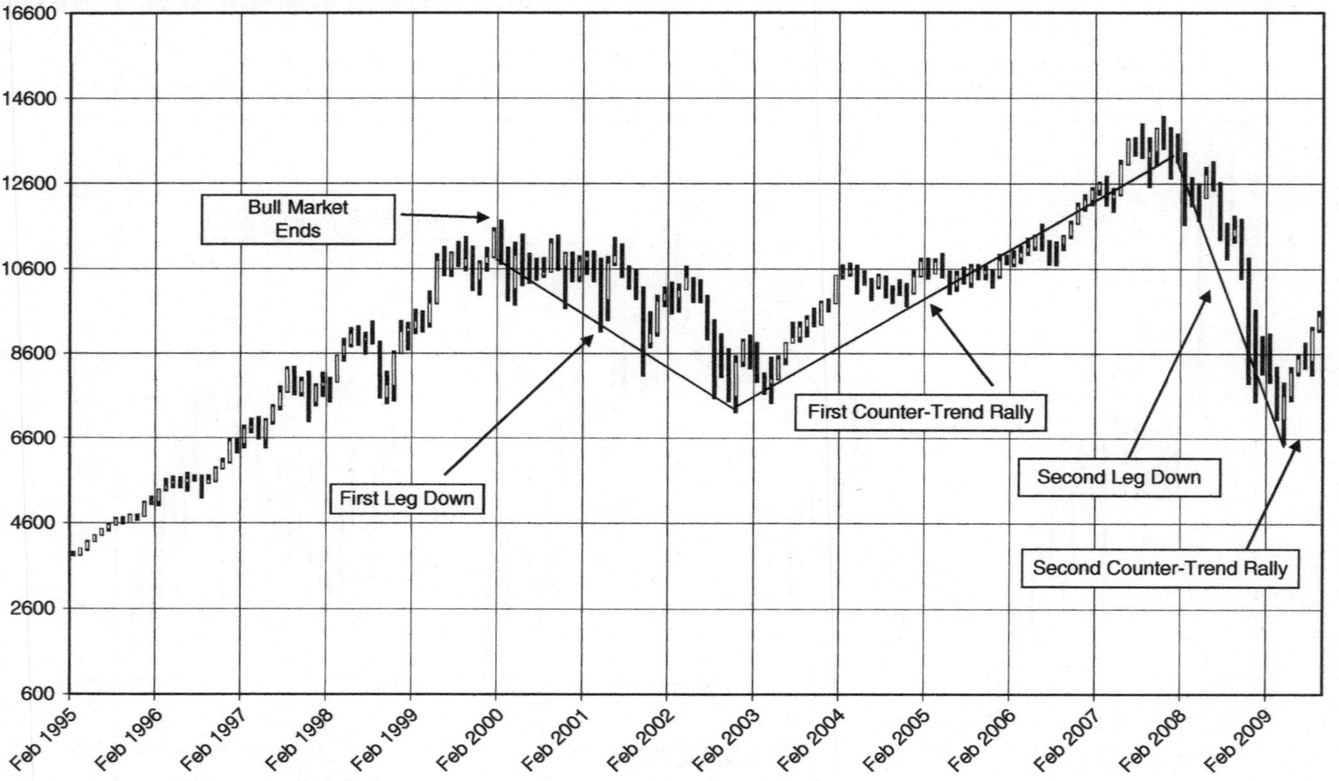

Figure 8.4 DJIA 1995 Through mid-September 2009 Bear Market

the one-two punch of extremely low interest rates and relaxed federal tax rates on capital gains and dividends.

In late 2003 through the fall of 2007, we see what happens when massive amounts of home equity, never-before-seen degrees of leverage by speculators, and institutions using lethal doses of derivatives can do to the stock market. When the Dow eclipsed its 2000 high in 2006, investors believed, just as they did in 1973, that a new bull market was underway. And, just like 1973, the market rolled over into another leg down.

The second leg down bottomed intra-day on March 9, 2009, with the dividend yield on the Dow reaching 4.90 percent, 10 basis points (10 one-hundredths of 1 percent) within 5.0 percent. Simultaneously our Blue Chip Trend Verifier recorded that 72 percent of our select blue chips were in the Undervalue category, indicating that the potential for a counter-trend rally was high.

As we know, a very powerful counter-trend rally has developed. If the pattern of this bear market mirrors that of bear markets in the past, the counter-trend rally should retrace at minimum 50 percent of the previous down leg, which would approximate 10,300 on the Dow. As you know now, counter-trend rallies can also return to the old high as in 1969, or can even breach that level as in 1973 and 2006.

Knowledge of these patterns allows investors to initiate new undervalued positions at important reversal points such as the March, 2009 lows and to recoup some lost ground on older positions that may have been held through the previous decline. If and when the counter-trend peaks and begins to decline again, it is time to take profits on overvalued stocks, place stop losses on below-rising trend stocks that have advanced significantly, and raise cash in anticipation of the next halt and reversal.

The Next Bull Market

In the case of the present cycle, I believe one more down leg remains ahead of us. When the 3.0 percent dividend-yield area on the Dow was violated in late 2008 and declined to almost 5.0 percent, it became clear to me that the era of irrational exuberance had come to an end. As such, it would be completely logical for the Dow to return to its historically repetitive extremes of undervalue and overvalue at dividend yields between 3.0 percent and 6.0 percent, respectively. At the very minimum, I would anticipate at least a retest of the March 2009 lows.

However the end game plays out, as night follows day there will be a new bull market. It should be quite profitable over its life but it will be different than bull markets of the past as the wind will no longer be at our backs. The perfect storm of low interest rates, an accommodative Fed, friendly personal and corporate tax rates, cheap money and ready liquidity, lax regulation and oversight, not to mention irrational exuberance, will be absent.

Not to worry though, because quality and value will be plentiful, which for value investors is the best environment one could hope for. Although it won't be as easy as in the past, it will be achievable. To quote the John Houseman line from the old Smith Barney commercials: ''We make money the old-fashioned way. We earn it.'' To modify the John Houseman line from the old Smith Barney commercial; ''We'll make money the old fashioned way, we'll earn it.''

PART III

WINNING IN THE STOCK MARKET

CHAPTER 9

Developing a Successful Stock Strategy

Chance favors only the mind that is prepared.

—Louis Pasteur

In the movie *Wall Street,* there is a scene in which the character Gordon Gekko tells the character Bud Fox that "a fool and his money are lucky to get together in the first place." This is a fairly cynical worldview but not altogether surprising considering that the Gekko character was a cheat and that his success in the stock market was due in large part to trading on inside information.

In my experience, you don't have to cheat to realize investment success. Investors also don't have to be particularly talented, but they *do* have to be disciplined. At the end of the day, if you work hard and are smart enough to save money, then you are entirely capable of managing it.

To be sure, there are avenues other than stocks and the stock market to build wealth. I know many people who have built fortunes in real estate or in one or more businesses. I have friends who have never owned a share of stock in their lives, but who have been very successful in the options and commodities markets. One of my closest friends is flat-out brilliant as a fixed-income manager.

Based on the fact that I wrote this book, publish an investment newsletter, and run an investment management company, however, it should come as no surprise that my preferred vehicle for the long-term building of wealth is high-quality, blue chip stocks. In my experience they provide the most potential with the least risk to accumulate wealth over a lifetime.

Investing in blue chip stocks requires discipline and patience. Although there isn't much I can do to help you in the patience department, in terms of discipline, there is a no more disciplined approach to value-based investing than the dividend-value strategy.

Whether you are young (or just feel young), single or married, kids or no kids, approaching retirement or already retired, the dividend-value strategy can be applied to any phase of life. You can use the strategy to identify fast-growing companies with lower dividend yields, more mature companies with higher dividend yields, or companies somewhere in between for overall total returns.

So no matter your station in life or your goals and objectives, the dividend-value strategy is geared to the most basic of investment fundamentals—getting a return on your investment dollar. Although the dividend-value strategy is not a short-term trading method, the discipline does have some short-term applications. From our experience, however, and from what other practitioners have shared with us, the primary appeal of the dividend-value strategy is that it rings true, it makes common sense, and it has worked for decades in every market environment imaginable.

In the final assessment, a portfolio that is built on a diversified selection of blue chip stocks that are purchased when they represent historically good value, held until they become overvalued, and then sold for a handsome profit makes the discipline and patience well worth the effort.

Take Care of Your Business

With investing, there is no such thing as one size fits all. Generic is something you buy at the drugstore. Just as every stock has its unique Profile of Value, each investor has his or her unique set of goals and objectives. Just as each stock must be evaluated individually, each investor must establish his or her specific goals and objectives based on individual needs.

If you haven't yet figured out what your needs are then you need to do some work. If this part of the discussion sounds like a foreign language to you, then you probably could use some help, which is okay. Everybody can use a little guidance from someone with more training or experience now and then.

If you do use a professional however, stay in control of the process. One of the first things people are taught in the financial services industry is how to take client control. Now, to give the industry the benefit of the doubt, this is often required because clients who are out of their element often need the organization and structure a firm can bring to the process. Just keep them on track and let them know what you are specifically interested in: a current and/or retirement budget, perhaps some cash flow analysis, or maybe some help with a personal balance sheet. Many times they will want to plug you into their system, which sounds more attractive than "We need to do some extensive data gathering," but they will need some information to get the ball rolling.

My partner and I knew a fellow who would gather vast amounts of personal and financial information from a potential client under the guise of "determining whether I can be of assistance to you before we enter into an agreement." He would then pore over everything in detail to find the most innocuous items and then in the follow-up interview ask the prospective client if he or she was aware of these issues and then would close in for the kill with this question: "Doesn't that concern you?"

Most professionals would never dream of using such tactics, but there are rotten apples in every barrel. Just remember three guiding principles: No one cares as much about you as you do; no one knows your personal situation better than you, so *you* should establish your investment goals and objectives; and no one will care for your assets greater than you will.

Plan today and tomorrow will work out.

Investment Goals

The dividend-value strategy is the big-picture part of the investment process. Now that you know how to identify quality and value, we need to discuss how to narrow your stock selections down further to a more goal-centered level.

The range of goals and objectives are probably as numerous as there are investors. Once after an educational presentation I gave at

The MoneyShow, a fellow approached me and said: "Kelley, I think I have hit on the perfect stock." "What would that be?" I asked. "It's a stock that always goes up, increases its dividend every year, the gains and dividends are tax free, and it is completely liquid." "I think you are right," I responded. "You wouldn't be willing to share the name of this stock with me, would you?" I asked. "I would be happy to, if I knew of such a stock," he said, "but I don't think it exists." I smiled and thanked the man and assured him he was correct on both fronts; he had indeed described the perfect stock but no, such a stock does not exist.

I share this vignette with you because it illustrates an important point. The attributes of the stock this man described encapsulate quite nicely the primary goals most investors are interested in: preservation of capital, growth of capital, income, growth of income, tax advantages, and liquidity.

Outside of a qualified retirement plan such as a 401-(k) or an Individual Retirement Account (IRA), there are limited tax advantages for common stocks. Under current law, dividends and capital gains do receive preferential tax treatment, but these are subject to the current whims of Congress, so we will put the tax issues aside.

Of the other attributes listed previously, the one that most investors will agree on is the need for liquidity (the ability to quickly convert an asset into cash). Even for the long-term investor, liquidity is an important attribute. Heaven forbid you find yourself in a situation in which you need to go to cash and you have no market to sell to.

Depending on the stage or circumstance of one's life, most investors will tend to focus on one or a combination of the other referenced attributes. At IQ Trends Private Client we have a hierarchy of investment goals as a firm that seems to attract a specific type of clientele. Although not every reader will appreciate our priorities, it nonetheless serves as an example of how to establish an orderly succession of goals.

As laid out in Chapter 3 in the section on the Criteria for Select Blue Chips, one of the six criteria is at least 5,000,000 shares outstanding. If you remember, I wrote that this relates to liquidity; we don't want to make an appointment to buy or sell a stock.

The following profiles of investors are presented to help readers think through investment goals. This is by no means an exhaustive list. Rather it is a collection of sketches designed to

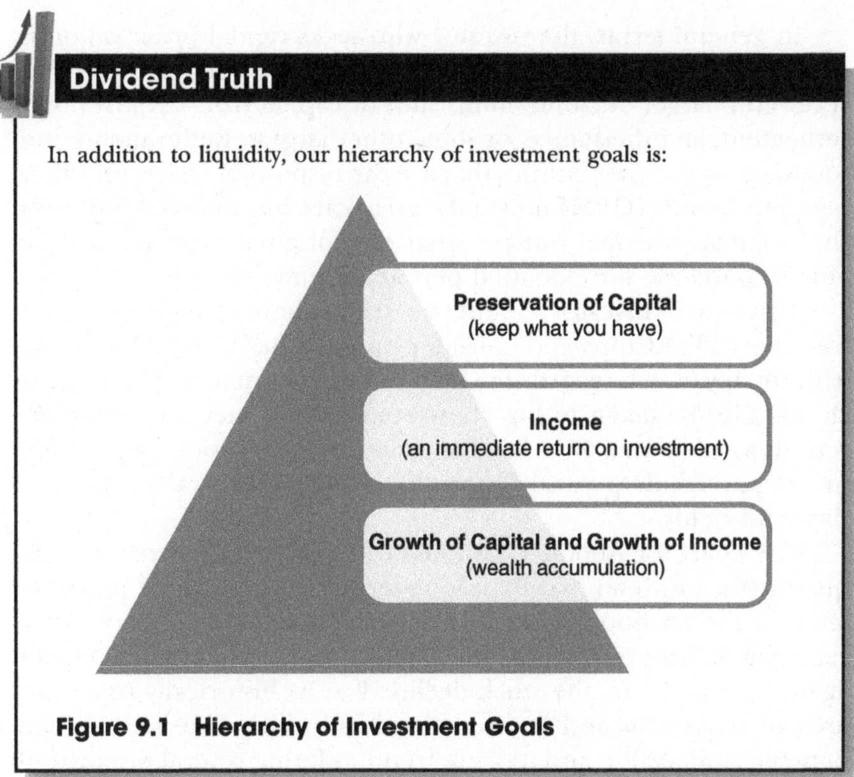

Dividend Truth
In addition to liquidity, our hierarchy of investment goals is:
Preservation of Capital
(keep what you have)
Income
(an immediate return on investment)
Growth of Capital and Growth of Income
(wealth accumulation)

Figure 9.1 Hierarchy of Investment Goals

capture a broad range of investment objectives, which not everyone will identify with. Investing is nothing if not a highly personal endeavor, and each investor is entitled to his or her own unique attitude and approach.

The Investor Who Needs to Preserve Capital

For some, to even talk about stocks and preservation of capital in the same breath is an oxymoron. It is easy to understand this line of thinking when you understand that stocks can and will fluctuate, sometimes to extremes. But preservation of capital is more than just avoiding price fluctuations. In the truest sense it is preserving what the capital can buy. In this vein, stocks are more likely to preserve purchasing power over long periods of time than will bonds or cash and cash equivalents.

In general terms, the investor who seeks capital preservation is retired or close to retirement age or perhaps is someone who has received a large, one-time lump sum of capital from an insurance settlement, an inheritance, or some other largess. Endowments and foundations or other entities that are the responsible party for other people's money (OPM) must take great care in preserving not only the original principal but for what that original principal will be able to purchase for extended periods of time.

This type of investor should pay strict adherence to the Criteria for Select Blue Chips and consider only the highest quality stocks with the best track records for long-term performance. Great pains should also be taken to buy these stocks when they are at depressed areas of undervalue for the maximum downside protection, maximum upside potential, and the highest historically repetitive dividend-yields.

The chart for Abbott Labs (ABT) in Figure 9.2 reflects a high-quality stock with an excellent long-term track record for performance in the traditionally defensive pharmaceutical industry. After reaching its historically repetitive area of *overvalue* in late 2000 and again in early 2002, the stock declined to its historically repetitive area of *undervalue* and has remained in a fairly consistent range between undervalue and a rising trend, offering several opportunities to add to the position and to compound the growing dividend stream. Even during the declining waterfall period the stock has remained above the lows in 2002, 2006, and has returned to the lows of 2008.

The Investor Who Needs Income

It is no secret that the stock market prefers lower interest rates than higher ones because a lower cost of capital is better for the bottom line, and, therefore, for earnings.

For the income investor, however, low interest rates results in lower coupons from more traditional income sources such as bonds. Certain investors, typically those with no employment or other income source, will necessarily turn to higher-yielding dividend stocks for current income.

Traditionally, investors will turn to stocks of gas and electric utilities or perhaps one of the legacy telecom companies for these higher yields.

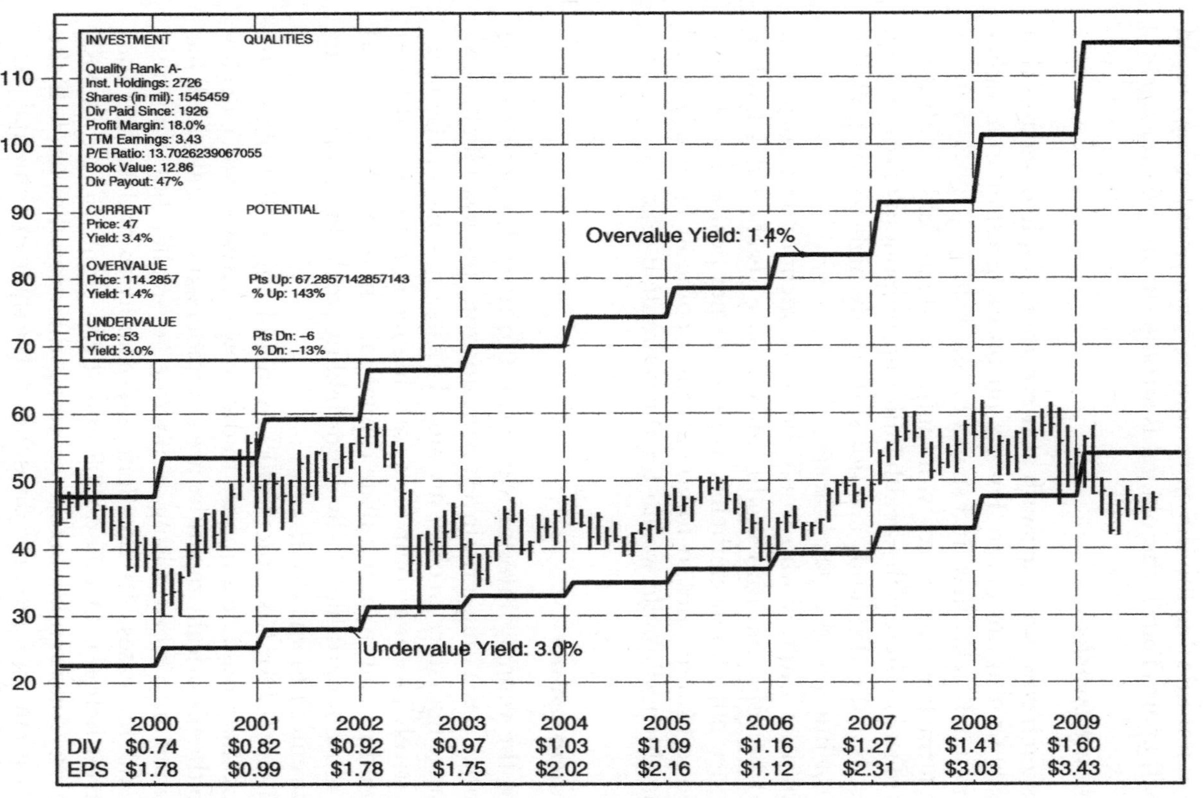

Figure 9.2 Abbott Laboratories (ABT)

Source: *Value Trend Analysis.*

Figure 9.3 of AT&T, Inc. (T) from late June 2009 reflects the type of higher-yielding stock an income investor would look for. As an aside, it is ironic that the U.S. government spent years tearing the old Ma Bell apart. Today, the old gal is stronger than she ever was.

The Growth Investor

This sketch covers a wide swath as there are multiple objectives that typically fit into this genre. For tax purposes, investors in a higher income tax bracket may find shares of low-yield/high-growth stocks more attractive than shares with higher dividend-yields. With these types of stocks there is the wealth-building component of rising stock prices, but the dividends are not sufficiently high to catapult the investor into a higher tax bracket.

Another investor who would be more inclined toward growth would be someone who might not yet have reached the level of affluence but who, nonetheless, is in his or her peak earning years; someone who decides to forgo current income in favor of capital gains, which will build wealth for the retirement years.

The Young Investor

Last is the younger investor who has yet to reach his peak earning potential, has a long-term investment horizon, and has a higher risk tolerance than does an older investor. This investor may opt for more aggressively growing companies with higher P/E ratios and lower dividend payouts to accumulate capital gains in the early years, and then move toward higher-dividend-yielding stocks in the later years as retirement looms closer.

Figure 9.4 for Nike, Inc. (NKE) from mid-August 2009 illustrates a stock that would be attractive to the growth investor. Since declining to the historically repetitive area of undervalue in 2000, NKE has remained in a steady rising trend due to smaller but consistent dividend increases. An excellent opportunity to add to positions occurred between October 2008 and the present. Note that NKE must rise considerably before reaching the overvalue level. If the company continues to raise dividends at the same incremental pace, the overvalue area will continue to move higher, which could result in the stock remaining in a rising trend for a considerable period of time.

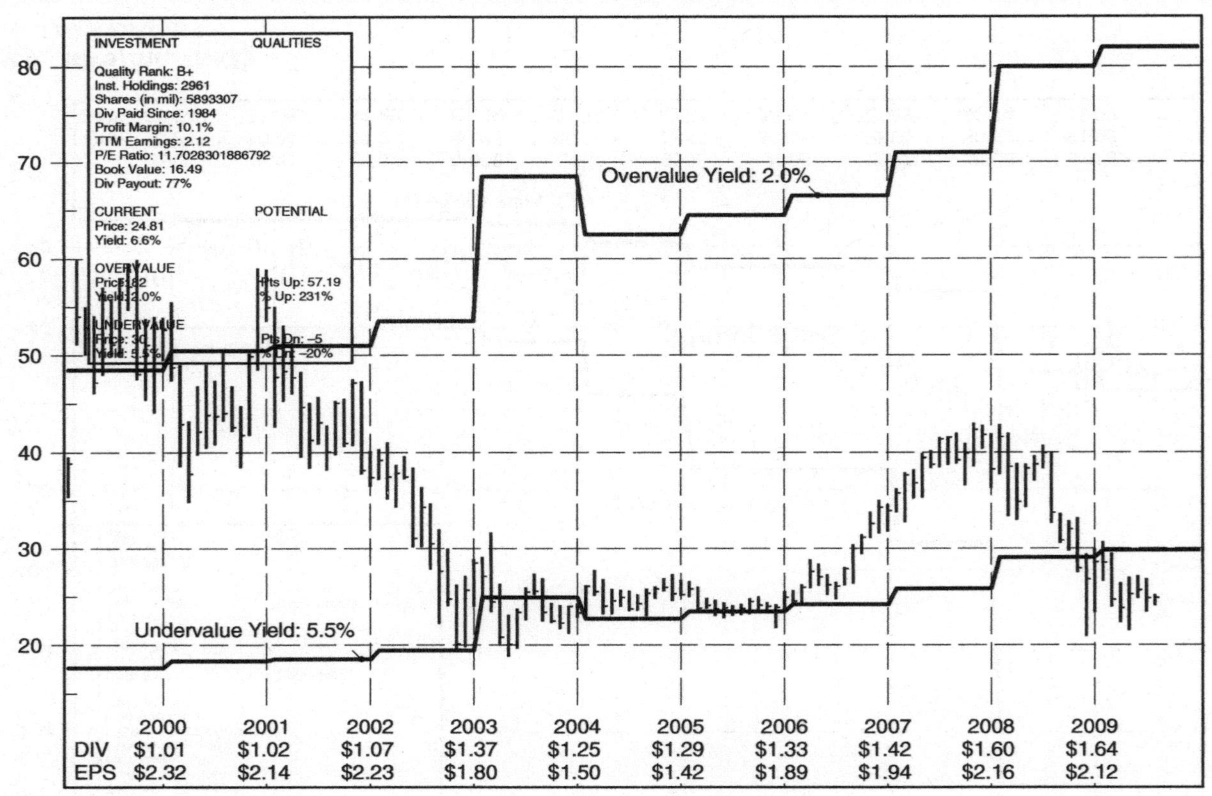

Figure 9.3 AT&T, Inc. (T)

Source: *Value Trend Analysis.*

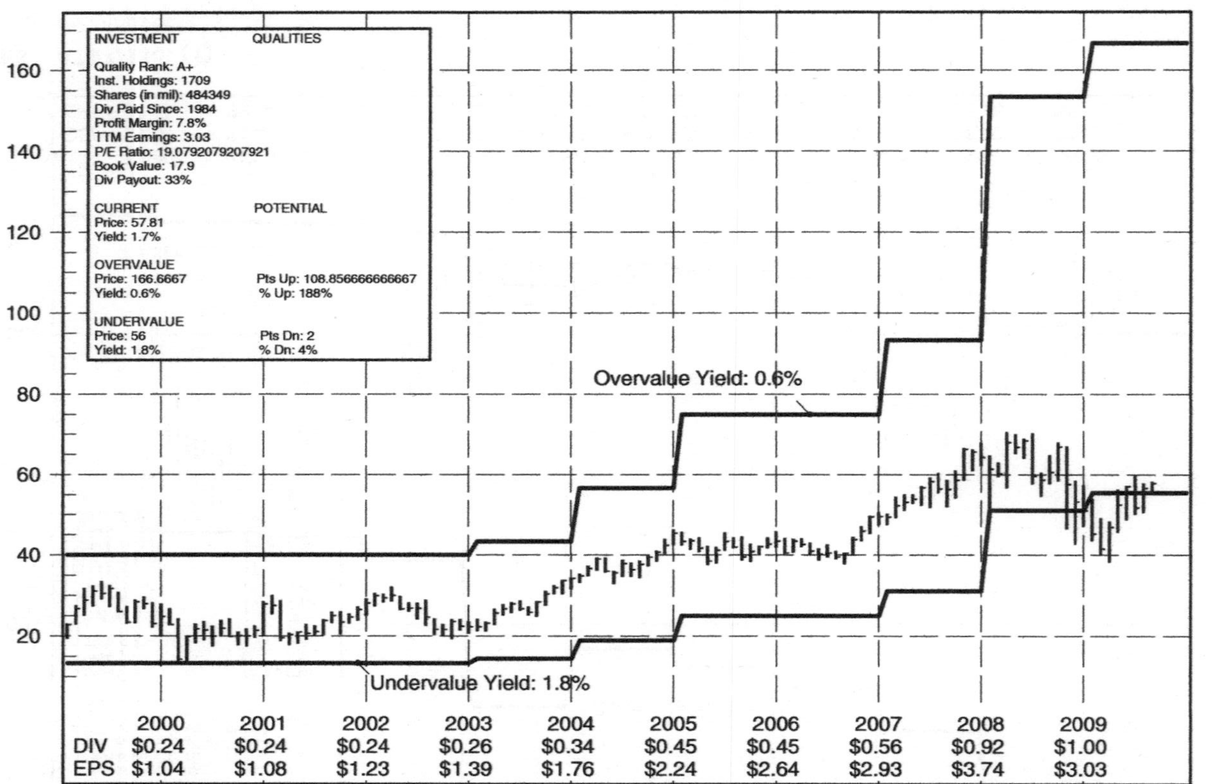

Figure 9.4 Nike, Inc. (NKE)

Source: *Value Trend Analysis.*

Know Your Limitations

I am going to go out on a limb here and guess this quote from Dirty Harry, A man's got to know his limitations, was not in reference to the stock market. That being said, the quote is apt when the topic turns to risk as it pertains to stock strategy.

Everybody is wired differently. What one investor would classify as risk may be totally dismissed by another. The reasons or motivations that compel an investor to embrace or reject risk could keep an army of psychotherapists busy until the end of time.

Since I have a deadline to meet, I am going to cut to the chase. If you are feeling pain, you have a risk problem. When Mike and I talk to clients about risk tolerance, we like to invoke the pillow test; if the last thought you have at night when your head hits the pillow is your investment portfolio, then you haven't passed the pillow test; you need to make some changes.

Risk tolerance can cut both ways; a portfolio producing insufficient growth of capital and income to meet future cash needs is as anxiety producing as a portfolio that contains too much short-term volatility for an investor with more immediate cash needs. This is why it is imperative to understand who, what, why, and when the portfolio is being created for. If you get this part wrong you can be the greatest stock picker the world has ever known and it can all come to naught.

The chart of Sigma-Aldrich (SIAL) in Figure 9.5 is about as close to value-stock Nirvana that an investor could find. Note how the stock price hugs the undervalue line as the dividends have been systematically increased. At first glance many investors might overlook this stock due to its relatively low-yield at undervalue. Oops, a very big mistake. Let me tell you why.

SIAL not only has an A+ quality ranking, it has also earned the IQ Trends "G" designation for outstanding dividend growth. Subscribers to IQ Trends who purchased SIAL at undervalue in 1999 at $11 per share are enjoying a 5.25 percent dividend-yield on cost today, not to mention close to 400 percent in price appreciation.

No matter what your investment goals and objectives, or whether you are concerned with too much volatility or too little growth, this is the type of stock all value investors should look for.

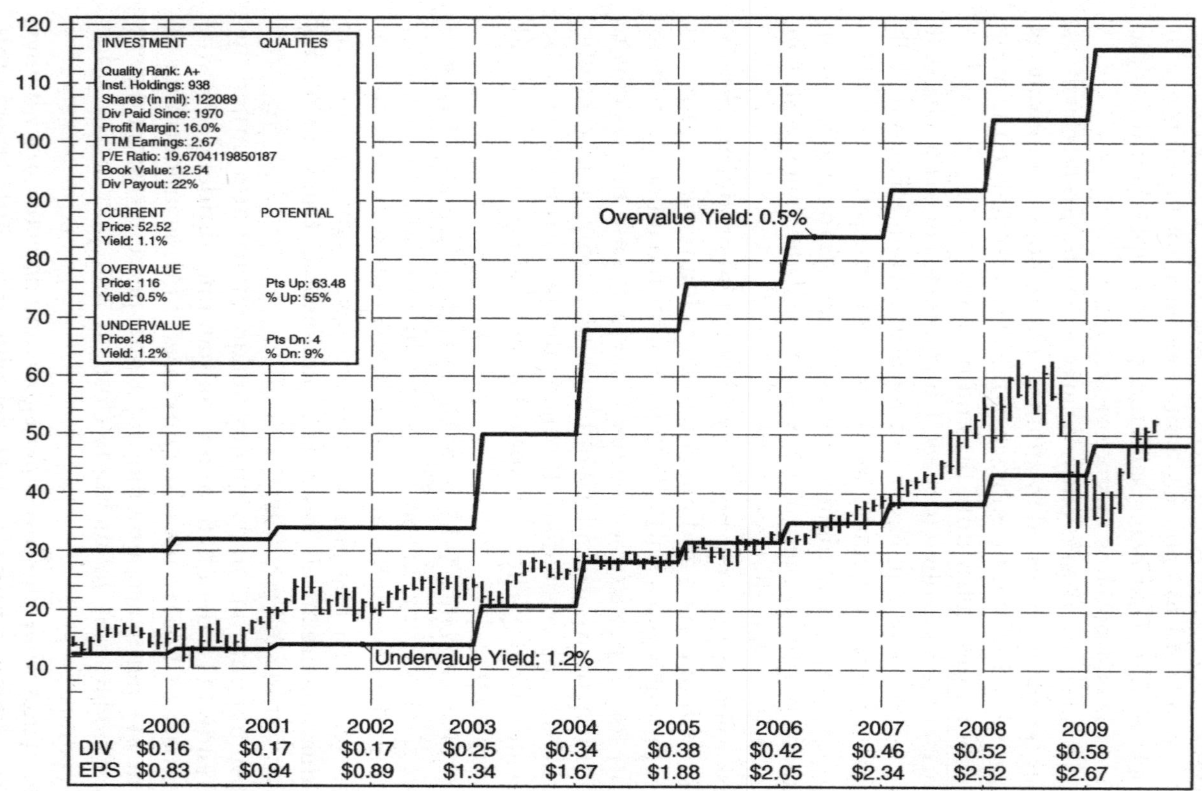

Figure 9.5 Sigma-Aldrich (SIAL)

Source: *Value Trend Analysis.*

Ideal Portfolio Size

Prior to the advent of the discount brokerage firm and the deregulation of trading commissions, the question of how many stocks should be in a portfolio was directly related to how much money an investor had to work with. When commissions were in the hundreds of dollars for a round lot (100 shares) or even more for an odd lot (less than 100 shares), it dramatically affected how many stocks one could hold in a portfolio.

Today most of the electronic brokers offer trading commissions between $7 and $20 per trade, depending on the amount of money in the account and/or the average number of trades per year. This is a significant development in the investment industry as minimizing trading costs can provide a meaningful boost to overall portfolio returns over the long-term.

Also, as investors are no longer penalized for trades of less than 100 shares, even an investor with a modest amount of capital can create a diversified portfolio of stocks. It wasn't all that long ago that an investor with a modest amount of capital was forced to use mutual funds to achieve adequate diversification. Thankfully, those days are behind us.

The number of stocks in a portfolio is subject to a number of variables such as the investment time horizon, the amount of capital available to invest, investor goals and objectives, and economic and market conditions.

When the Dow is overvalued or the primary trend is down, it may be prudent to hold a smaller number of stocks in anticipation of greater selection and values when the Dow represents good historic value or there are a greater number of stocks that represent good historic values.

When the Dow is undervalued or in an early rising trend, the number of stocks can be increased for more broad participation in the expanding economy. As a general rule of thumb, however, we suggest limiting a portfolio to 25 stocks.

25 stocks is a sufficient number to allow for wide diversification, but it is not too many to track effectively. Also, by limiting the portfolio to 25 excellent stocks, there is a higher probability for outperforming the broad market. This is an important advantage of the dividend-value strategy you don't want to give up; if you hold too many stocks you might as well own an index fund.

By example, in the First January 2000 issue of *Investment Quality Trends,* we introduced a portfolio of 13 stocks to aid subscribers in the portfolio construction process. The text below is taken directly from the IQ Trends web site that describes this portfolio:

Investment Quality Trends provides information targeted toward subscribers with varying levels of investment experience and portfolio construction. Unlike many other newsletter services, we do not construct and maintain model portfolios. Because we follow such a wide variety of companies that are dynamically moving in price, along with a steady influx of new subscribers, such an approach would be impractical for our particular application.

For tracking purposes, however, *The Hulbert Financial Digest* has maintained a portfolio for *Investment Quality Trends* since 1986. This portfolio consists of all the companies in the Undervalued and Rising-Trend categories, which, at any given time, could total as many as 100 companies or more; clearly too large a number to be practical.

Additionally, many studies have shown that the optimum number of stocks for an individual portfolio is 25. That number is appropriate for diversification while not allowing the portfolio to become unwieldy. Accordingly, investors must be selective and fashion a diversified portfolio of Undervalued and Rising-Trend stocks based on personal preferences, investment objectives, financial conditions, and tolerance for risk.

To assist subscribers in this endeavor (and at popular urging), we decided in January of 2000 that instead of engaging in the traditional (albeit generally futile) attempt to forecast the year ahead, to construct a portfolio of stocks that offered extraordinary value for your investment consideration.

The portfolio, which has become known affectionately as The Lucky 13, as shown in Figure 9.6, was designed to emphasize sectors of the market that, while perhaps were currently out of favor, nonetheless offered exemplary fundamentals and attractive dividend yields. Thirteen stocks were also sufficient to establish the foundation for a portfolio while leaving room for expansion when opportunities become available throughout the year.

Since its inception in January 2000, through year-end 2008, the Lucky 13 has had an average annual total return of 10.88 percent, as shown in Figure 9.6, which is a marked premium above the major

Name	Symbol	Shares	Buy Price	Last Price	Dividends To Date	Value	Gain/ Loss	% Gain
Abbott Labs	ABT	1	$52.17	$49.47	$1.16	$50.63	($1.54)	−2.95%
Atmos Energy Corp.	ATO	1	$23.32	$28.18	$0.99	$29.17	$5.85	25.09%
Emerson Electric	EMR	1	$34.29	$40.08	$0.99	$41.07	$6.78	19.77%
Johnson & Johnson	JNJ	1	$58.15	$60.89	$1.44	$62.33	$4.18	7.19%
Coca-Cola Co.	KO	1	$44.41	$53.70	$1.23	$54.93	$10.52	23.69%
McCormick & Co.	MKC	1	$31.09	$33.94	$0.72	$34.66	$3.57	11.48%
Altria Group Inc.	MO	1	$15.19	$17.81	$0.96	$18.77	$3.58	23.57%
Nike Inc.	NKE	1	$48.94	$64.70	$1.00	$65.70	$16.76	34.25%
Procter & Gamble	PG	1	$60.20	$57.92	$1.28	$59.20	($1.00)	-1.66%
Philip Morris Int'l	PM	1	$43.16	$48.74	$1.62	$50.36	$7.20	16.68%
Sigma-Aldrich	SIAL	1	$40.60	$53.96	$0.44	$54.40	$13.80	33.99%
Union Pacific Corp.	UNP	1	$46.08	$58.35	$1.08	$59.43	$13.35	28.97%
United Technologies	UTX	1	$51.33	$60.93	$1.16	$62.09	$10.76	20.96%
			$548.93	**$628.67**	**$14.07**	**$642.74**	**$93.81**	**17.09%**

Percent Gain: **17.09%**
9/30/2009

Figure 9.6 The Lucky 13

indexes. So even a smaller portfolio, when properly configured, can provide excellent total returns.

Diversify, Diversify, Diversify

Throughout this book I have emphasized the importance of the twin pillars of quality and value. At this juncture I have to add a third leg to the investment stool: diversification.

If you do everything right, have well-defined goals and objectives, choose asset classes that are appropriate for your time horizon and risk tolerance, select only the highest-quality stocks that represent historically good value, but fail to diversify across a broad number of industries and/or sectors, it can totally negate all of your preparation and hard work.

Throughout the history of the stock market there are cycles where various industries and sectors have suffered major declines due to an exhausting list of reasons. Although there is often fair warning that trouble may be looming on the horizon for an industry or group of industries, there is an equal number of instances in which trouble has appeared out of the blue.

Although limiting investment considerations to high-quality blue chips that represent historically good values can often reduce any downside to a relatively minor degree for a short amount of time, there are instances, such as the complete meltdown of the financial sector over the last 18 months, that no system of value identification could anticipate or predict. As such, it is important to limit your exposure to any one industry or sector.

In a perfect world, a portfolio of 25 stocks diversified across 25 separate industries or sectors would limit the overall portfolio exposure to only 4 percent in any one industry or sector. Under this scenario an investor could suffer a total loss (an improbable but not impossible occurrence) in any one position and emerge relatively unscathed.

Of course, we don't live in a perfect world and it isn't always possible to diversify across that many industries or sectors because they may not all offer simultaneous good historic values. By example, let's say the utilities sector offers historically good value and there are six or seven that are currently undervalued. As utility stocks tend to have higher dividend-yields, particularly at undervalue, an investor might be tempted to snap up all six or seven. What would be more prudent though is to choose perhaps one gas utility and one electric utility that are based in different geographic regions. In this example the investor has gained exposure to the sector but he has diversified by type of utility and by region.

Of course, there won't always be such a clear-cut distinction by type and region as there is in the utilities example. Among individual investors and in the professional community there are some age-old battle lines drawn when it comes to certain industries and companies: Procter & Gamble versus Colgate-Palmolive, Coca-Cola or Pepsi, Wal-Mart or Target, and so forth.

In these situations investors must return to individual analyses and compare the fundamentals and strengths: Are they both at undervalue; what are the quality rankings; does one offer a more attractive price or dividend yield; does one have a lower payout ratio or debt level; and so forth. Often times one company will stand out over the other; in an equal number of cases there may be a draw. At the end of the day an investor may choose the course of Solomon and divide the allocation among both companies.

In any event and no matter the decision, the fundamental concept behind diversification is to spread overall portfolio risk as far as is reasonably possible so that the unexpected will not cause irreparable harm to the value of the portfolio.

CHAPTER 10

Building and Managing the Dividend-Value Portfolio

First, have a definite, clear practical ideal; a goal, an objective. Second, have the necessary means to achieve your ends; wisdom, money, materials, and methods. Third, adjust all your means to the end.

—Aristotle

When I first began mapping out this book, my initial thought was that this would be the easiest chapter to write, as a good portion of each workday is directed toward research, analysis, stock selection, and portfolio management decisions. Now that I have reached this place in the book, I am beginning to think I was perhaps a little cavalier in that assessment.

Obviously I would hope at this point you realize it isn't that I don't have a grasp of the material. Much of this I do on an autonomic level just like breathing. The truth be told, after 25-plus years in this business, much of this process is so automatic for me I don't have to stop and think about the order of analytical steps and the myriad variables to consider in the decision-making process; I just do it.

As there are no existing mechanisms that allow me to download the data that resides on the hard drive between my ears directly to yours, I am relegated to transcribing the data in as precise and complete a manner possible through the medium in your hands. Although a linear presentation will not appeal to readers whose modality is perhaps more abstract, my thought is that it is the most logical way to progress through the material.

As such I have divided the material into two distinct parts. The first is to lay the academic foundation to the approach that I advocate and follow—one might say the textbook part, which is what has been covered to this point. Although not particularly entertaining, the academics are of vital importance because one must have an intellectual framework to work from.

The second part is the equally if not more important aspect of practical application in the real world. Theory without application may be intellectually stimulating, but it does little in the way of building profits in a portfolio. It occurred to me, though, that the process of practical application is not a linear exercise that follows a sequential series of steps; each action must be filtered through the prism of experience, which can lead to a host of possibilities and further decisions.

In short, it is not possible to tell you exactly what I would do every time in a given situation. To use a sports analogy, with investing you often have to make some game-time decisions, which will vary based on the circumstances and situation of the moment.

Now that I have taken you over the hills and through the woods to grandmother's house to make my point, I will summarize it for you this way. On an intellectual level I know it is impossible to remember and write about everything I have learned and pass it on to you so that you don't make some of the same mistakes that I have. That just isn't realistic. What I can do is to try and cover as much as possible the factors to consider as you go about implementing the concepts in this book into your investment decisions.

I appreciate your indulgence on this divergence. I am just so passionate about investing and our approach that I want to do everything possible to help be successful and to reach your goals and objectives.

In this chapter, we first consider various types of market climates. Next, we apply the concepts explained previously to the process of structuring a dividend-centered, value-based stock portfolio. This process will include examinations about how to monitor both the individual portfolio components as well as the portfolio as a whole, and how to make adjustments to the portfolio as both the individual components and the market progress through various cycles and phases of value.

For the purposes of this chapter, when I use the term *portfolio,* I am referring to that portion of your investment capital that you have allocated to the stock market.

Macro versus Micro

Whether by design or evolution, there are two sides to everything associated with stocks and the market: Bull and bear; long and short; fundamental and technical; *overvalue* and *undervalue,* and so on. It should come as no surprise then that there are two primary approaches to stock selection: top-down and bottom-up.

With the top-down approach, investors place a higher priority on identifying the trends in the macro economy before selecting the industries and the companies within those industries that have a tendency to benefit from those trends.

By example, if an investor thinks that inflation will remain low, he or she might consider the retailing industry, as consumer spending power is typically enhanced during periods of low inflation. Using that premise as a guide, the investor may look at Wal-Mart, Target, or other retailers and then try to determine which company has the best earnings prospects in the near term.

Staying with the example of inflation, another macro viewpoint would be the anticipation for a period of higher inflation, in which case the investor might then find the mining industry to be attractive. Once again using that premise as a guide, the investor may look at Barrick Gold, Freeport McMoRan, or other mining companies to determine which is better positioned to benefit from a trend of rising prices.

A more colloquial way of thinking about the top-down approach is that this type of investor is looking first at the forest and then at the trees. Such investors believe it is better to identify the major themes in the market first and then select individual companies second. The logic behind this line of thinking is that if current economic conditions are not supportive of the industry in which a company operates, it could prove to be difficult for the company to generate sufficient earnings to motivate investors to propel the stock price higher. The investor is vulnerable in this approach as he or she may overlook good companies that are still performing well, even in a depressed sector.

With the bottom-up approach investors place a higher priority on analyzing individual companies than the trends of the macro economy. The thought here is if the company's fundamentals are strong and there is evidence of good value, cycles within the economy, the market, or the industry are transitory in nature and the fundamentals will eventually be recognized. Indeed, value investors as well as contrarians welcome the later stages of a market downturn as stocks are typically trading at depressed levels, which provide substantial upside potential once the market decline halts and reverses direction.

As such, the bottom-up investor may begin to acquire positions before trends in the macro economy show improvement or industry outlooks start to firm. The thought here is that, although an industry may be out of favor, investors who defer a purchase until confirmation of improving earnings may miss the opportunity to purchase a historically well-managed company with a long-term performance record for a price that is well below its intrinsic value. However, the investor is vulnerable in this approach because his or her investment capital may be exhausted too soon, before the end of the market decline.

As you can see, these two approaches to investing are quite different. Although proponents of both approaches can be overly zealous, the fact is that both approaches have something to offer. As the dividend-yield strategy marries aspects of both fundamental and technical analysis, it also utilizes aspects from both the bottom-up and top-down approaches.

From the top-down approach we believe it is prudent to be aware of the primary trend of the macro economy as economic activity does affect the way stocks behave. However, economic indicators have no value when determining when a stock is overvalued and should be sold or when it is undervalued and should be bought. That determination can only be made by comparing the current dividend yield against its historically repetitive boundaries, information one would gain from a company specific, bottom-up approach.

Observing how economic activity or inactivity affects the mood of the market can lead investors toward certain industry groups and away from others. These observations can also help investors gauge whether it is a propitious time to be taking new undervalue positions or perhaps time to raise cash by liquidating oversold positions.

This is not to suggest that we engage in market timing as a primary determinant in when and what to buy, sell, or hold. What we are trying to do is to take the myriad macro and micro factors that can affect stocks and the market into consideration for the purpose of refining the purchase of undervalued blue chips at a lower price or the selling of overvalued positions at a higher price. This is not to imply that we can buy every bottom and sell every top, but we can expand the meat in the middle. In the long run, if we can capture a few points in price here or there and lock down the highest dividend yields possible for a longer period of time, the miracle of compound returns can work its magic.

Expansion and Contraction

I don't know if they are still around, but when I was a kid the Slinky was all the rage. For those too young to remember (or those in denial about their age), the Slinky is a helical spring that stretches and shrinks with the aid of gravity and its own momentum.

If I were to show it to one to my kids today, they would just look at me and then head off to play Wii or a computer game. How technology has changed the world!

The economy is much like the old Slinky; it expands and contracts. If it gets pulled too far, it snaps; without any tension it lies inert. The cycles of expansion and contraction vary in length, but on average each cycle lasts about four years.

Dividend Truth

These cycles of expansion and contraction in the economy are similar to the cycles in stock prices and dividend yields. The explanation for this fluctuation in both economic and stock cycles is the same primary force: simple supply and demand.

Kaboom and Kabust

If you think back to the latter half of the 1990s there was a tremendous demand for all things technological: computers, chips, monitors, bandwidth, and so forth. At the early stages of this demand, prices were high as supplies were scarce and earnings were through the roof. Not wanting to miss out on the action, everybody and their brother got into the tech and dot-com act, production was ramped up, and the next thing we knew we had a full blown boom on our hands.

As we all know, the tech and dot-com craze went to an extreme and eventually there was too much supply. To reduce inventories, producers slashed prices, and in so doing they also slashed their earnings. Unable to reduce inventories sufficiently, producers stopped producing, unemployment began to rise, and eventually the economy and the markets went into decline.

A variation of this theme played out with the housing industry in this decade, albeit with a slight twist. Whereas the technology boom was the result of demand for technology products and services, demand was created by government monetary policy (read stimulus), and the housing boom was the result.

When the Fed dramatically lowered the interest rate on Fed Funds, the interest rate on all fixed-income instruments declined as well, including mortgage-backed bonds. As a result, borrowers determined they could buy more expensive homes than their current one because the principal and interest payments were often equal to if not less than the payment on their current mortgages.

As if by some miracle, simultaneous to the decline in interest rates, the requirements to qualify for a mortgage were significantly relaxed, which allowed many more borrowers to qualify to purchase a home. With this new-found purchasing power, the demand for homes quickly erased the supply of existing homes, which motivated home builders to ramp up the construction of new homes across America.

With all booms come the inevitable groups of speculators who attempt to profit from the craze de jour. In the tech and dot-com bubble, we saw this with the day traders. In the housing boom, we saw this with the flippers. Whether a speculation is in stocks, real estate, or another asset, the principle is the same; get in and get out.

Getting in is always easy during the manic phase of a boom. When getting out becomes difficult or next to impossible, the party is over. Whether speculators understand it intellectually or not, the speculative game is played according to the greater fool theory; the boom will last to infinity as long as there is a greater fool to sell to. Unfortunately, at some point in every boom the music stops playing and someone is left without a chair. In the housing boom, the music stopped when prices reached unsustainable levels and there were no greater fools to sell to.

When a boom takes over an economy, such as tech did in the 1990s and housing did in this decade, it spawns massive growth in ancillary or supporting businesses. When the source of growth runs out of gas, so do these other businesses. As these businesses contract or fail altogether, employment drops and incomes fall.

Just as a boom can create rising profits, therefore rising stock prices, a contraction can have the opposite effect. If a contraction is severe and lasts for a prolonged period, the economy can slide into recession.

Recessions

The technical indicator of a recession is two consecutive quarters of negative economic growth as measured by a country's Gross Domestic Product (GDP). GDP is the total market value of all final goods and services produced in a country in a given year.

A recession becomes official when announced by the National Bureau of Economic Research or NBER. However, most investors do not need an official announcement to know when a recession is underway. Often, but not always, a recession is preceded by the end of a bull market, rising unemployment, or a marked slowdown in consumer spending.

Over the past 60 years there have been 11 official recessions. All but one, in 1980, occurred within one year of the onset of a bear market. As mentioned previously, the stock market continually discounts future events as investors expect them to develop. In this regard, investors and the markets have proved to be rather prescient.

Although unpleasant, recessions are part of the natural order. When an economic boom or bull market reaches levels of excess, which they generally do, a recession is the corrective process that removes excesses from the system in order for the natural functions of supply and demand to return to normalcy.

It is generally deemed prudent to focus on noncyclical or so-called defensive stocks during a recession, things that are generally considered necessities: food; water, gas, and electric utilities; and personal items such as shampoo, soap, and toothpaste.

Although defensive stocks are not immune to the forces of a declining trend, the fact that these products and services are considered necessities provides for a more consistent stream of earnings and, therefore, protection for the dividends.

Recessions do not represent the end of the world, just a notice to change your focus.

Recovery

As night follows day, an economic rebound follows a recession. Where noncyclical stocks are the order of the day during recessions, cyclical industries and stocks are often the leaders out of the recovery gate.

Of the 11 most commonly recognized industry sectors, 9 are considered to be cyclical. These are transportation, capital goods, technology, financial, consumer cyclical, communications, basic materials, health care, and energy. The reason why they are called cyclical is because they move up or down due to the direction of businesses cycles. If a particular business is going up, then this sector is likely going up as well.

Cyclical industries are comprised of a wide range of products and services, which are in demand at various stages of the business cycle. As such they are commonly divided into three distinct categories: early cycle, midcycle, and late cycle.

Dividend Truth

It is important to remember that even though a sector or a company within that sector may be widely viewed as timely or favorable, these are subjective perceptions. Values can only be defined by repetitive patterns of dividend yield. Therefore, no stock should be purchased unless it represents historically good value as defined by its undervalued boundary of dividend yield.

Politics and Markets

I don't remember who told me this, but allegedly many years ago, the late Richard Nixon was asked what he'd be doing if he weren't president. He said that he'd probably be on Wall Street buying stocks. One old-time Wall Streeter chimed in that if Nixon weren't president, he too would be buying stocks.

Public policy is important and can affect stocks and the market in numerous ways. Generally, however, these effects typically reveal themselves less in the manner conventional wisdom expects and more often through the law of unintended consequences. Depending on which side of the aisle your bread gets buttered, then, the public policy of the moment can be a good or bad thing. Since policy swings back and forth from election to election, everyone usually has something to be upset about, which means it all evens out in the wash.

Putting partisan politics aside, there does appear a propensity for the markets to have positive returns during presidential election years. The explanations for this phenomenon are varied, depending on whether they originate from academia or conspiracy theorists. In any event, as you can see in Table 10.1, in the 21 presidential

Table 10.1 Election-Year Returns

Election Year	S&P 500 Return, %
2008	−37.00
2004	10.90
2000	−9.10
1996	23.10
1992	7.70
1988	16.80
1984	6.30
1980	32.40
1976	23.80
1972	19.00
1968	11.10
1964	16.50
1960	0.50
1956	6.60
1952	18.40
1948	5.50
1944	19.80
1940	−9.80
1936	33.90
1932	−8.20
1928	43.60

election years since 1928, the S&P 500 had a positive return in 17 of the 21 periods, or 81 percent of the time.

Don't Fight the Fed

As my grandfather would often say, "money makes the mare go, son." In Wall Street speak we would say that monetary conditions have enormous influence on stock prices. The fact is that liquidity is the lifeblood of the market. When liquidity is plentiful the market moves up; when liquidity is constrained, the market moves down.

The major determinant of the direction of interest rates is Federal Reserve policy, which all interest rates react to. In general, when interest rates are rising, it is bearish for stocks. Conversely, when interest rates are declining, it is bullish for stocks.

When interest rates are low or declining, the competition for stocks by other instruments, particularly short-term fixed-income investments such as T-bills, CDs, and money markets, are less attractive. Think about it; which would you prefer, a high-quality blue chip at undervalue prices yielding 4 percent, or a fixed-income instrument with a coupon of 2 percent or perhaps less? You don't have to think too long about that one.

Also important is that when interest rates are low or declining, corporations can borrow at lower rates. Debt can be a costly expense, and when an expense is reduced, it clears the way for higher earnings. When Wall Street has an expectation for higher earnings, stock prices will generally be bid higher. In a high or rising-interest-rate environment, the exact opposite occurs and stock prices decline.

When the market declines because of a hike in interest rates or because of the perception that a rate hike is imminent, it isn't so much that a quarter point will make all the difference in the world, it is what the rate hike signals to Wall Street—a change in trend. Once the trend changes from a low-to-declining environment to a rising-trend environment, Wall Street discounts that the upward trend will remain in place until the Fed achieves its goals, which generally is a slowdown in the economy, which generally results in lower earnings.

This will initially be most evident in interest-rate-sensitive stocks, such as banks, insurance companies, and utilities. Industrial companies with a high debt-to-equity ratio will also suffer because a slowing economy that results in lower earnings will put even more pressure on a debt-laden company.

Dividend Truth

Blue chips with low debt levels and higher returns on equity will be more stable in terms of share price during periods of rising interest rates.

A Yen for Dollars, or Pounds, or Euros

When you make an investment in a stock that trades in a foreign currency, the total return is based on two factors: the return in local currency plus any currency fluctuations. By example, let's say you buy a stock in the Euro Zone and the price increases 10 percent in one year in terms of euros. If during that same year the euro increases in value by 5 percent as compared to the U.S. dollar, the total return would be 15 percent; 10 percent from investment return plus 5 percent from currency return. On the other hand, if the euro were to decrease in value by 5 percent against the dollar, the total return would be just 5 percent; 10 percent from investment return and –5 percent in currency return.

When the U.S. dollar declines compared to the other currency, the return on investment increases as more dollars are required to purchase the stock. An increase in the U.S. dollar compared to the other currency means the return on investment will be less.

Many U.S. companies are what we call multinationals, meaning that they have both domestic and foreign operations. The foreign operations will typically receive its revenues in the foreign currency, and, depending on when the currency is converted into dollars, the amount can be higher or lower, as just detailed.

Some investors attempt to offset the risk of these currency fluctuations through currency hedging, which entails using options, futures, or forward contracts. This is a specific skill set that the average investor may have trouble with because of the inherent complexities. Since Wall Street is nothing if not creative, mutual funds and ETFs are available that do the hedging for you and are referred to as being currency neutral.

We do not follow foreign stocks at *Investment Quality Trends* because most of the companies that meet our criteria have very complex dividend-conversion policies that make it difficult to pinpoint the dividend yield at any given time. As such, we have difficulty establishing undervalue and overvalue boundaries, which as you know is central to the dividend-value strategy.

Putting It All Together

It would be a wonderful coincidence if the current market environment was one with the investment winds at our back and a new bull market was underway. If that were the case I could write darn near anything and end up looking like a genius.

Sadly, this is not the case, *so I will approach this section as if I were building a portfolio today* to show you my thought process. Of course, there will be a few months' lag time between the completion of this book and the time it reaches the bookshelves, so the environment could be very, very different.

Be that as it may, I would still approach the process in the same way, although the number of stocks and percentage of the portfolio invested might be different. Because it would border on the impossible to contemplate all the potential investment scenarios, I will nonetheless try to give you some guiding rules of thumb to follow.

What Is the Primary Trend?

The primary trend is down. When the Dow violated the 3 percent dividend-yield level and tumbled through and below the 10,000 level, a bear market was confirmed. Since March 2009, the Dow has been in a counter-trend rally, which is also known as cyclical bull market or a retracement.

Counter-trend rallies or retracements will typically recover one-third to one-half of the previous decline. In Figure 8.3 in Chapter 8, however, we see that a counter-trend rally can recover the entire decline or in the case in 1973, even make a new high. Once a retracement has recovered 50 percent of the previous decline, though, I tend to become more cautious.

What Is the Current Phase of Value?

The Dow is in a declining trend. As the market is currently enjoying a counter-trend rally, many might think the Dow has entered into a rising trend. In order to enter a rising trend *from the current level,* the Dow would need to record a new high price.

What Is the Reading of the Blue Chip Trend Verifier?

As of the mid-September issue of *Investment Quality Trends,* the Undervalued category represents 30.8 percent of the Select Blue Chip universe. The percentage has declined significantly from the March 2009 reading of 72 percent, which was in line with the Dow having reached support at the 5.0 percent dividend-yield area.

That the current reading has declined significantly since March confirms that the secondary trend is bullish and a cyclical retracement is in force. If the current rally continues, we should see this reading drop to the 17 percent overvalue area.

What Is the Interest Rate Trend?

In response to the global financial crisis, the Federal Reserve has reduced the interest rate on Fed Funds to a level between 0 percent and 0.25 percent. In theory, the Fed could drop all pretenses and fix the rate at 0 percent, but it would hardly be worth the trouble and would probably cause more harm than good because the credit markets would panic. For all intents and purposes, this is the lowest Fed Fund rate we will ever see. Although it is unlikely the Fed will make any change in the Funds rate until midyear 2010, the next change in trend will definitely be up.

For purposes of our current analysis however, there is no investment competition from high-quality fixed-income instruments.

Expansion, Contraction, or Recession?

To date there has been no official announcement from the National Bureau of Economic Research that the recession that began officially in December 2007 has ended. Federal Reserve Chairman Ben Bernanke has opined that the recession is over, as have many economists and members of the financial media.

Although fears of an economic depression have subsided, there is no concrete evidence of sustainable economic growth without government assistance.

Portfolio Tactics

The first order of business is to summarize the preceding information into a big-picture point of view:

- The primary trend is down, but the secondary trend is in force. Depending on the index, however, the market has retraced close to or above 50 percent of the previous decline.
- The Dow is in a declining trend.
- The Blue Chip Trend Verifier shows a reading of 30.8 percent. This is above the overvalue area of 17 percent but well below the undervalue area between 70 percent and 80 percent.
- The interest rate environment is a positive for stocks and the market and should remain so for close to another year. The next change in trend will be up.
- The recession is most likely over, but the economy is still fragile. Without continued government assistance there is a possibility for a slide back into recession.

I have seen worse, but I have also seen much better. In my opinion the downside risks outweigh the upside potential, so I believe prudence and caution is the way to proceed. Defensive stocks make the most sense right now, so depending on your risk tolerance, I would allocate between 25 percent and 50 percent of capital, but I would be more comfortable with 25 percent.

No matter the investment climate, I always start investment considerations with the Undervalued category. Next, I want to find the stocks with the highest quality rankings, an outstanding track record for increasing dividends, a modest to lower payout ratio, low debt, a moderate P/E ratio, and a reasonable book value.

Figure 7.3 in Chapter 7 shows a listing of the Undervalued category from the mid-September 2009 issue of *Investment Quality Trends.* I have used this list to screen for stocks according to the preceding criteria, and have selected 22 stocks, which are listed in Figure 10.1. We will use this list to build a sample portfolio.

Stock			Price	Dividend	Yield	Pts Dn	% Down	Undervalue LoPr/ HiYld		Pts Up	% Up	Overvalue HiPr/ LoYld		S&P	52-wk Lo	52-wk Hi	Bk Val	12-mo Earn	P/E	Pay out	Div in Dgr	Debt	BC	Tic
Abbott Labs	G	U	47	1.60	3.38%	−6	−13%	53	3.00%	67	141%	114	1.40%	A–	41	60	13	3.43	14	47%		45%	6	ABT
Altria Group	G	U	18	1.36	7.77%	−10	−55%	27	5.00%	28	159%	45	3.00%	A	14	21	2	1.52	12	89%		260%	6	MO
Archer Daniels	G	U	27	0.56	2.05%	−1	−3%	28	2.00%	29	105%	56	1.00%	A+	14	32	21	2.65	10	21%		46%	6	ADM
AT&T Inc.		U	27	1.64	6.08%	−3	−11%	30	5.50%	55	204%	82	2.00%	B+	21	31	17	2.02	13	81%		57%	4	T
Automatic Data	G	U	39	1.32	3.39%	−31	−79%	69	1.90%	150	385%	189	0.70%	A+	31	44	11	2.64	15	50%		1%	6	ADP
Becton Dickinson	G	U	69	1.32	1.93%	3	4%	66	2.00%	97	141%	165	0.80%	A	58	83	22	4.82	14	27%		20%	6	BDX
Chevron Corp.	G	U	71	2.72	3.85%	−7	−10%	78	3.50%	65	92%	136	2.00%	A–	56	87	44	8.13	9	33%		8%	6	CVX
Coca-Cola	G	U	53	1.64	3.10%	−2	−3%	55	3.00%	152	287%	205	0.80%	A	37	55	10	2.70	20	61%		12%	6	KO
Colgate-Palmolive	G	U	77	1.76	2.30%	3	4%	73	2.40%	84	109%	160	1.10%	A+	54	78	5	3.91	20	45%		165%	6	CL
CVS Caremark Corp.	G	U	35	0.30	0.85%	−2	−7%	38	0.80%	40	113%	75	0.40%	A+	23	38	25	2.25	16	13%		26%	5	CVS
Exelon Corp.	G	U	50	2.10	4.21%	4	8%	46	4.60%	50	101%	100	2.10%	B+	38	69	18	4.20	12	50%		134%	5	EXC
Johnson & Johnson	G	U	61	1.96	3.23%	5	8%	56	3.50%	48	80%	109	1.80%	A+	46	70	17	4.55	13	43%		19%	6	JNJ
McDonald's	G	U	57	**2.20**	3.86%	−4	−7%	61	3.60%	53	93%	110	2.00%	A–	46	64	12	3.77	15	58%		71%	6	MCD
Nike Inc Cl B	G	U	59	1.00	1.71%	3	5%	56	1.80%	108	184%	167	0.60%	A+	38	68	18	3.03	19	33%		6%	6	NKE
Overseas Shipholding	G	U	38	1.75	4.60%	3	8%	35	5.00%	65	171%	103	1.70%	B+	20	64	71	8.35	5	21%		83%	5	OSG
PepsiCo	G	U	59	1.80	3.07%	−23	−39%	82	2.20%	91	156%	150	1.20%	A+	44	72	9	3.23	18	56%		36%	6	PEP
Philip Morris Intl Inc.	G	U	48	**2.32**	4.87%	1	3%	46	5.00%	30	62%	77	3.00%	A+	32	52	3	3.25	15	71%		45%	6	PM
Procter & Gamble	G	U	58	1.76	3.03%	−12	−21%	70	2.50%	102	176%	160	1.10%	A+	44	72	21	4.26	14	41%		34%	6	PG
Sigma-Aldrich	G	U	52	0.58	1.11%	4	8%	48	1.20%	64	121%	116	0.50%	A+	31	56	13	2.67	20	22%		12%	6	SIAL
TJX Companies	G	U	37	0.48	1.30%	0	0%	37	1.30%	59	161%	96	0.50%	A+	18	39	7	2.22	17	22%		40%	6	TJX
United Technologies	G	U	62	1.54	2.50%	−8	−14%	70	2.20%	67	109%	128	1.20%	A+	37	64	18	4.40	14	35%		37%	6	UTX
Wal-Mart Stores	G	U	49	1.09	2.20%	−5	−10%	55	2.00%	60	120%	109	1.00%	A+	46	61	17	3.41	15	32%		57%	6	WMT

Figure 10.1 Twenty-Two Stocks

The first stock is Abbott Labs (ABT): It has an A– quality ranking; the *Investment Quality Trends* "G" designation for average annual dividend increases of at least 10 percent per year for the last 12 years. The payout ratio and debt are less than 50 percent; and the P/E is 14. I'm not going to worry too much about the book value because it is difficult to value some of the intellectual property such as patents. As ABT is in the pharmaceutical sector, it is definitely a defensive position.

The next stock is Altria Group (MO): An A quality ranking; a "G"; the P/E is 12; uh oh, a payout ratio of 89 percent and a debt of 260 percent! I know, you think I've lost my mind. This is where you have to do some additional homework. You may not like this industry, but tobacco is a classic sin stock, and as such it will most likely always be in business.

MO is what we call a cash cow; they practically print money. The debt level seems outrageous until you learn they bought one of their major competitors, U.S. Tobacco, at the end of 2008. The beauty of the U.S. Tobacco acquisition is that it adds one of the fastest growing segments of the tobacco industry to the MO lineup—smokeless tobacco.

I know, you are thinking that is a great story but what about the numbers? Here is where you want to look at the return-on-equity or ROE. ROE is the amount of net income returned as a percentage of shareholders' equity and is expressed as a percentage. Return on equity measures a corporation's profitability by revealing how much profit a company generates with the money shareholders have invested. A business that has a high return on equity is more likely to be one that is capable of generating cash internally.

ROE is reported over various time frames, so you can see some volatility in the numbers. As a general rule of thumb, however, I like to see the longer-term measures show some signs of consistency. In the case of MO, the longer-term ROEs come in about 20 percent on average. This is a number I can more than live with.

As we move down the list, you can see the remaining stocks I have chosen: Archer-Daniels-Midland (ADM); AT&T, Inc. (T); I really like Automatic Data Processing (ADP), but it will do much better in a rising interest rate environment. So make a note of that and we will set this stock aside; Becton, Dickinson (BDX); Chevron (CVX); Coca-Cola (KO); Colgate-Palmolive (CO); CVS Caremark (CVS); Exelon (EXC); Johnson & Johnson (JNJ); McDonald's (MCD); Nike, Inc.

(NKE); Overseas Shipholding Group (OSG); PepsiCo (PEP); Philip Morris International (PM); Procter & Gamble (PG); Sigma-Aldrich (SIAL); TJX Companies (TJX); United Technologies (UTX); and Wal-Mart Stores (WMT). For this example then I have selected 21 companies, enough to find good diversification but below the 25 stock maximum.

Now, let's see if we are too concentrated in any one industry. Abbott Labs (ABT) and Johnson & Johnson (JNJ) are both giant pharmaceuticals, but they focus on different areas. If the industry as whole were to take a hit, then both would probably decline as well, at least temporarily. As both are at historic levels of undervalue though, any declines should be minor because the dividends are well supported by earnings.

Becton, Dickinson (BDX) is also a healthcare related stock, but it does not manufacture drugs. Becton, Dickinson (BDX) is a medical technology company that makes and sells a range of medical supplies, devices, laboratory equipment, and diagnostic products used by healthcare institutions, life-science researchers, clinical laboratories, and the general public.

Sigma-Aldrich (SIAL) is a specialty chemical maker that makes the chemical building blocks that pharmaceutical, biopharma, and biotech companies need to make their medications and remedies. Sigma-Aldrich (SIAL) doesn't need a giant drug to be successful; they just need to sell their chemical compounds, which they do better than any other chemical company.

CVS Caremark (CVS) fills prescriptions and provides related healthcare services through approximately 6,900 CVS/Pharmacy and Longs Drug retail stores. The company also provides pharmacy benefit management, one of the fastest growing segments in the industry.

Colgate-Palmolive (CO) and Procter & Gamble (PG) share some of the same space, as do Coca-Cola (KO) and PepsiCo (PEP). Pepsi, however, is also a snack-food company, which diversifies their earnings stream.

Chevron (CVX) is a major oil company, and Overseas Shipholding Group (OSG) is a bulk shipping company engaged primarily in the ocean transportation of crude oil and petroleum products. I like this combination—a producer and a transporter.

Exelon (EXC) is an electric utility; you always need one of those. McDonald's (MCD) just flat out produces so I like that. Wal-Mart

(WMT) and TJX Companies (TJX) are both retailers but in entirely different segments of that market. Nike, Inc.(NKE) rules the shoe world; we could be in a depression and kids would still find a way to buy a pair of Nike tennis shoes.

Everyone or nearly everyone owns a cell phone, so I like AT&T, Inc. (T) (not to mention the yield). United Technologies (UTX) has operations in six segments: elevators and escalators; heating, ventilation, and air conditioning; fire suppression; jet engines and turbines; aerospace; and helicopters. This leaves us with Archer-Daniels-Midland (ADM), which is a long-term commodity play, and the two tobacco companies, Altria Group (MO) and Philip Morris International (PM). Altria Group is domestic and Philip Morris is international so I like that diversification.

Alright, not too bad for a defensive portfolio. If the market heads lower, most of these should hold up nicely. If the market heads higher, there is still enough growth potential for capital appreciation. In either event we still have between 50 percent and 75 percent of our capital to work with.

Okay, now we need to think about the two most likely scenarios.

Scenario 1

Since the secondary trend is up, the market has an upward bias. Since I'm not the only one who knows this is a primary bear market, though, don't be surprised to see some money rotate into more defensive sectors, like some of those represented by the stocks I just mentioned. As such, some of these stocks could move into rising trends.

If the market starts to break down and roll over, you need to make a decision. Do you keep your positions and add to them later, knowing you bought at historically repetitive areas of undervalue, or do you put in some stop loss orders, take your profits, and come back in at lower levels with a most likely larger universe to choose from?

Scenario 2

The market has retraced around 50 percent of the previous decline. As the primary trend is down, the Dow is in a declining trend, and the economy is still relatively weak, the rally could end tomorrow and head for a third leg down. We know most bear markets end when the Dow is yielding at or around the 6.0 percent dividend-yield level. We also know there is historical precedent for a halt and reversal at the 5.0 percent dividend-yield level, which could mean just a retest of the March 2009 lows.

Whether another leg down or a retest, what do you want to do? Your choices are to dollar-cost average down, sell outright, or do nothing. Once again, your decision should be based on your own tolerance for risk, your investment time horizon, your goals and objectives, and any potential tax consequences.

Dollar-cost averaging is the technique of buying a fixed dollar amount of a particular investment on a regular schedule, regardless of the share price. More shares are purchased when prices are low, and fewer shares are bought when prices are high. Eventually, the average cost per share of the security will become smaller and smaller. Dollar-cost averaging lessens the risk of investing a large amount in a single investment at the wrong time.

For example, you decide to purchase $100 worth of ABC each month for three months. In October, ABC is worth $33, so you buy three shares. In November, ABC is worth $25, so you buy four additional shares this time. Finally, in December, ABC is worth $20, so you buy five shares. In total, you purchased 12 shares for an average price of approximately $25 each.

As food for thought, here are a few things to consider:

1. This bear market is probably two-thirds over, but the last third could be rough.
2. When this market does bottom, it will probably represent the greatest buying opportunity of your lifetime.
3. Some stocks have probably already established bear-market lows; an equal number probably haven't. Which ones? I can't tell you; the market doesn't always play fair.
4. Only liars pick the absolute tops and the bottoms. If you get the meat in the middle you will do just fine.
5. If you buy right but a position turns against you, don't panic. This too shall pass.

Your decision should be based on your own tolerance for risk, your investment time horizon, your goals and objectives, and any potential tax consequences.

CHAPTER 11

The Stock Market and the Economy

You will go most safely by the middle way.

—Ovid

As written earlier, nobody has tomorrow's newspaper, therefore, the future is uncertain. As a market observer, commentator, and money manager, however, prognostication, as futile as it may be, is nonetheless expected.

As opposed to staking out any hard and fast territory, what I offer in this chapter is a mixture of observations, some historical context, and an educated guess or two, which have been filtered through the prism of a career of study and experience. My intention is that these musings will provide you some grist for your own contemplation and analysis.

The Stock Market

As of late September 2009, the broad equity indexes have rallied close to or more than 50 percent above the March 2009 lows. This being the case, some believe a new bull market is underway. As this is the first major retracement of declines in the stock market since the high-price watermark was established in October/November 2007, it is of no surprise that this has become a popular position to adopt.

For reasons outlined clearly in earlier chapters, however, I am of the opinion we are merely experiencing a garden-variety bear market rally. Also, from all the research I have conducted, no bear market in history has ended in a V bottom. For readers who are not stock-chart aficionados, a V bottom is a pattern created when a decline at a steep angle halts, pivots, and starts to ascend at an equally steep angle, thus creating the shape of the letter V.

An excellent example of a V bottom can be found in Figure 8.3 in Chapter 8. Note that the first and second down legs halted and reversed into a V-shaped pattern.

In the American lexicon there is a wonderful colloquial phrase that suggests there is a first time for everything. Just because no bear market in history has ever ended in a V bottom is not a guarantee that this one will not be the first; Mr. Market can do whatever he pleases. Considering the extreme levels of overvaluation the markets reached between the years 1995–2007, however, I wouldn't want to bet the ranch the lows for this bear cycle have been established. I stand willing and able to cheerfully and graciously admit my error if I am proven wrong though, because it will mean that a new bull market and a period of rising equity prices is underway.

At the end of the last major bear market in 1974, the markets entered what was essentially a sideways, trading-range pattern between dividend-yield extremes of 5 percent and 6 percent on the Dow, until the next bull market was launched in 1982. Although it would be difficult to find widespread enthusiasm for a reprise of that period, it did allow for the creation of a tremendous pool of value as measured by low-price/high-dividend-yield extremes. Based on the extraordinary degree of excess that was built up over the aforementioned period between 1995 and 2007, a similar, albeit hopefully shorter, period of consolidation would not be a surprise to your author.

If this scenario does indeed develop, I would suggest it will represent the greatest buying opportunity for my and many of your lifetimes.

Industries and Stocks to Watch

As I stated in Chapter 9, the dividend-value strategy uses aspects of both the bottom-up and top-down investment approaches. As I peruse the Undervalued category from the mid-September 2009 edition of *Investment Quality Trends,* it is abundantly clear that the majority of these stocks would be considered to be in defensive industries.

Apparently investors have chosen to throw their lot in with more cyclical industries and stocks, which is entirely to be expected as the market is in the throes of a very strong rally. Little if any of the current affection for cyclical issues is based on historic good value; rather, it is based on speculation that the recession has ended and the earnings for cyclical stocks will rebound as the economy strengthens. We will know soon.

The largest group of defensive stocks at current levels of undervalue is those related to health care: pharmaceuticals and medical devices, instruments, and services. The obvious explanation for this is that the largest overhaul of the healthcare and medical insurance industries in history is currently being debated in Congress. Although speculation is rampant about what will emerge, if anything, from this debate, investors have obviously chosen to sit this one out until the view is significantly less murky.

Based on our experience and the propensity for the dividend-value strategy to isolate opportunities when they are less obvious to the large majority of investors, I would suggest that regardless of what does or does not develop with healthcare overhaul, companies like Abbott Labs (ABT), Becton-Dickinson (BDX) (as shown in Figure 11.1), CVS Caremark (CVS), and Johnson & Johnson (JNJ) (as shown in Figure 11.2) will not only survive but prosper. The largest demographic age group in America is still the baby-boomers, and they have shown no signs of wanting to give up their medications, therapies, and ancillary healthcare services.

McDonald's (MCD), which was highlighted in Chapter 3, announced another 10 percent dividend increase in 2009, which means the prices for its *undervalue* and *overvalue* boundaries will rise, again.

Tobacco giant Altria Group (MO) and its spinoff, Philip Morris International (PM), both offer historically good value and relatively rich dividend yields. Other blue chip stalwarts mentioned in various places throughout this book, such as AT&T, Inc.(T); Nike, Inc. (NKE); Sigma-Aldrich (SIAL); and Wal-Mart Stores (WMT) also represent historic good values. Stocks not previously mentioned, but nonetheless are of equal blue chip quality such as soft-drink icons Coca-Cola (KO) and PepsiCo (PEP), personal care products companies like Colgate-Palmolive (CO) and Procter & Gamble (PG), offer excellent historic value.

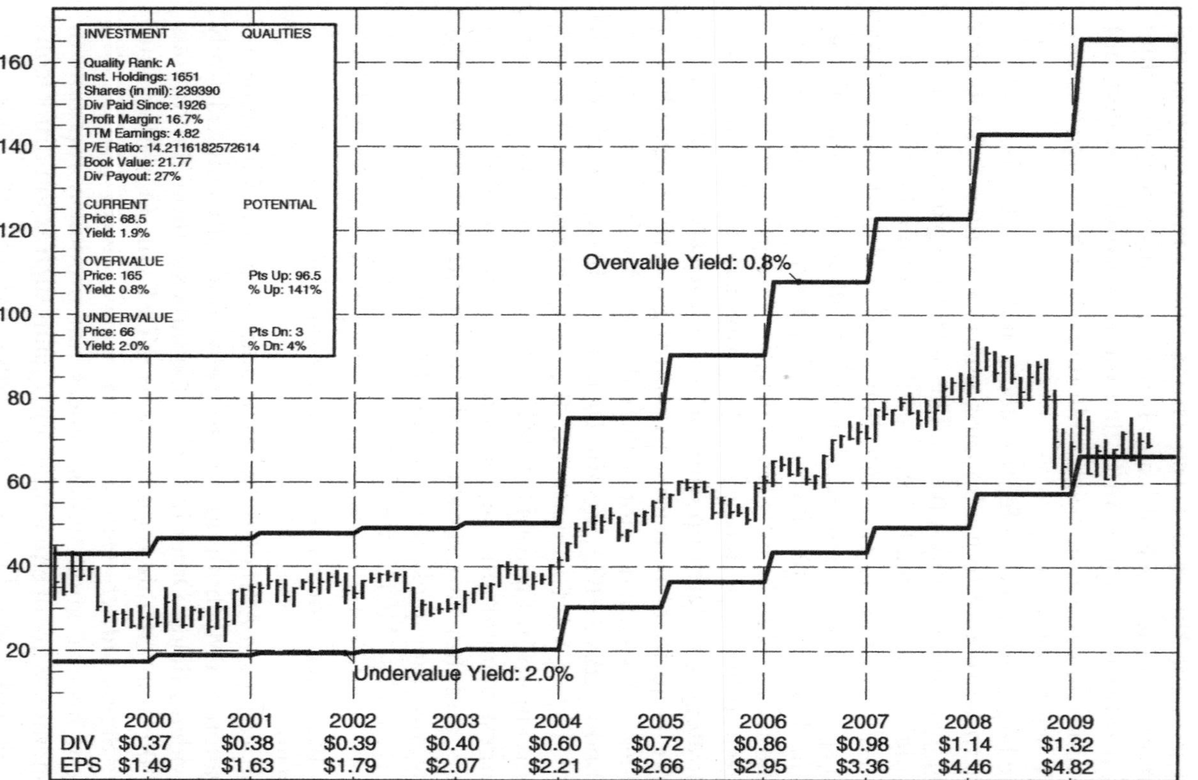

Figure 11.1 Becton, Dickinson (BDX)

Source: *Value Trend Analysis*

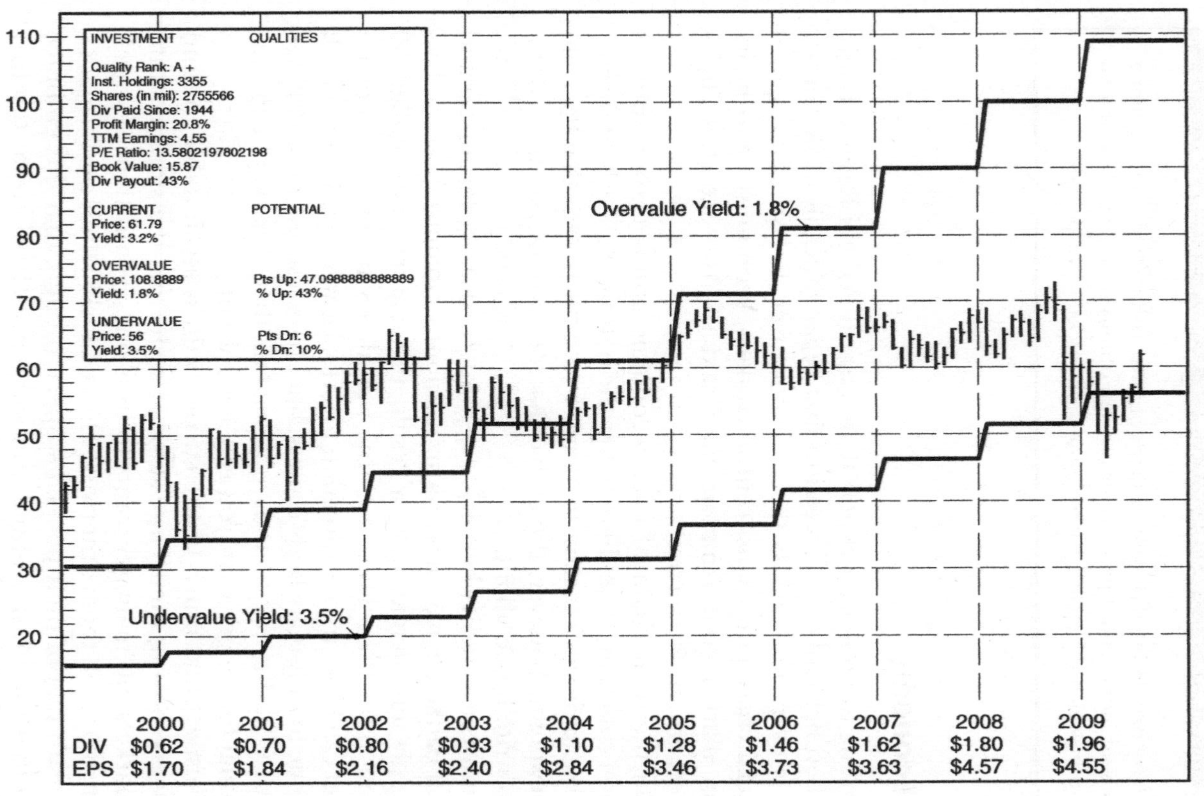

Figure 11.2 Johnson & Johnson (JNJ)

Source: *Value Trend Analysis*

Dividend Truth

The companies listed previously may not enter rising trends in the coming weeks or months but they do offer the opportunity for long-term, real total returns, which is exactly what we want from stocks in our portfolio.

The Economy

According to no less an expert than current Federal Reserve Chairman Ben Bernanke, the recession that began officially in December 2007 is over. Not only is the recession over, but so is the global financial crisis; politicians, central bankers, economists, and mainstream market commentators have said so. You see, the equity markets are up 50 percent.

On the food chain of macroeconomic opinion, your author's opinion comes in somewhere below the bottom. So, far be it for me, merely a lowly stock picker, to disagree with the powers that be; from my viewpoint, however, the global macroeconomic picture is nothing to write home about.

I must give credit where it is due though; so far, governments and central bankers have somehow miraculously circumvented the laws of supply and demand. As a result, the markets have rallied 50 percent from their lows, but this was always to be expected; no market can move in one direction forever. How long this market will continue to rally is anybody's guess, but I have a suspicion we will see a display of Keynes famous observation that "markets can stay irrational for longer than you can stay solvent."

I suspect that much of the current rally is attributable to fund managers moving their large stash of cash from the sidelines into the markets; no manager wants to miss out, even if their research and instincts tell them otherwise. Heaven forbid their performance is beneath that of their peers. I suspect, though, that this embrace of equities will be short-lived and will move elsewhere at the first hint of trouble.

There has been no real economic improvement aside from the results of government handouts and stimuli. Unless I have somehow missed it, I don't recall that any major infrastructure investment and manufacturing capacity is still far below trend. As for job creation, there has been little except in the public sector.

The banks are making money due to the steep yield curve, but there are still land mines galore such as major credit-card defaults, adjustable-rate mortgage refinancing problems in tranches not related to subprime, and looming commercial property refinancing issues that could present a larger problem than that in the residential market.

Also disconcerting is the problem with the U.S. dollar. Our largest creditor, China, is getting squeamish about the depreciating value of its dollar-denominated assets and is beginning to diversify into other currencies and tangible assets. In particular, China has become enamored with gold and for the first time is actually encouraging its citizens to store a portion of their new-found wealth into coins and smaller weight bars.

The Chinese seem to be on to the fact that the United States in particular is facing some daunting economic times and has some very steep hills to climb. This isn't the first time the United States has been challenged and it most certainly won't be the last. America is a creative and resilient country, though, and has many assets and advantages that are still the envy of the world.

In short, the economy will present many challenges in the years ahead. The stock market, as it has always done, will create opportunities from these challenges. Our job will be to deal with the challenges and take advantage of the opportunities.

CHAPTER 12

Questions and Answers

Live the questions now. Perhaps then someday far in the future, you will gradually, without even noticing it, live your way into the answer.

—Rainer Maria Rilke

Having published an investment newsletter in excess of four decades, we have received and answered hundreds of questions from subscribers, not to mention an equal if not greater number from attendees at investment workshops and speaking engagements. In addition, there are two previous books and countless commentaries in *Investment Quality Trends* and other publications that have addressed the dividend-value strategy in every way imaginable.

Be that as it may, it seems there is no such thing as too much information, as the title of this chapter would suggest. To our delight, the readers of *Investment Quality Trends* have demonstrated a talent for looking at investment problems from a very interesting angle. All of the following questions were posed by those readers.

Dividends

Q: *How can I tell when a dividend is in danger?*

A: As my grandfather told me many times, ''you can't draw water from an empty well.'' Dividends are paid out of earnings. When a company's dividend payment equals or exceeds its earnings, the well is dry and there is nothing left to operate and expand the company. A company can pay the dividend for a time out of cash flow or savings, but this is a temporary solution to what could be a serious financial problem. It is akin to putting a Band-Aid on a deep laceration before a doctor can attend to it.

For this reason we look at a company's payout ratio. The payout ratio is calculated by dividing the dividend by the trailing 12-month earnings and then multiplying by 100. By example, if the dividend is \$1.60 per share and the trailing 12 months earnings are \$3.43 per share, the formula would look like this: \$1.60/\$3.43 = 0.466. We then multiply 0.466 by 100, which equals 46.6, and is expressed as a percentage, 46.6 percent. In this case the payout ratio is 46.6 percent.

As a general rule of thumb we prefer the payout ratio to be 50 percent or less for an industrial company, and because of its different capital structure, 75 percent for a utility company. When the payout ratio is too high, it can limit a company's ability to invest in future growth. This isn't such a great concern if a company maintains a high return on equity (ROE), but all things being equal, we prefer to see a company grow its dividend while maintaining a healthy balance between net profits and dividend payouts.

Q: *How can I tell when a dividend is likely to be increased?*

A: Companies that have a more rapid rate of growth will often maintain a lower payout ratio than a more mature company that has a slower rate of growth but a more developed earnings stream. In that case, the shareholder is typically rewarded with greater capital appreciation than dividend income.

What we look for are companies that can grow earnings and increase dividends at the same time. In *Investment Quality Trends*, these companies often are awarded our "G" designation, which reflects a record of average annual dividend increases of 10 percent per year over the last 12 years.

In our experience, when such a company has a payout ratio of 30 percent or less, it often is an indicator that the dividend will likely be increased.

Q: *According to some reports, the preferential tax treatment afforded to dividends in the Tax Reform Act of 2003 may sunset in 2011. What impact would this have on the share prices for dividend-paying stocks?*

A: Have you ever looked at the federal income tax code? If you have, you are either an accountant or an insomniac. The number of pages and regulatory changes is never ending. This is because the tax code is Congress's private little fiefdom and it changes constantly regardless of the party in power.

If you look throughout history, the federal tax rate on dividends has been raised and lowered many times. Initially the market reacts in a kneejerk way to any changes, but eventually adjusts to the underlying reality of values.

The simple fact is that as an investor, you have a partner in Uncle Sam. The degree to which his hand is in your pocket will vary from time to time, but his hand will always be in your pocket. As my partner Mike often says, "It is what it is." The mistake many investors make is letting the tax-tail wag the investment-dog. If you try to adjust your investment program to the ever-changing tax code, you will lose; it can't have any long-term success.

Just stick with the principles of good investing as described in this book. The capital and dividend growth from blue chips will prove more than sufficient to grow your wealth and provide for your cash needs.

Q: *Do you believe stock buybacks add value to a stock?*

A: Technically, a stock buyback does increase the value of a stock. With fewer shares outstanding, earnings per share rise and P/E ratios shrink. As an enlightened investor, though, you know you should buy shares only when they are at historically repetitive areas of undervalue. The management of many companies has not yet learned that lesson.

Earlier in this decade, share buybacks were all the corporate rage. Unfortunately many of the buybacks occurred when the companies were deep into rising trends or, in the worst of cases, at overvalued levels. In these cases it was a needless waste of shareholder money. I would have preferred that the money spent on buybacks been paid to the shareholders directly to either spend or to invest in shares of another undervalued company.

Stocks

Q: *Do stocks ever move from Declining Trends into the Rising-Trends category?*

A: The only time a Declining Trend stock can directly reenter the Rising-Trends category is if the stock scores a new high price and dividend increases have lifted the price at overvalue, boosting the upside potential and giving the stock additional upside potential. However, when this happens (especially if it happens early in the new cycle), the upside potential rarely justifies the downside risk, and the shareholder is best advised to sell into the Rising Trend.

Q: *Do you advise buying stocks that are in the Rising-Trends category?*

A: The trend is your friend until it isn't. If the upside potential to *overvalue* exceeds the downside risk back to *undervalue,* stocks in Rising Trends are attractive, **in a bull market.** However, stock trends are greatly influenced by major market trends. As such, in a bear market, stocks in Rising Trends are likely to fall back into the Undervalued category. Once a bear market has been identified, we suggest that you limit your investment considerations to stocks in the Undervalued category. Rising Trend stocks can be held if the downside risk back to undervalue is not large. If Rising Trend stocks fall back into the Undervalued category in a correction, they are often investment opportunities.

Q: *Are stocks that fall into your Faded Blues category "bad companies" as it pertains to quality?*

A: Terms like *bad* and *good* are subjective interpretations. This is why we use the Criteria for Select Blue Chips to eliminate emotion and subjectivity so we may view a stock solely on a qualitative basis. A major benefit of using the criteria is that it brings clarity to the universe of over 13,000 publicly traded stocks by eliminating approximately 96 percent of them from investment consideration.

This clarity is distilled even further by assigning each Select Blue Chip to its respective category of current value based on its historic dividend yield profile. This allows us to concentrate only on the undervalued stocks when we undertake investment considerations for your hard earned capital.

The result of this disciplined approach is that we invest in only the best of the best. This also supports our three primary investment objectives: protect your principal, earn an immediate return on investment from dividends and dividend increases, and harvest long-term capital gains at overvalued levels to realize real total return.

When a stock is moved to the faded-blues category, it is because it no longer meets our strict criteria. Although many of these companies continue to perform without incident, the loss of Select Blue Chip status is often a harbinger of trouble for others. In our opinion, the potential risks outweigh the potential returns in these situations.

Q: *Should I sell a stock when it is moved to the Faded Blues category?*

A: In general terms, a move to the Faded Blues category raises the yellow flag of caution. What is required at this point is some discernment about the cause of the downgrade. For some stocks, a downgrade to the Faded Blues is a transitory event, because the company quickly addresses the issue(s) that prompted the downgrade. For other stocks, the downgrade can be the first in a string of negative events.

We would suggest a review of recent history to assist in the discernment process. By example, if, prior to the downgrade, a stock is earmarked as a dividend in danger (the dividend exceeds the trailing 12-months earnings) for an extended period of time and its level of debt has been persistently elevated, it may be prudent to eliminate the position. Remember, there is no profitable substitute for quality.

Q: *When analyzing the Undervalue category, can you discuss what weight you place on each of the table headings?*

When considering the stocks in the Undervalue category, our analysis begins with the Standard & Poor's Earnings and Dividends Quality Ranking. This measurement by S&P is a very comprehensive assessment of a company's ability to consistently generate earnings, which allows them to fund and maintain their dividend. Optimally, we prefer a ranking of A+, which is not awarded lightly and suggests a superior company.

Time and space do not permit a thorough discussion of all the components that are considered by S&P in this assessment, but subscribers who are so inclined can obtain a white paper directly from S&P that discusses each component in detail.

Closely following the S&P ranking is the "G" designation, which denotes a remarkable 10 percent average annual dividend growth over the past 12 years. Stocks that maintain this record are excellent compounding vehicles and generally realize consistent price appreciation.

The "BC" number, which represents how many of the six criteria in our Criteria for Select Blue Chips the stock meets, is a number we look at closely. Obviously, we prefer that a stock maintain all six, but many outstanding companies vacillate between five and six.

A payout percentage at or below 50 percent (75 percent for utilities) suggests that a company can both maintain their dividend and still have room to raise the dividend as earnings increase. Debt is another measure we look at closely. It is important to note that, when used correctly, debt can be an important tool. When debt reaches an abnormally high level for a sustained amount of time, however, it can become a problem and an indicator of potential trouble. We generally prefer that companies keep their debt level below 50 percent (75 percent for utilities).

The Dividend-Value Strategy

Q: *When a takeover occurs, do the undervalued and overvalued yield lines change for the dominant company?*

A: The acquiring company is typically larger than the acquired company in terms of capitalization and number of shares outstanding. Therefore, the dominant company has the most influence on the patterns of undervalue and overvalue, and the boundaries of dividend-yield will typically follow the pattern of the dominant partner.

Investors will adjust these boundaries if the earnings and/or dividend patterns change once the acquisition has been completely digested.

Q: *How should I adjust my portfolio once a bear market has been identified?*

A: When the market is undervalued or early in a rising trend, up to 90 percent of the investment capital that is allocated to stocks should be invested. I never invest 100 percent of my capital because an unforeseen circumstance might arise in which I need to access some cash, or an unexpected investment opportunity may become available.

When the market reaches the overvalue area, however, the rules change dramatically. In general, I want to sell any overvalued positions that are in the portfolio. If an overvalued stock is still showing signs of strength, however, I may elect to use a rising stop-loss order to milk the gains. If I have any rising trend stocks that are less than 50 percent from the overvalue area, I will use a stop loss for these positions as well. The important point to understand is that it is prudent to protect against a sudden reversal and decline.

My primary goal when the market reaches overvalue and shows signs of topping out is preservation of capital. When the market is overvalued or in a primary declining trend, preservation of capital is more important than appreciation of capital. That is, the return of capital is more important than the return on capital.

When the market is overvalued or in a primary declining trend, I don't want to have more than 25 percent of my capital invested. That 25 percent should also be limited strictly to undervalued blue chips. As the Dow declines from overvalue, it will typically find support in the 4 percent dividend-yield range and reverse into a counter-trend rally. At this point, another 25 percent can be invested in undervalued blue chips. Once the counter-trend rally has retraced 50 percent of the previous decline, it is time to place stop-loss orders once again.

As the second leg down gathers momentum, the stop losses will get hit and the second 25 percent tranche will most likely be liquidated, leaving you with 25 percent still invested. The second leg down should find support at the 5 percent yield area on the Dow, halt, and reverse into a second counter-trend rally. At this juncture I would place another 50 percent of my capital, for a total of 75 percent, into undervalued blue chips. Once the second counter-trend rally has retraced 50 percent of the previous decline, I would place very tight stop loss orders and prepare for the third leg down.

The third leg down is often the most severe, which means you should return to a 25/75 split again as the result of your stop loss orders. The third leg down will typically find support at the 6 percent yield area on the Dow. This is also typically the area that the bear market will end. At this juncture I want to move my 75 percent in cash into undervalued blue chip stocks in 25 percent increments until I am at 90 percent to 95 percent invested.

In Figure 12.1, you will find the DJIA from 1896–2008. Note that the periods in which the dividend yield was 6 percent or greater have been coincident with bear market bottoms.

Year	Dow At Start of Year	Year's High Close	Date		Year's Low Close	Date		Year's Close	Change Points	%	Book Value	Earns	P/E	Divs	% Yields
2008	13043.96	13058.20	May	2	7552.29	Nov.	20	8776.39	– 4488.43	–33.84	N.A.	N.A.	N.A.	316.40	3.61
2007	12474.52	14164.53	Oct.	9	12050.41	Mar.	5	13264.82	+801.67	+6.43	3115.48	199.87	66.4	298.99	2.25
2006	10847.41	12510.57	Dec.	27	10667.39	Jan.	20	12463.15	+1745.65	+16.29	3323.94	r728.02	17.1	267.75	2.15
2005	10729.43	10940.50	Mar.	4	10012.36	Apr.	20	10717.50	–65.51	–0.61	3510.65	476.39	22.5	246.85	2.30
2004	10409.85	10854.54	Dec.	28	9749.99	Oct.	25	10783.01	+329.09	+3.15	3359.70	588.96	18.3	239.27	2.22
2003	8607.52	10453.92	Dec.	31	7524.06	Mar.	11	10453.92	+2112.29	+25.32	2918.09	519.96	20.1	209.42	2.00
2002	10073.40	10635.25	Mar.	19	7286.27	Oct.	9	8341.63	–1679.87	–16.76	2286.69	385.58	21.6	189.68	2.27
2001	10646.15	11337.92	May	21	8235.81	Sept.	21	10021.50	–765.35	–7.10	2463.72	369.51	27.1	181.07	1.81
2000	11357.51	11722.98	Jan.	14	9796.03	Mar.	7	10786.85	–710.27	–6.18	1315.16	485.14	22.2	172.08	1.60
1999	9184.27	11497.12	Dec.	31	9120.67	Jan.	22	11497.12	+2315.69	+25.22	1638.10	477.22	24.1	168.52	1.47
1998	7965.04	9374.27	Nov.	23	7539.07	Aug.	31	9181.43	+1273.18	+16.10	1691.68	383.35	24.0	151.13	1.65
1997	6442.49	8259.31	Aug.	6	6391.69	Apr.	11	7908.25	+1459.98	+22.64	1594.14	391.29	20.2	136.10	1.72
1996	5177.45	6560.91	Dec.	27	5032.94	Jan.	10	6448.27	+1331.15	+26.01	1414.04	353.88	18.2	131.14	2.03
1995	3838.48	5216.47	Dec.	13	3832.08	Jan.	30	5117.12	+1282.68	+33.45	1337.33	311.02	16.4	116.56	2.27
1994	3756.60	3978.36	Jan.	31	3593.35	Apr.	4	3834.44	+80.35	+2.14	1305.32	256.13	15.0	105.66	2.75
1993	3309.22	3794.33	Dec.	29	3241.95	Jan.	20	3754.09	+452.98	+13.72	1117.81	146.84	25.6	99.66	2.65
1992	3172.41	3413.21	June	1	3136.58	Oct.	9	3301.11	+132.28	+4.17	1146.03	108.25	30.5	100.72	3.05
1991	2610.64	3168.83	Dec.	31	2470.30	Jan.	9	3168.83	+535.17	+20.32	1301.31	49.27	64.3	95.18	3.00

1990	2810.15	2999.75	July	16	2365.10	Oct.	11	2633.66	−119.54	−4.34	1331.52	172.05	15.3	103.70	3.94
1989	2144.64	2791.41	Oct.	9	2144.64	Jan.	3	2753.20	+584.63	+26.96	1276.14	221.48	12.4	103.00	3.74
1988	2015.25	2183.50	Oct.	21	1879.14	Jan.	20	2168.57	+229.74	+11.85	1075.47	215.46	10.1	79.53	3.67
1987	1927.31	2722.42	Aug.	25	1738.74	Oct.	19	1938.83	+42.88	+2.26	1008.95	133.05	14.6	71.20	3.67
1986	1537.73	1955.57	Dec.	2	1502.29	Jan.	22	1895.95	+349.28	+22.58	986.48	115.59	16.4	67.04	3.54
1985	1198.87	1553.10	Dec.	16	1184.96	Jan.	4	1546.67	+335.10	+27.66	944.97	96.11	16.1	62.03	4.01
1984	1252.74	1286.64	Jan.	6	1086.57	July	24	1211.57	−47.07	−3.74	916.70	113.58	10.7	60.63	5.00
1983	1027.04	1287.20	Nov.	29	1027.04	Jan.	3	1258.64	+212.10	+20.27	888.21	72.45	17.4	56.33	4.47
1982	882.52	1070.55	Dec.	27	776.92	Aug.	12	1046.54	+171.54	+19.60	881.51	9.15	114.4	54.14	5.17
1981	972.78	1024.05	Apr.	27	824.01	Sept.	25	875.00	−88.99	−9.23	975.59	113.71	7.7	56.22	6.42
1980	824.57	1000.17	Nov.	20	759.13	Apr.	21	963.99	+125.25	+14.93	928.50	121.86	7.9	54.36	5.64
1979	811.42	897.61	Oct.	5	796.67	Nov.	7	838.74	+33.73	+4.19	859.41	124.46	6.7	50.98	6.08
1978	817.74	907.74	Sept.	8	742.12	Feb.	28	805.01	−26.16	−3.15	890.69	112.79	7.1	48.52	6.03
1977	999.75	999.75	Jan.	3	800.85	Nov.	2	831.17	−173.48	−17.27	841.76	89.10	9.3	45.84	5.51
1976	858.71	1014.79	Sept.	21	858.71	Jan.	2	1004.65	+152.24	+17.86	798.20	96.72	10.4	41.40	4.12
1975	632.04	881.81	July	15	632.04	Jan.	2	852.41	+236.17	+38.32	783.61	75.66	11.3	37.46	4.39
1974	855.32	891.66	Mar.	13	577.60	Dec.	6	616.24	−234.62	−27.57	746.95	99.04	6.2	37.72	6.12
1973	1031.68	1051.70	Jan.	11	788.31	Dec.	5	850.86	−169.16	−16.58	690.23	86.17	9.9	35.33	4.15
1972	889.30	1036.27	Dec.	11	889.15	Jan.	26	1020.02	+129.82	+14.58	642.87	67.11	15.2	32.27	3.16
1971	830.57	950.82	Apr.	28	797.97	Nov.	23	890.20	+51.28	+6.11	607.61	55.09	16.2	30.86	3.47
1970	809.20	842.00	Dec.	29	631.16	May	26	838.92	+38.56	+4.82	573.15	51.02	16.4	31.53	3.76

Figure 12.1 DJIA 1896–2008

Year	Dow At Start of Year	Year's High Close	Date		Year's Low Close	Date		Year's Close	Change Points	%	Book Value	Earns	P/E	Divs	% Yields
1969	947.73	968.85	May	14	769.93	Dec.	17	800.36	−143.39	−15.19	542.25	57.02	14.0	33.90	4.24
1968	906.84	985.21	Dec.	3	825.13	Mar.	21	943.75	+38.64	+4.27	521.08	57.89	16.3	31.34	3.32
1967	786.41	943.08	Sept.	25	786.41	Jan.	3	905.11	+119.42	+15.20	476.50	53.87	16.8	30.19	3.33
1966	968.54	995.15	Feb.	9	744.32	Oct.	7	785.69	−183.57	−18.94	475.92	57.68	13.6	31.89	4.06
1965	869.78	969.26	Dec.	31	840.59	June	28	969.26	+95.13	+10.88	453.27	53.67	18.1	28.61	2.95
1964	766.08	891.71	Nov.	18	766.08	Jan.	2	874.13	+111.18	+14.57	417.39	46.43	18.8	31.24	3.57
1963	646.79	767.21	Dec.	18	646.79	Jan.	2	762.95	+110.85	+17.00	425.90	41.21	18.5	23.41	3.07
1962	724.71	726.01	Jan.	3	535.76	June	26	652.10	−79.04	−10.81	400.97	36.43	17.9	23.30	3.57
1961	610.25	734.91	Dec.	13	610.25	Jan.	3	731.14	+115.25	+18.71	385.82	31.91	22.9	22.71	3.11
1960	679.06	685.47	Jan.	5	566.05	Oct.	25	615.89	−63.47	−9.34	369.87	32.21	19.1	21.36	3.47
1959	587.59	679.36	Dec.	31	574.46	Feb.	9	679.36	+95.71	+16.40	339.02	34.31	19.8	20.74	3.05
1958	439.27	583.65	Dec.	31	436.89	Feb.	25	583.65	+147.96	+33.96	310.97	27.95	20.9	20.00	3.43
1957	496.03	520.77	July	12	419.79	Oct.	22	435.69	−63.78	−12.77	298.69	36.08	12.1	21.61	4.96
1956	485.78	521.05	Apr.	6	462.35	Jan.	23	499.47	+11.07	+2.27	284.78	33.34	15.0	22.99	4.60
1955	408.89	488.40	Dec.	30	388.20	Jan.	17	488.40	+84.01	+20.77	271.77	35.78	13.7	21.58	4.42
1954	282.89	404.39	Dec.	31	279.87	Jan.	11	404.39	+123.49	+43.96	248.96	28.18	14.4	17.47	4.32
1953	292.14	293.79	Jan.	5	255.49	Sept.	14	280.90	−11.00	−3.77	244.26	27.23	10.3	16.11	5.73
1952	269.86	292.00	Dec.	30	256.35	May	1	291.90	+22.67	+8.42	213.39	24.78	11.8	15.43	5.29

1951	239.92	276.37	Sept.	13	238.99	Jan.	3	269.23	+33.82	+14.37	202.60	26.59	10.1	16.34	6.07
1950	198.89	235.47	Nov.	24	196.81	Jan.	13	235.41	+35.28	+17.63	194.19	30.70	7.7	16.13	6.85
1949	175.03	200.52	Dec.	30	161.60	June	13	200.13	+22.83	+12.88	170.12	23.54	8.5	12.79	6.39
1948	181.04	193.16	June	15	165.39	Mar.	16	177.30	−3.86	−2.13	159.67	23.07	7.7	11.50	6.49
1947	176.39	186.85	July	24	163.21	May	17	181.16	+3.96	+2.23	149.08	18.80	9.6	9.21	5.08
1946	191.66	212.50	May	29	163.12	Oct.	9	177.20	−15.71	−8.14	131.40	13.63	13.0	7.50	4.23
1945	152.58	195.82	Dec.	11	151.35	Jan.	24	192.91	+40.59	+26.65	122.74	10.56	18.3	6.69	3.47
1944	135.92	152.53	Dec.	16	134.22	Feb.	7	152.32	+16.43	+12.09	118.33	10.07	15.1	6.57	4.31
1943	119.93	145.82	July	14	119.26	Jan.	8	135.89	+16.49	+13.81	113.03	9.74	14.0	6.30	4.64
1942	112.77	119.71	Dec.	26	92.92	Apr.	28	119.40	+8.44	+7.61	107.50	9.22	13.0	6.40	5.36
1941	130.57	133.59	Jan.	10	106.34	Dec.	23	110.96	−20.17	−15.38	102.33	11.64	9.5	7.59	6.84
1940	151.43	152.80	Jan.	3	111.84	June	10	131.13	−19.11	−12.72	98.75	10.92	12.0	7.06	5.38
1939	153.64	155.92	Sept.	12	121.44	Apr.	8	150.24	−4.52	−2.92	95.58	9.11	16.5	6.11	4.07
1938	120.57	158.41	Nov.	12	98.95	Mar	31	154.76	+33.91	+28.06	87.13	6.01	25.8	4.98	3.22
1937	178.52	194.40	Mar.	10	113.64	Nov.	24	120.85	−59.05	−32.82	88.30	11.49	10.5	8.78	7.26
1936	144.13	184.90	Nov.	17	143.11	Jan.	6	179.90	+35.77	+24.82	85.55	10.07	17.9	7.05	3.92
1935	104.51	148.44	Nov.	19	96.71	Mar.	14	144.13	+40.09	+38.53	N.A.	6.34	22.7	4.55	3.16
1934	100.36	110.74	Feb.	5	85.51	July	26	104.04	+4.14	+4.14	N.A.	3.91	26.6	3.66	3.52
1933	59.29	108.67	July	18	50.16	Feb.	27	99.90	+39.97	+66.69	N.A.	2.11	47.3	3.40	3.40
1932	74.62	88.78	Mar.	8	41.22	July	8	59.93	−17.97	−23.07	N.A.	-0.51	N.A.	4.62	7.71
1931	169.84	194.36	Feb.	24	73.79	Dec.	17	77.90	−86.68	−52.67	N.A.	4.09	19.0	8.40	10.78

Figure 12.1 DJIA 1896–2008 (*Continued*)

Year	Dow At Start of Year	Year's High Close	Date		Year's Low Close	Date		Year's Close	Change Points	%	Book Value	Earns	P/E	Divs	% Yields
1930	244.20	294.07	Apr.	17	157.51	Dec.	16	164.58	−83.90	−33.76	N.A.	11.02	14.9	11.13	6.76
1929	307.01	381.17	Sept.	3	198.69	Nov.	13	248.48	−51.52	−17.17	N.A.	19.94	12.5	12.75	5.13
1928	203.35	300.00	Dec.	31	191.33	Feb.	20	300.00	+97.60	+48.22	N.A.	N.A.	N.A.	N.A.	N.A.
1927	155.16	202.40	Dec.	31	152.73	Jan.	25	202.40	+45.20	+28.75	N.A.	N.A.	N.A.	N.A.	N.A.
1926	158.54	166.64	Aug.	14	135.20	Mar.	30	157.20	+0.54	+0.34	N.A.	N.A.	N.A.	N.A.	N.A.
1925	121.25	159.39	Nov.	6	115.00	Mar.	30	156.66	+36.15	+30.00	N.A.	N.A.	N.A.	N.A.	N.A.
1924	95.65	120.51	Dec.	31	88.33	May	20	120.51	+24.99	+26.16	N.A.	N.A.	N.A.	N.A.	N.A.
1923	98.77	105.38	Mar.	20	85.76	Oct.	27	95.52	−3.21	−3.25	N.A.	N.A.	N.A.	N.A.	N.A.
1922	78.91	103.43	Oct.	14	78.59	Jan.	10	98.73	+17.63	+21.74	N.A.	N.A.	N.A.	N.A.	N.A.
1921	72.67	81.50	Dec.	15	63.90	Aug.	24	81.10	+9.15	+12.72	N.A.	N.A.	N.A.	N.A.	N.A.
1920	108.76	109.88	Jan.	3	66.75	Dec.	21	71.95	−35.28	−32.90	N.A.	N.A.	N.A.	N.A.	N.A.
1919	82.60	119.62	Nov.	3	79.15	Feb.	8	107.23	+25.03	+30.45	N.A.	N.A.	N.A.	N.A.	N.A.
1918	76.68	89.07	Oct.	18	73.38	Jan.	15	82.20	+7.82	+10.51	N.A.	N.A.	N.A.	N.A.	N.A.
1917	96.15	99.18	Jan.	3	65.95	Dec.	19	74.38	−20.62	−21.70	N.A.	N.A.	N.A.	N.A.	N.A.
1916	98.81	110.15	Nov.	21	84.96	Apr.	22	95.00	−4.15	−4.19	N.A.	N.A.	N.A.	N.A.	N.A.
1915	54.63	99.21	Dec.	27	54.22	Feb.	24	99.15	+24.42	+32.68	N.A.	N.A.	N.A.	N.A.	N.A.
1914	78.59	83.43	Mar.	20	71.42	July	30	74.73	−4.05	−5.14	N.A.	N.A.	N.A.	N.A.	N.A.
1913	88.42	88.57	Jan.	9	72.11	June	11	78.78	−9.09	−10.34	N.A.	N.A.	N.A.	N.A.	N.A.

1912	82.36	94.15	Sept.	30	80.15	Feb.	10	87.87	+6.19	+7.58	N.A.	N.A.	N.A.	N.A.	N.A.
1911	82.11	87.06	June	19	72.94	Sept.	25	81.68	+0.32	+0.39	N.A.	N.A.	N.A.	N.A.	N.A.
1910	98.34	98.34	Jan.	3	73.62	July	26	81.36	−17.69	−17.86	N.A.	N.A.	N.A.	N.A.	N.A.
1909	86.27	100.53	Nov.	19	79.91	Feb.	23	99.05	+12.90	+14.97	N.A.	N.A.	N.A.	N.A.	N.A.
1908	59.61	99.38	Nov.	13	58.62	Feb.	13	86.15	+27.40	+46.64	N.A.	N.A.	N.A.	N.A.	N.A.
1907	94.25	96.37	Jan.	7	53.00	Nov.	15	58.75	−35.60	−37.73	N.A.	N.A.	N.A.	N.A.	N.A.
1906	95.00	103.00	Jan.	19	85.18	July	13	94.35	−1.85	−1.92	N.A.	N.A.	N.A.	N.A.	N.A.
1905	70.39	96.56	Dec.	29	68.76	Jan.	25	96.20	+26.59	+38.20	N.A.	N.A.	N.A.	N.A.	N.A.
1904	47.38	73.22	Dec.	5	46.41	Mar.	12	69.61	+20.50	+41.74	N.A.	N.A.	N.A.	N.A.	N.A.
1903	64.60	67.70	Feb.	16	42.15	Nov.	9	49.11	−15.18	−23.61	N.A.	N.A.	N.A.	N.A.	N.A.
1902	64.95	68.44	Apr.	24	59.57	Dec.	15	64.29	−0.27	−0.42	N.A.	N.A.	N.A.	N.A.	N.A.
1901	70.44	78.26	June	17	61.52	Dec.	24	64.56	−6.15	−8.70	N.A.	N.A.	N.A.	N.A.	N.A.
1900	68.13	71.04	Dec.	27	52.96	Sept.	24	70.71	+4.63	+7.01	N.A.	N.A.	N.A.	N.A.	N.A.
1899	60.41	77.61	Sept.	7	58.27	Dec.	18	66.08	+5.56	+9.19	N.A.	N.A.	N.A.	N.A.	N.A.
1898	49.31	60.97	Aug.	26	42.00	Mar.	25	60.52	+11.11	+22.48	N.A.	N.A.	N.A.	N.A.	N.A.
1897	40.74	55.82	Sept.	10	38.49	Apr.	23	49.41	+8.96	+22.15	N.A.	N.A.	N.A.	N.A.	N.A.
1896	40.94	44.90	Nov.	12	28.48	Aug.	8	40.45	N.A.	N.A.	N.A.	N.A.	N.A.	N.A.	N.A.

Figure 12.1 DJIA 1896–2008 (*Continued*)

Q: *Regarding the Timely-Ten feature, if I bought a stock that made the list in the last issue but it isn't in the current issue, should I sell that stock and replace it with another stock that made the current list?*

A: This is an excellent question that obviously needs to be addressed. In short, the answer is no. In accordance with our long-term policy, our buying considerations are generally made from the stocks listed in the Undervalued category. I know that some long-term subscribers are already preparing e-mails to remind us that, on occasion, we deviate from that policy, but those occasions are rare, are based on my discretion and intuition, and are generally accompanied by a well-worded caveat.

Also, a long-held policy is that it is always a good time to buy a good undervalued stock. We approach the Timely Ten then, as if the reader is looking at IQ Trends for the first time. The 10 stocks that make up the current list are the ones we would start a portfolio with as of this issue, make additions to a partially invested portfolio as of this issue, or, to compare to a fully invested portfolio when the investor may be looking to replace one or two of their least favorite positions as of this issue.

If a stock is dropped from one issue to the next, it is generally because the stock has entered its Rising Trend and is no longer appropriate for buying consideration. If a stock is dropped from one issue to the next but is still undervalued, we have determined that another selection is simply more attractive as of this issue, but it does not mean that you should liquidate the position.

Stocks that are purchased at undervalue are appropriate to hold until they complete their Rising Trend and reach overvalued levels.

CHAPTER 13

Conclusion

In character, in manner, in style, in all things, the supreme excellence is simplicity.

—Henry Wadsworth Longfellow

The one question I have been asked more than any other is, "Does the dividend-value strategy really work?" Whether the person asking the question realizes it or not, what he or she is actually asking is, "Will it work for me?"

The short answer is absolutely, if you work it. The long answer is, well, longer.

I have referenced my grandfather often throughout this book. I do so because he had a profound impact on my formation. The lessons he taught me were based on his experience, the wisdom of which wasn't fully appreciated until I had my own experience.

My grandfather was not formally educated. He attended some grammar school. But in the agrarian-based culture of eastern Kentucky in the early 1900s, boys in particular were needed for work on the family farm or business. He would often say that he was a graduate of the School of Hard Knocks.

He left his home as a very young man to find a better life than that of his parents and siblings. Work was hard to find, but being resourceful he managed to scrape by. When the Great Depression hit, he returned home to help out my great-grandparents.

My grandfather had many talents, one of which was public speaking. As my great-grandparents were religious, my grandfather was very familiar with the Bible, which he combined with his proclivity for public speaking, and he would preach on the street corners and then pass the hat to pick up some pennies and nickels.

These street-corner collections were then used to finance another of his talents—playing pool for money. When he had sufficient earnings after cleaning up at various pool halls, my grandfather would make his way to the racetrack, where he was quite successful as a horse picker. This was how he supported the family through much of the Great Depression.

One of the odd jobs he had worked at when previously out on the road was commercial painting. When the economy began to improve, my grandfather and his brothers started a commercial painting company and eventually opened a paint and hardware store as well. My grandfather would bid on all the jobs that no one else wanted to take. With little competition, his business grew to be one of the largest in eastern Kentucky.

Although not wise in the ways of the stock market, my grandfather nonetheless understood that his money needed to earn more than it could in the bank, so he began to invest in stocks. Although it is obvious he was not afraid of gambling, he learned through trial and error that speculating on stocks was, as he would later tell me, "a tough row to hoe." It was through this cauldron of trial and error, though, that he began to learn the necessity of identifying value and the importance of dividends. The stories about the lessons he learned comprised much of my early education.

When I was in college, I took a statistics course. In one of the segments, we used the stock market as a data source for some of the exercises. It was during this time that I stumbled on Benjamin Graham and first read *The Intelligent Investor.* I remember laughing out loud at various points in the book, because some of what Graham espoused had been taught to me by my grandfather.

I was sharing this with one of the guys in my study group who said, "If you like Graham, you should read Charles Dow." I took his suggestion and was surprised, once again, that much of Dow's writings about values was in synch with what my grandfather had learned experientially and passed onto me.

I entered this business in 1984 to follow the passion that had been sown and cultivated by my grandfather for stocks and the stock market. As anyone with intellectual curiosity may expect, I wandered off the dividend-value trail a number of times, engaging in brief flirtations with a number of the "cutting edge" approaches to economics and finance that were born from financial academia. Thankfully, these dalliances were short, but the lessons have been long remembered.

I read my first issue of *Investment Quality Trends* in 1984 when the owner of the brokerage firm I worked for in La Jolla gave me his copy to read. He told me if I had any sense I would follow Geraldine Weiss' advice and I would do right by my clients.

When *Dividends Don't Lie* was published in 1989, I committed large portions to memory. When I first met Geraldine in 2002 it was a thrill. After all, she is the diva of dividends. Today I have the privilege to be the editor of *Investment Quality Trends,* as well as the chief investment officer and portfolio manager of IQ Trends Private Client Asset Management.

So back to the question of whether our approach works. The short answer is *still* yes.

Successful investing in the stock market is not rocket science. It does, however, require discipline, patience, and an appreciation for quality and value. No matter what your goals and objectives, there are high-quality, dividend-paying blue chips to fulfill every need. When purchased at *undervalued* levels and sold at *overvalued* levels, your capital and income will grow, which is the sole reason for investing.

I will close as Geraldine always does:

> We wish you lifelong investment success, with many happy dividends along the way.

May you and yours know the blessings of the Almighty.

Recommended Reading

Books

Dividends Don't Lie: Finding Value in Blue-Chip Stocks

Geraldine Weiss and Janet Lowe, 1988. Published by Dearborn Financial Publishing.

Dow Theory Unplugged: Charles Dow's Original Editorials and Their Relevance Today

Laura Sether, 2009. Published by W&A Publishing.

Elliott Wave Principle: Key to Market Behavior

A.J. Frost and Robert Prechter, 2001. Published by John Wiley & Sons.

Market Wizards: Interviews With Top Traders

Jack D. Schwager, 1989. Published by the New York Institute of Finance

Reminiscences of a Stock Operator

Edward Lefevre, 2009. Published by John Wiley & Sons.

Security Analysis: Sixth Edition

Benjamin Graham and David L. Dodd, 2005. Published by McGraw-Hill Trade.

The Art of War

Sun Tzu; Translated by Thomas Cleary, 1988. Published by Shambhala Publications.

The Dividend Connection: How Dividends Create Value in the Stock Market

Geraldine Weiss and Gregory Weiss, 1995. Published by Dearborn Financial Publishing.

The Dow Theory

Robert Rhea, 1994. Published by Fraser Publishing.

The Intelligent Investor: The Definitive Book on Value Investing

Benjamin Graham, 2005. Published by HarperCollins.

Winning on Wall Street

Martin E. Zweig, 1986. Published by Warner Books.

Magazines, Newsletters, and Newspapers

Barron's

Dow Theory Letters

Forbes

Hulbert Financial Digest

Investment Quality Trends

Stocks, Futures and Options Magazine

The Economist

The Financial Times

The Wall Street Journal

USA Today

Web Sites

Hussman Funds: Weekly Market Comment, http://hussmanfunds.com/WeeklyMarketComment.html

Investment Quality Trends, www.iqtrends.com

MSN Money, www.moneycentral.msn.com

About the Author

Kelley Wright is chief investment officer and portfolio manager for IQ Trends Private Client Asset Management, a registered investment advisory company. Additionally, he is managing editor of the *Investment Quality Trends* newsletter.

Kelley's interest in stocks and investing was the result of his relationship with his grandfather, a small business owner whose investment philosophy was formed by his experiences during the Great Depression. With everyday life as a classroom, Kelley learned the building blocks of business and how to discern quality offered at good value. From construction sites to the family vegetable garden, the experience of one generation was passed with love to the next.

In college Kelley made a connection between the lessons of his youth and his course work in business and economics. It was during the introduction to securities analysis that Kelley discovered that the lessons from his grandfather were similar to the basics of value investing as taught by Charles Dow and Benjamin Graham. This link from the past to the present was the linchpin that cemented his interest in all things associated with stocks and investing.

His career in the financial services industry began in 1984 as a registered representative and registered principal for both major wire houses and private boutiques. Since 1989 Kelley has been a private money manager and has served as chief investment officer to three investment management firms.

In 2002 Kelley was handpicked by the legendary Geraldine Weiss to succeed her as managing editor of the number-one rated *Investment Quality Trends* newsletter she started in 1966.

Kelley is an active lecturer nationwide at trade shows and investment conferences, a contributor to *MSN Money Hot Stocks Blog*, and frequent guest on both television and radio. He has been published in *Barron's; Bottom Line; Personal; BusinessWeek; Forbes.com; The Economist; MarketWatch.com; Stocks, Futures and Options Magazine;* and many other business and financial periodicals.

Kelley lives in San Diego North County with his bride of twenty-two years, Kathy, and their five children: Trinity, Keegan, Jillian, Evan, and Christian.

Index

"No one knows value like IQ Trends.*"*

–Forbes.com

"The Bible for value investors."

–The Economist

"IQ Trends *is high-test text."*

–Barron's

Founded in 1966, **Investment Quality Trends** has become the voice of authority on blue chip stocks and on the importance of dividends in determining stock market value. Published twice monthly, *IQ Trends* offers a prudent and profitable long-term approach to investing, based on quality and value in the stock market.

Mark Hulbert, founder of the *Hulbert Financial Digest,* writes that "*IQ Trends* is a simple, yet elegant application of the belief that dividends and dividend yield represent the most basic of investment fundamentals; earning a return on your investment dollar. By that score *IQ Trends* stands head and shoulders above its peers, consistently earning our highest rankings for risk-adjusted newsletters."

To judge this service for yourself, send for a **FREE** sample . . . **OR** enter your order for **online access** to a two-month, four-month, six-month or 12-month subscription.

FREE ISSUE!

Investment Quality Trends

2888 Loker Avenue East, Suite 116

Carlsbad, CA 92010

Name ______________________________

Address ______________________________

____

City ______________ **State** ______________

ZIP ______________________________

E-Mail Address ______________________________

Please enter my online subscription now.

( ) 2-Month Trial, Online	**$ 45.00**
( ) 2-Month Trial, Hardcopy	**$ 55.00**
( ) Quarterly, Online (Jan, Apr, July, Oct)	**$115.00**
( ) Quarterly, Hardcopy	**$145.00**
( ) 6-Month, Online (2 issues/month)	**$175.00**
( ) 6-Month, Hardcopy	**$200.00**
( ) Annual, Online (2 issues/month)	**$265.00**
( ) Annual, Hardcopy	**$310.00**